EXPLAINING OUR ACTIONS

We often explain our actions and those of others using a common-sense framework of perceptions, beliefs, desires, emotions, decisions, and intentions. In his thoughtful new book, Peter Carruthers scrutinizes this everyday explanation for our actions, while also examining the explanatory framework through the lens of cutting-edge cognitive science. He shows that the "standard model" of belief-desire psychology (developed, in fact, with scant regard for science) is only partly valid; that there are more types of action and action-explanation than the model allows; and that both ordinary folk and armchair-philosophers are importantly mistaken about the types of mental state that the human mind contains. His book will be of great value to all those who rely in their work on assumptions drawn from common-sense psychology, whether in philosophy of mind, epistemology, moral psychology, ethics, or psychology itself. It will also be attractive to anyone with an interest in human motivation.

PETER CARRUTHERS is Distinguished University Professor of Philosophy at the University of Maryland. His publications include *Human and Animal Minds* (2019) and *Human Motives: Hedonism, Altruism, and the Science of Affect* (2024).

"A thorough tour of the philosophy of psychology, from the standard model of common-sense psychology on which philosophers have long relied through to the picture provided by the best of contemporary cognitive science. As a pioneer of research in this area, Carruthers serves as an ideal guide. He offers a comprehensive assessment of the challenges and opportunities for philosophers in the interdisciplinary activity of explaining action. An essential read for anyone wanting a sense of philosophy of psychology, where it's been, and where it's headed."

Sarah Robins, Purdue University

"A mammoth achievement: *Explaining our Actions* draws together findings from disparate fields in psychology and shows how they fit together into a comprehensive theory of action. In a refreshingly concise treatment, the book ranges from rapid Pavlovian responses, through habits, reinforcement learning, and the emotions, to planning, intentions, and judgment. It will be an indispensable resource for philosophers of any stripe working on agency."

Nicholas Shea, University of London

EXPLAINING OUR ACTIONS

A Critique of Common-Sense Theorizing

PETER CARRUTHERS

University of Maryland, College Park

CAMBRIDGE
UNIVERSITY PRESS

CAMBRIDGE
UNIVERSITY PRESS

Shaftesbury Road, Cambridge CB2 8EA, United Kingdom

One Liberty Plaza, 20th Floor, New York, NY 10006, USA

477 Williamstown Road, Port Melbourne, VIC 3207, Australia

314–321, 3rd Floor, Plot 3, Splendor Forum, Jasola District Centre,
New Delhi – 110025, India

103 Penang Road, #05–06/07, Visioncrest Commercial, Singapore 238467

Cambridge University Press is part of Cambridge University Press & Assessment,
a department of the University of Cambridge.

We share the University's mission to contribute to society through the pursuit
of education, learning and research at the highest international levels of excellence.

www.cambridge.org
Information on this title: www.cambridge.org/9781009585767

DOI: 10.1017/9781009585781

When citing this work, please include a reference to the DOI 10.1017/9781009585781

First published 2025

Printed in the United Kingdom by CPI Group Ltd, Croydon CR0 4YY 2025

A catalogue record for this publication is available from the British Library

Library of Congress Cataloging-in-Publication Data
NAMES: Carruthers, Peter, 1952– author.
TITLE: Explaining our actions : a critique of common-sense theorizing / Peter Carruthers, University of Maryland, College Park.
DESCRIPTION: Cambridge, United Kingdom ; New York, NY, USA : Cambridge University Press, 2025. | Includes bibliographical references and index.
IDENTIFIERS: LCCN 2025002729 | ISBN 9781009585767 (hardback) | ISBN 9781009585774 (paperback) | ISBN 9781009585781 (ebook)
SUBJECTS: LCSH: Psychology – Philosophy. | Common sense.
CLASSIFICATION: LCC BF38 .C376 2025 | DDC 150.1–dc23/eng/20250212
LC record available at https://lccn.loc.gov/2025002729

ISBN 978-1-009-58576-7 Hardback

for little Dara
– always on the move –

Contents

Preface *page* ix

1 Introduction and Background Assumptions 1
1.1 The Standard Model and Variations 1
1.2 A Brief Look at the Way Ahead 4
1.3 Assumption (1): Realism 6
1.4 Assumption (2): Physicalism 8
1.5 Assumption (3): Representationalism 10
1.6 Philosophical Challenges 15
1.7 Conclusion 18

2 Habits, Skills, and Know-How 20
2.1 Habits 20
2.2 Online Control of Action 24
2.3 Fast Acting 27
2.4 Skilled Performance 29
2.5 Speech as Skilled Action 34
2.6 Skills as Distinctively Human 37
2.7 Philosophers on Know-How 39
2.8 Conclusion 45

3 Affect-Caused Action 46
3.1 The Science of Affect: A Primer 46
3.2 Expressive Action 51
3.3 Seemingly Instrumental Action 54
3.4 Model-Based versus Model-Free Action 59
3.5 Instrumentally Learned Affect-Caused Action 62
3.6 The Abstract Nature of Affective Action-Urges 63
3.7 Actions With and Without Intentions 65
3.8 Conclusion 69

4 Mental Actions 70
4.1 What Are Actions? 70
4.2 Mental Rehearsal and Inner Speech 72

4.3 Imagination, Memory Search, and Attention 75
4.4 Controlled Thinking 79
4.5 Mind-Wandering and Creative Thought 82
4.6 Judgments and Decisions Are Not Actions 87
4.7 Conclusion 90

5 Decision-Making and Goals 91
5.1 The Fragmentation of Desire 91
5.2 Irreducible Intentions 95
5.3 Prospection 100
5.4 Neuroeconomics 104
5.5 Verbal Decision-Making 108
5.6 How Intentions and Desires Interact 110
5.7 Conclusion 113

6 Pleasure and (Affective Forms of) Desire 114
6.1 The Nature of Pleasure 114
6.2 The Nature of Desire 118
6.3 Desires Are Not Propositional Attitudes 121
6.4 Philosophers on Pleasure (1): Intrinsic Feeling 124
6.5 Philosophers on Pleasure (2): Object of Desire 126
6.6 Philosophers on Desire: Partial Insights 129
6.7 Conclusion 134

7 Belief, Judgment, and Knowledge 135
7.1 Beliefs Are Real and Structured 135
7.2 Belief: Semantic and Episodic 139
7.3 What Is Memory For? 143
7.4 The Motivational Role of Evaluative Belief 146
7.5 Judgments and Commitments 148
7.6 Knowledge Is Not a Mental State 152
7.7 Conclusion 157

8 Do Attitudes Come in Degrees? 158
8.1 Intrinsic versus Extrinsic Degrees 158
8.2 The Push-Push Theory of Decision-Making 160
8.3 Strength of Desire 162
8.4 Degrees of Arousal 164
8.5 Strength of Belief: Credences 165
8.6 Strength of Will 173
8.7 Conclusion 178

9 Summary and Conclusions 179
9.1 Summary of Findings 179
9.2 Methodological Morals 180

References 185
Index 218

Preface

This book grew out of what had originally been intended as a collection of new and previously published papers, to be entitled *Real Minds: They Aren't What You Think*. But a pair of very thoughtful readers convinced me that the project wasn't really viable. I am grateful to them for their advice. The volume as it stood was too uneven in its pacing and it tried to cover too many topics, among other problems. In consequence, I decided to drop the re-printing of the previously published papers and instead to expand and add to some of the newly written material. The result is this book.

The book's goal is to outline what our best science tells us about the nature and variety of kinds of action, the ways in which they should properly be explained, and the kinds of mental state that do the explaining. In doing so it critiques theories that have been advanced by so-called "armchair" philosophers, who mostly rely upon some combination of common-sense belief, introspection, and their own intuitions when theorizing about the mind. The book shows that there are many ways in which such common-sense theorizing slices things too thickly or too thinly, gets the order of explanation back-to-front, offers explanations of action that are mistaken, mischaracterizes the nature of the explanatory mental states involved, and so on. The methodological moral of the book is that standard ("armchair") philosophical methods are bankrupt, at least in this domain.

This is not a book about the commitments of common-sense – or "folk" – psychology as such, however. That would require expertise in experimental philosophy and psychology that I don't possess, as well as a very different sort of book. Rather, I leave it to my readers to judge which of the book's conclusions they do or do not find surprising or challenging. I can, however, draw on decades of experience of listening to and reading the work of armchair-philosophers of mind, and it is their claims that provide the book's main foil.

In previous books I have discussed other areas in which common-sense theories and cognitive science clash. Specifically, I have shown how our access to many of our own mental states is interpretative in nature (not wholly unlike our access to the mental states of other people), contrasting this with the claim that we have direct self-knowledge of our own thoughts (which is assumed by common sense and widely endorsed among philosophers; Carruthers 2011). And I have argued that the range of types of conscious mental states is actually more limited than either common sense or most philosophers will allow (Carruthers 2015). The focus of the current project is on what cognitive science reveals about the variety of kinds of action, as well as the nature of the mental states and processes that should be called upon to explain them.

The philosophy of action is often seen as closely connected to the question of free will. But I will say nothing substantial about the latter in this book. While I am myself a compatibilist about free will, I don't propose to argue for that here; and I remain agnostic among the specific forms that compatibilism can take. All the same, knowledge of the differing kinds of action and their scientific explanations, of the sort that this book provides, may be useful fodder for those interested in issues having to do with free will and moral responsibility. But beyond making a few remarks in passing here and there, I propose to leave it to others to work out the implications of our best science for those topics.

I have tried throughout to describe the current scientific consensus on the issues I discuss, or at least the dominant or best-supported view. But in some cases I have been forced to extrapolate from existing findings, and in others I rely on integrating and generalizing from scientific literatures that are often kept separate. I try to be judicious in giving citations, and where possible I cite meta-analyses or review papers in top scientific journals. I also try to avoid scientific technicalities wherever I can, and provide explanations of neuroscientific terms when I am forced to employ them. And of course, given the scope and range of the topics to be discussed, I have had to paint with a broad brush. Moreover, on matters of terminology I have sometimes had to make choices, since there is little consistency in the field. This is especially true of terms employed in affective science and neuroscience, such as, "affect," "emotion," "valence," "value," "goal," "appraisal," and others. My use of terminology throughout should be regarded as stipulative. I don't believe anything substantive turns on my choices.

I am grateful to Victor Barcellos, Christopher Masciari, Klas Osvärn, Shen Pan, Pat Scannell, Elizabeth Schechter, Julius Schönherr, Nicholas

Shea, Amitai Shenhav, Chandra Sripada, Louis Trost, and Evan Westra for discussion or feedback on some of the ideas contained in this book. I also wish to thank three very thoughtful and insightful reviewers for Cambridge University Press. The foundational research that is reflected in this book was done while I was supported by a Scholars' Award from NSF's *Science and Technology Studies* program (award # 2143473) covering the academic year 2022–23. I am grateful to them for their support.

CHAPTER 1

Introduction and Background Assumptions

This chapter begins by sketching the standard model of action and action-explanation employed by most philosophers, while also noting some variations. Of necessity, given the immense literature on the topic, this will be presented at a high level of generality, abstracting over many local disagreements. The model and its variations will provide the main set of foils for the scientifically grounded accounts to be discussed in later chapters, which are briefly previewed in Section 1.2. The remaining sections of the chapter then go on to explain and quickly motivate three major assumptions that are taken for granted throughout the remainder of the book (and that are agreed upon by many philosophers and almost all cognitive scientists, it should be said): realism, physicalism, and representationalism.

1.1 The Standard Model and Variations

The sub-discipline of philosophy called "the philosophy of action" is almost exclusively about what philosophers call "intentional action" (Mele 2003; Wilson & Shpall 2012; Piñeros Glasscock & Tenenbaum 2023). These are actions done with a goal or intention in mind, and are done for reasons. In their most general form, the reasons that motivate actions ("motivating reasons") are things toward which one holds a "pro-attitude" of some sort (a desire) or a "con-attitude" (a repulsion), together with beliefs about the states of the world that might enable one to achieve or avoid the things in question (Searle 1983). This is so-called "belief-desire psychology." Actions are taken to achieve things one wants in light of one's beliefs about the means of getting them. For example, Mary wants to go to medical school and believes she needs to study hard to get there, which is why she is studying.

Most philosophers have followed Davidson (1963) in thinking that reasons motivate actions by causing them. When one acts *because* one wants something and believes that the action will achieve what one wants, the desires and beliefs in question are the causes of one's subsequent action. So action-explanation is a species of causal explanation. As for the nature of the explaining attitudes themselves (beliefs and desires), there are varying opinions, as we will see. But it is nevertheless agreed that they are *propositional* attitudes. They have contents that can be correctly expressed using a that-clause. Mary wants *that* she should get accepted into medical school and believes *that* she needs to study hard to get in. And these states (in the presence of a host of enabling conditions) causally explain the fact that she is studying.

Moreover, beliefs and desires are thought to be distinguished from each other by their functional roles. It is common to use the phrase "direction of fit" in this connection (Searle 1983). Thus beliefs have a mind-to-world direction of fit: their role is to "fit" or "match" the state of the world, and to guide action-selection appropriately in the light of that fit. Desires, in contrast, have world-to-mind direction of fit: their role is to change the world in such a way as to "fit" or "match" the content of the desire. Thus beliefs have correctness-conditions whereas desires have satisfaction-conditions. Mary's belief that she needs to study hard to get into medical school is true if she really does need to do that, false otherwise. Her desire is satisfied if she succeeds in getting into medical school, frustrated if she fails. And it is the desire that motivates studying/causes her to study, given her belief.

While Davidson (1963) assumed that beliefs and desires are the only categories of mental state that are needed to explain action (in addition to perceptual states, of course), most of the field has since become convinced by Bratman (1987, 1999) and others that one also needs to appeal to plans or intentions. Beliefs and desires inform planning and decision-making, and action itself is subsequently controlled and guided by the plans decided upon. These intentions, once formed, are thought to constrain one's reasoning thereafter, pre-empting further decision-making and motivating the intended actions. Intentions, too, are thought to be propositional attitudes. Knowing that there is a test coming up tomorrow, Mary might decide *that* she should study until late tonight, thereby forming an intention that guides and constrains her plans for the evening. (For example, she might turn down an invitation to a party.)

Much less attention has been paid to forms of action other than intentional action. As Frankfurt (1978) points out, however, there is a sense in which a spider making its way across the floor is *acting*. Its movements are controlled ones, and might be guided by a simple aim, such as to reach the darkness under the bed. But it is thought that most human actions are distinctively different. (In part this may be because of a reluctance to attribute propositional attitudes or even simple forms of practical reason to spiders and other animals. If so, this is surely a mistake; Carruthers 2009, 2019.) Human actions, insofar as they conform to the standard model, are thought to reflect our distinctive rational capacities. And while philosophers of action might occasionally notice that some human actions can be habitual ones, rather than intentional, these are apt to be set aside as not really paradigmatic cases of action. (This may be because people vastly underestimate the extent to which human life is governed by habits, as we will see in Chapter 2.) Indeed, some say that we are *passive* with respect to such actions (Wu 2023): they are things that happen to us, rather than things that we genuinely *do*. Only intentional actions are thought to be truly expressive of *our selves*.

While discussion of intentional action in the 1960s and 1970s had little to say about the role of emotion in motivating action, this has changed in recent decades. But many of the resulting theories still cleave to the basics of the belief-desire model. Thus on some views emotions are identified with a special class of judgments (Solomon 1976; Nussbaum 2001). To be afraid of the spider is to judge that it is dangerous, or at least to entertain the thought that it is (Greenspan 1988). Others have maintained that emotions are combinations of judgments with desires (Marks 1982; Gordon 1987), together with some degree of bodily arousal, perhaps. So to fear the spider is to think of it as dangerous and to want to get away from it. But some argue that emotions are more like a form of evaluative perception (Tappolet 2016). So to fear the spider is to *see* it as dangerous, in some kind of simple nonconceptual manner. But still the motivational role of emotion is thought to involve desire (in this case, the desire to get away).

While everyone in the field agrees that desires admit of degrees, and can come in a variety of different strengths, belief-desire theorists are more divided on the question of degrees of belief. Some think that beliefs of all kinds are graded in nature, referred to in much of the literature as "credences" (Jeffrey 1970; Levi 1991). Others think that while some beliefs are graded there is another set of beliefs that are categorical or "all or nothing" (Pollock 1983; Sosa 2011). And yet others think that all beliefs are categorical but can embed degrees of likelihood in their contents (Harman 1986; Schiffer 2003). We will return to these issues in Chapter 8, along with the question of degrees of intention-strength, or "strength of will."

According to the dominant version of the standard model in philosophy, then, intentional actions are caused and controlled by intentions. Intentional actions are thought to either constitute the vast majority of human actions, or to be distinctively human actions, or to be the actions that are of special philosophical interest insofar as they reflect and express one's agency or *self* – or some combination of the above. Intentions, in turn, result from decision-making influenced causally by one's beliefs and desires. And all three categories of state (intention, belief, and desire) are propositional attitudes, some at least of which admit of degrees, or variations in strength. Moreover, both intentions and desires have satisfaction-conditions and world-to-mind direction of fit, whereas beliefs have truth-conditions and mind-to-world direction of fit.

1.2 A Brief Look at the Way Ahead

The goal of this book is to evaluate the standard model and its variants, confronting it with our best science. While some aspects of the model turn out to be correct, much proves to be erroneous. The philosophy of action is in need of a substantial make-over, as we will see. Here I will give just a brief indication of what is to come.

Chapters 2 through 4 discuss a range of action-types that fall outside the standard model altogether, and require a different sort of explanation. Chapter 2 discusses habitual, speeded, and skilled actions, which together make up a very large proportion of our daily activities. None are caused and controlled in the manner envisaged by the standard model. The chapter also critiques intellectualist accounts of so-called "know-how" that have been advanced by some philosophers. Chapter 3 then discusses actions that are a direct product of affective (emotional and emotion-like) states, both expressive and seemingly (but not really) instrumental. These, too, fail to conform to the standard model.

Chapter 4 turns to discussion of mental actions, notably mental rehearsals of action, prospection of the future, inner speech, attention, memory search, mind-wandering, and creative insight. Many of these also fail to conform to a (suitably internalized) version of the standard model, and need to be explained differently. But at the same time, two categories of (alleged) mental action widely accepted by philosophers – judgments and decisions – turn out not to be action-like at all.

Chapter 5 moves on to the very heartland of the standard model: reflective forms of decision-making. It first shows that cognitive science vindicates a separate category of intentions, before outlining the evidence that valence (pleasure and displeasure when conscious) is the common currency of all, or almost all, decision-making. Finally, it explains how intentions and desires interact with one another, in such a way that while intentions generally exclude and pre-empt pursuit of conflicting desires, sometimes they do not, and one decides to set aside one's goal in favor of a new desire instead.

The remaining chapters concern the nature of the attitudes appealed to by the standard model, especially beliefs and desires. Chapter 6 explains the true (scientifically informed) nature of desire, and its relationship to pleasure. In contrast to claims made by philosophers, pleasure is neither a motivating intrinsic feeling nor is it a desired experience. It is, rather, an analog-magnitude / nonconceptual representation of value.[1] And desires themselves are neither propositional attitudes, nor do they have world-to-mind direction of fit. On the contrary, they have correctness-conditions, since they represent the object of desire as to some degree (nonconceptually) good.

Chapter 7 is about the nature of belief, demonstrating the reality of at least two forms of belief – episodic and semantic memory. In contrast, many of the states that result from what philosophers regard as the very paradigm of belief-formation – making up one's mind after considering the evidence – aren't really beliefs at all, but are, rather, intention-like. They are commitments to think and act in the future as if the proposition were true. The chapter also critiques a view that has become quite popular among philosophers, that knowledge is a basic kind of factive mental state. This finds no place in cognitive science; indeed, it is inconsistent with the latter's core commitments.

Chapter 8 then addresses the question of degrees. It argues that neither beliefs nor desires admit of degrees of attitude-strength. Rather, degrees are built into the *contents* of those attitudes – analog-magnitude representations of value, in the case of desire, and analog-magnitude representations of likelihood, in the case of belief. In contrast, there is at least one good sense in which intentions can vary in strength, albeit not in the sort of way that common sense suggests.

[1] An analog-magnitude property (in the world) is one that is continuously graded. Color is an analog-magnitude property of surfaces, and length and mass are analog-magnitude properties of objects. An analog-magnitude *representation* is one that represents an analog-magnitude property through the use of an analog-magnitude symbol of some sort (such as a rate of neural firing). The height of the mercury in a classical mercury thermometer, for example, provides an analog-magnitude representation of the ambient temperature.

Chapter 9 then briefly summarizes the main conclusions of the book. The standard belief-desire model both ignores and is incapable of explaining vast swaths of human action. And even within its proprietary domain (so-called "intentional action"), the standard model mischaracterizes many of the explanatory states involved. It is right about the nature and role of intentions (except that not all intentions have propositional contents). But it treats states as beliefs that are actually more intention-like, while falsely assuming that all beliefs are propositional attitudes; and it is deeply mistaken about the nature of desire. What will emerge is that, although some aspects of the standard model can pass scientific muster, many cannot. And many of the ancillary claims that have been defended by some armchair-philosophers are false, too (e.g. that skills are a form of propositional knowledge, that knowledge is a basic kind of mental state, and that credences – degrees of belief – are real).

Chapter 9 concludes by drawing some methodological morals for the way in which philosophy of mind should properly be conducted. If philosophers are to take the nature of action and action-explanation seriously, then they need to engage with the science much more seriously than most of them currently do.

In what remains of this chapter I propose to lay out and briefly motivate three assumptions that are foundational to all, or almost all, cognitive science. These will be taken for granted in the remainder of the book. While these assumptions are consistent with the standard model, they aren't components or entailments of it. Moreover, many philosophers accept them, although by no means all do. Readers already familiar with the issues can, if they wish, jump straight to Chapter 2 without much loss.

1.3 Assumption (1): Realism

Most philosophers who endorse some version of the standard belief-desire model of action-explanation are realists about the states that do the explaining. Following Davidson (1963) and many others, they think that beliefs and desires are discrete mental states that can be acquired or lost on an individual basis, and which causally explain the behaviors to which they give rise. But not everyone agrees. Dennett (1971, 1987), in particular, denies that belief-desire psychology makes any real-world commitments. Rather, it is a useful – indeed, indispensable – *instrument* for predicting human behavior, as well as for explaining it in the weak sense of rendering it predictable.

According to Dennett, when we attribute mental states to people we adopt a particular stance toward them and their behavior – the *intentional stance*. We make a background assumption of rationality, and then make predictions based on what a rational and well-designed organism with such-and-such access to the world and so-and-so previous experiences of the world would be likely to do. On this view, for it to be the case that an organism believes that *P* or desires that *Q* is just for its overall behavior to be reliably and voluminously predicted via a package of state-attributions that includes the belief that *P* or the desire that *Q*. There is no deeper reality to possessing a particular belief than for one's overall behavior to be best predicted by attributing to one that belief. So there is nothing, here, to be scientifically falsified or corrected. Provided the intentional strategy works (as plainly it does, in general) there is nothing to prevent us from continuing to use it; indeed, practically speaking, we *cannot* stop using it; it is practically indispensable.

Dennett (1991b) insists that the patterns in people's behavior are real, of course. But that is all they are: patterns that the intentional stance enables us to see and predict. The terms we use when we adopt that stance have no deeper reality than this. In embracing such a position, however, Dennett violates one of the core methodological assumptions of both science and ordinary everyday theory choice. This is to prefer theories that causally explain observable patterns of events over theories that don't (Carruthers 2006; Emery 2023). This is what realism about belief-desire psychology enables us to do. Beliefs, desires, and other types of mental state interact causally during decision-making to select and issue in actions. So the patterns that mental-state-attribution enables us to discern in people's behavior aren't just predictable, they are causally explicable.

Moreover, there seems little doubt that ordinary folk are committed to the real existence of the attitudes and perceptual states they ascribe to themselves and others. Indeed, any suggestion to the contrary will be met with an incredulous stare. In part this is because one is often aware, in one's own case, of specific mental events that seem to be causes of one's subsequent behavior. One is aware of the longing one feels at the sight of a piece of chocolate cake before one grabs it; and one is aware of judging that a shelf is too high to reach before turning to get a footstool to climb up on. Now, one doesn't have to believe in any sort of Cartesian introspective infallibility to take such data seriously. Similar points can be made even from the standpoint of self-interpretative theories of self-knowledge (Carruthers 2011). While one might indeed take an "interpretative stance" toward oneself, among the data for interpretation are conscious mental events of various kinds.

Moreover, ordinary folk are quite prepared to entertain the idea that someone paralyzed throughout their life, or people with severe cerebral palsy who have only minimal control of their movements, might nevertheless have a rich internal mental life, with many of the experiences, thoughts, and desires that others possess. But there is no behavior here to be voluminously predicted and made sense of from the intentional stance; and the assumption of optimal design is plainly not operative. So if the common-sense psychology of the folk were really just a stance, then we would expect them to withhold mentality in such circumstances.[2]

In any case, whatever might be true of the folk, there is no doubt that cognitive science is committed to the reality and causal efficacy of the states with which it deals. And this is what we will assume going forward.

1.4 Assumption (2): Physicalism

While ordinary folk and most philosophers are agreed in being realists about the mental states they appeal to when explaining people's actions, they differ about the ontological status of those states. While a bare majority of philosophers have embraced physicalism about the mind (Bourget & Chalmers 2023), most ordinary people have not: they are ontological dualists. Indeed, belief in an ontological separation of mind and body appears to be almost a human universal (Boyer 2001; Cohen et al. 2011; Roazzi et al. 2013). All of the world's major religions (as well as most of its minor ones) involve a belief in some sort of life after death. According to some, the afterlife is purely ethereal or non-physical; according to others it will involve being reincarnated into a new body; and for yet others it will involve the resurrection of one's original body, with an attenuated self that exists in a kind of limbo in the interim. Moreover, throughout history and across cultures, people have believed in spirits and gods – minded agents who aren't subject to ordinary physical constraints (Brown 2001). Many people today continue to possess such beliefs – or at least believe that an afterlife is *possible* – although with the advance of science and consequent

[2] It is very hard to *see* the behavior of people with cerebral palsy as imbued with mentality, of course, and interacting with such people can be difficult – which is why they often face prejudice and discrimination. But the point is that ordinary people are nevertheless quite prepared to *believe* (rightly) that there can still be a rich mental life behind the mask of disability.

decline of religion in much of the developed world, such beliefs may be becoming less common.

Although belief in an afterlife isn't endorsed by everyone, it appears that some form of mind/body dualism is either a human universal, or close to being one. Indeed, it can persist even among highly educated academics. Moreover, there is good evidence of dualist intuitions even among people who explicitly endorse physicalism. As with other implicit folk theories, it seems that people can retain intuitions that conflict with what they explicitly accept (Shtulman & Valcarcel 2012; Kelemen et al. 2013). Thus dualist responses to imagined scenarios become significantly greater when people are placed under cognitive load (and are thus unable to answer reflectively), and also when they are primed to adopt an intuitive rather than an analytical mindset (Forstmann & Burgmer 2015). Moreover, Chudek et al. (2018) used a simple animated-shapes task with adults and children (some as young as two) from North America and Fiji designed to elicit body-swap intuitions. They found compelling evidence of the presence of such intuitions across cultures. This is especially striking since social norms in indigenous iTaukei Fijian culture discourage discourse about people's mental states altogether.

There should be no doubt, then, that common sense is committed to the non-physical nature of mental states (whether explicitly or implicitly), as are many philosophers. But there should also be no doubt that ontological dualism is false. The mind is physical through-and-through. I won't argue for this in any detail here, except to make the following brief points.

- Decades of work with patients who have undergone brain damage demonstrate how the brain is necessary for mentality. Thus damage to primary visual cortex causes blindness, damage to auditory cortex causes deafness, and so on. And this is not just true of the inputs to the mind. Damage to the prefrontal cortex causes an array of deficits of reasoning and decision-making (Manes et al. 2002), and in extreme cases can cause people to become completely unresponsive to stimuli (Knight & Grabowecky 1995).
- We already know enough about the brain to know that there are no physical processes within it that are initiated in the absence of any physical cause. So there is no way for non-physical states or processes to have a causal impact on behavior (as mental states seem obviously to do).
- Scientific inquiry assumes that the natural world is layered, with higher-level properties and processes being realized in lower-level ones.

(So neuroscience is realized in biochemistry, which in turn is realized in chemistry, and so on.) If mental processes are real, we should expect them to be realized in neurological ones.

- The physically layered nature of the natural world has been the guiding methodological assumption of science for centuries. The ongoing success of scientific inquiry provides good reason to think that the assumption is true.

That having been said, in the remainder of this book I propose just to take physicalism about the mind for granted, as do many philosophers and almost all cognitive scientists.

1.5 Assumption (3): Representationalism

It is widely accepted among philosophers that many (perhaps all) mental states possess the property of *intentionality* – they are *about* something. And this is essential to their predictive and explanatory roles. It is because one has a desire that is *about* coffee, and a belief that is *about* coffee being in the mug, that one reaches for it. And it is because one sees the coffee mug (is in a perceptual state that is about the coffee mug and its position on the desk) that one knows where to reach. Turing (1950), reflecting on the significance of newly invented computing machines, was among the first to suggest how such facts about the mental can be physically realized; ideas that were later developed in detail by Fodor (1975) and many others – especially influential among whom is Marr (1982).

The proposal is that one can physically explain the aboutness of mental states, and also how aboutness contributes to their causal roles in selecting and guiding behavior, by dividing the problem into two components. One is to suggest that the mind/brain computes over physical symbols of some sort; and the second involves an account of how these symbols come to be about anything (relying especially on the concept of *information*). Roughly, it is because the physical symbols carry information about the world, and because the brain computes over them in ways appropriate for the informational content that they carry, that behavior can be caused and explained by mental states that are about the world. This is accepted by many philosophers and is the guiding framework of all (or almost all) cognitive science.

Although mostly interested in vision, Marr (1982) famously suggests that a complete explanation of any given mental phenomenon should proceed on three levels, ultimately integrating all three. At the top is a representational, content-involving, specification of the process or phenomenon in question.

(Marr calls this the "computational level," which is somewhat confusing since it is also a representation-involving level; Ritchie 2019.) Below that (the "algorithmic level") is an account of the algorithms that execute the content-involving process, transforming physical symbols of some sort into other such symbols. And then at the bottom is the detailed neurological implementation of those algorithms and symbols. Our focus for the moment will be on algorithmic explanation (more generally described in terms of computations over symbols), later returning to discuss representational content and its place in cognitive science.

Early iterations of cognitive science postulated a "language of thought" involving discrete componentially structured symbols (Fodor 1975) – somewhat like a language with its sentential syntax and component words – together with formal (logic-like) transformations and inferences over those symbols. There then followed a period of competition between this approach and various kinds of distributed connectionist modeling (Fodor & Pylyshyn 1988; Smolensky 1988; Elman et al. 1999; Smolensky & Legendre 2006). Given the extraordinary advances in both the computing power and speed of modern-day computers, the fields of artificial intelligence and machine learning have increasingly (almost exclusively) gone in the direction of distributed multi-layered neural networks. But much actual cognitive modeling designed to explain human performance has continued to operate with discrete symbols, albeit using probabilistic representations – especially employing Bayesian statistical inferences (Goodman et al. 2008; Erdogan et al. 2015; Piantadosi & Jacobs 2016; Overlan et al. 2017).

There is a persuasive case for claiming that many cognitive representations have a discrete compositional (language-like) structure (Quilty-Dunn et al. 2023). For example, as we will see in Chapter 7, semantic memory is organized around individual-object files and object-kind files, which have a noun-like file-header combined with embedded information about the object or kind in question. In this respect representations in semantic memory have structures much like natural-language generics, such as "Birds fly," or sentences about individual people, like "John is tall." But many cognitive processes compute over analog-magnitude representations, too – which approximately map some real-world continuous quantity such as time, color, direction of motion, or approximate number – employing a continuously varying internal magnitude of some sort as a symbol. Thus many foraging animals can compute a rate of return from a given foraging site, which requires them to integrate an analog-magnitude representation of the approximate number of items foraged with an analog-magnitude representation of an approximate time-interval, dividing the former by the latter (Gallistel & Gibbon 2001). Other cognitive processes compute over iconic (or picture-like) representations (Kosslyn et al. 2006; Toribio 2011).

Less is known about the way cognitive representations as a whole are neurally realized. But some kinds are well studied. In connection with spatial navigation, for example, we know that individual cells in the hippocampal formation represent particular places (becoming especially active when and only when the animal is in a particular place in the environment), whereas others represent particular head-directions (O'Keefe 1976; Grieves & Jeffery 2017). Analog magnitudes, in contrast, are generally represented via the activity of populations of neurons, using so-called "population coding" (Deneve et al. 1999; Pouget et al. 2000; Averbeck et al. 2006). For example, there are a great many neurons in an area of visual cortex known as MT that increase their firing-rate for a range of directions of motion, with their activity taking the form of a bell-curve centered on a particular direction, and responding with greater or lesser precision. An animal's judgment of the actual direction of a motion-stimulus is computed across this population. And where precise discrimination is required, reliance is placed on the set of neurons with the greatest precision (Purushothaman & Bradley 2005).

There seems little doubt, then, that mental states with their property of *aboutness* can be scientifically vindicated by explanatory frameworks that postulate computations over content-bearing symbols or representations, provided that an account can be given of what makes a given symbol be about a particular thing or property, and provided that the representational contents in question play an important role in cognitive-science explanations.

All naturalistic theories of representation are either built around the notion of *information* (Millikan 1984, 1989; Papineau 1987; Dretske 1988, 1995; Fodor 1990; Neander 2017; Rupert 2018), or else the idea of a structure-preserving mapping – an isomorphism – between representations and their content (Cummins 1996; Gallistel & King 2010), or both (Shea 2018). I am happy to join Shea in endorsing both, accepting that representations can acquire content in a number of different ways. We consider informational content first.

When one type of thing causes, or is apt to cause, another, the latter event carries information about the former. Roughly speaking, knowing the latter, one can deduce, with some degree of confidence, that the former event has occurred. So when events in the mind/brain are caused by properties or events in the world or body, the mind/brain events carry information about the world or body. But this is not enough, as yet, for them to qualify as representational. Someone's blistering skin carries the information that their skin has been exposed to the sun for a significant amount of time, but the blisters don't *represent* previous sun exposure. For that, there has to be some downstream consuming system or process that can make use of that information – that is, one that responds to, uses, or computes with the information-carrying state in a manner that is somehow appropriate for, or dependent on, the information carried.

As a first approximation, one can say information-carrying states of the mind/brain qualify as representations provided that they cause downstream effects (whether other mind/brain events or overt behavior) that are sensitive to the information carried. This means that, in one way or another, those downstream effects occur as they do *because of* the distal cause of the state. Teleological theories cash this out in terms of evolution by natural selection (Millikan 1984; Papineau 1987; Neander 2017). The downstream effects occur as they do because they are an adaptive response to the distal cause, selected through evolutionary processes. But other approaches can instead (or better, also) emphasize learning as the process that gives rise to adaptive responses to information (Dretske 1988; Shea 2018).

Any representational state will carry much more information than is actually represented, of course. Consider the state caused by perceiving a raccoon. In addition to carrying information about the presence of a raccoon, it carries information about a complex pattern of stimulation on the retina, about light passing through the intervening space, as well as about the fact that a raccoon-mating event and a kit-birthing event occurred sometime in the past (in that temporal order). But it *represents* none of the latter set of things. In addition, a raccoon-representing perceptual state can be caused by a cat seen at twilight, when one mistakes a cat for a raccoon. But it doesn't represent the disjunctive property raccoon-or-cat-at-twilight, either. On the contrary, if one takes the cat to be a raccoon, then that is a *mis*representation, and is false or incorrect.

What, then, picks out the *represented* information from among the total set of causes and possible causes of the state in question? Many of the writers cited above offer detailed and subtly different answers to this question. Those details won't matter for our purposes. Here I propose to follow the account provided by Shea (2018), which is designed specifically to explain the notion of representation employed in cognitive science. He argues that what makes it the case that something is an information-based representation is that it plays a computational / functional role in some cognitive process. And what fixes the content (or correctness-condition) for a representation from among all the information that it carries is what causally *stabilized* the role of that representation in the computations that it enters into, either through natural selection, or through learning, or through its contribution to individual survival. The content of the representation is the information carried that we need to appeal to in explaining the role that the representation plays in determining the behavior of the organism.

When applied to the case of visually representing a raccoon, this account delivers the right answers. What explains the evolution of animate-object perception in general is the proximal stimulus-object (e.g. a raccoon); for it is this that underlies the success of subsequent actions (such as approaching or avoiding the creature in question). Carrying information about temporally distal events (an earlier raccoon mating) played no role in stabilizing the success of the system; nor did the patterns of stimulation on the retina (except insofar as they carry information about the distal object). And when perceptual learning leads one to distinguish raccoons from other living creatures, it is the presence of raccoons (and only raccoons) that explains the successful accumulation of knowledge about raccoons in the resulting animate-object kind-file.

Consider, now, representation via structural mapping. The simplest example concerns representation within the visual system. Neurons in primary and secondary visual cortex (and indeed, in other regions of cortex further downstream as well) are arranged retinotopically. That is to say, neurons that are adjacent to one another in visual cortex carry information about (and represent) information received from adjacent neurons in the retina. Lines, edges, and shapes represented in the visual system are constructed through the firing-patterns of adjacent neurons that carry information about adjacent patterns of stimulation on the retina, and thereby information about adjacent items in the perceived world. In effect (and simplifying hugely), the visual system uses spatial relations within itself to represent spatial relations in the world.

For a different, more complex, example of structural mapping, recall hippocampal place-cells, which fire when and only when the organism is in a particular location in the environment. So each place-cell, when firing, carries the information that the organism is in a particular place. But this is not yet to *represent* that it is in that place. For unless that place can be positioned in relation to others in a mental map, the information is useless. What transforms place-cells into representations of places are the associative links between them. Activations of one place-cell will tend to co-activate others in proportion to their adjacency in the environment. (These associative links get set up as the animal explores.) As a result, organisms can (and do) plan to get to place A from place B via activation of the links between the connecting nodes. Here the relation of associative co-activation is in structural correspondence with spatial distances and directions, and animals can use prospectively generated sequences of such activations when planning routes through their environments.

As Shea (2018) makes clear, the intentional contents of the symbol-like representations that cognitive processes compute over (i.e. their truth-conditions, correctness-conditions, or satisfaction-conditions) play an essential role in cognitive-science explanations. For the correctness-condition of a numerosity-representation, for example, is the information that it carries about approximate number. And it is this that explains how the inferences and behaviors that it guides have become stabilized by evolution or learning (such as when taking foraging decisions). In order to understand why cognitive processes work as they do, and to explain patterns of success and failure, scientists need to appeal to the worldly contents that are represented by the symbols and structures undergoing those processes. In which case, one central defining feature of the mind (*aboutness*) is vindicated by the cognitive sciences, not undermined.

1.6 Philosophical Challenges

Some philosophers have mounted challenges to computational / representational forms of cognitive science (Chemero 2009; Hutto & Myin 2013). The most general umbrella term for the view of the mind that is intended as a replacement is that minds are "embodied" (Shapiro & Spaulding 2021).[3] The mind is said to be constituted by interactions between the organism and its environment in a way that leaves no room for (or at least, that has no need of) explanation in terms of computations over representations. What is urged on us by these philosophers is a radical new direction for the sciences of the mind. Meanwhile, tens of thousands of real cognitive scientists continue to make new findings and offer successful explanations within a variety of

[3] The thesis of the *extended* mind is often treated alongside the idea of the embodied mind. (The former claims that the mind literally incorporates external objects and processes such as notebooks and pencil-and-paper calculations; Clark & Chalmers 1998; Clark 2008.) But in fact the extended mind presents no challenge to traditional forms of cognitive science. Rather, it proposes an extension of the scope of the latter to include external representational processes. For my own discussion and critique of the extended-mind idea, see Carruthers (2015).

computational / representational frameworks, and carry on advancing our scientific understanding of the mind.

That mind and body, as well as mind and action, interact with each other is no surprise, of course. And many phenomena of this general sort have been known about and studied for decades within standard cognitive-science frameworks. Vision scientists have always known, for example, that visual processing cannot involve an isolated set of computations proceeding from retinal stimulation to perception of the world. For one's eyes are constantly in motion, causing shifting patterns of stimulation on the retina. In fact so-called "efference copies" of the motor instructions that initiate these movements are among the main inputs to the visual system, where they are integrated with information deriving from the retina to enable perception of a stable world. Likewise for head movements and the motion of one's body through the environment. If this makes visual processes "embodied," so be it. But there is nothing radical here; nor is there any challenge to regular forms of cognitive science.

It is also widely recognized that even a core cognitive-science construct like *attention* is actually action-like, and operates in close interaction with affective valuational systems (Hickey & Peelen 2015; Vuilleumier 2015; Anderson 2016). Patterns of scanning across the visual scene, for example, partly depend on contextually cued habits (including tendencies to look toward faces), but partly on patterns of previous reward and punishment. One looks at and attends to things anticipating that they may be relevant, or that they might be important sources of knowledge. So here, too, there is constant feedback and interaction between vision, action, attentional networks, and value systems. Surprising, perhaps; but fully accountable for within standard cognitive-science frameworks.

Likewise, we have known for decades that thought and planning about the future utilize the resources of bodily motor-control systems. As we will see in more detail in later chapters, efference-copies of motor instructions (with overt execution thereafter suppressed) are used to generate "sensory forward models" of what it would feel like and look like if the action were executed. People and other animals are constantly simulating and evaluating the various possible actions that are open to them (and their likely outcomes) during decision-making (Seligman et al. 2016). And the uses of these sensory forward models in fine-grained motor control, too, have been well known and well studied for decades, not only in humans (Wolpert & Kawato 1998; Jeannerod 2006), but even in dragonflies (Mischiati et al. 2014), as we will see.

Again, that the body and mind interact and depend on one another is no news to standard cognitive science.[4]

It might be thought that the thesis of "embodied concepts" (Barsalou 1999) provides support for embodied cognition more generally. On this view, concepts are stored as networks of sensorimotor representations, not as abstract, amodal, symbols. But this would be to misunderstand computational cognitive science, which need not be committed to the thesis that all computations operate over abstract symbols like the "0"s and "1"s in a digital computer. All it really requires is that there are processes that create and transform structured physical symbols of some sort. And that is true of the modality-specific computations that take place within the visual system just as much as those that take place elsewhere. That said, the evidence adduced in support of embodied concepts is less than convincing, and can be better explained in terms of bi-directional spreading activation between amodal concepts and associated sensory and motor representations (Mahon & Caramazza 2008). And even if it were true that many concepts *are* sensorimotor in nature, we have good reason to think that plenty are not, including representations of mental states, action-concepts, and representations of shape, space, and physical causality (Carruthers 2015; Spelke 2022).

Those who defend embodied-cognition approaches have drawn their inspiration from robotics and forms of artificial intelligence that operate without internal representations (Chemero 2009; Hutto & Myin 2013). Early iterations of robotics had some success with this idea (Brooks 1991). And of course we now have deep-learning systems that can hold conversations, compose essays, and drive cars. But there are compelling reasons to think that the ways in which these multi-layered deep-learning networks operate and achieve their success is quite different from the manner in which human and animal minds work. One is that they require huge numbers of training runs, generally in the hundreds of millions or hundreds of billions (Schrittwieser et al. 2020), and large-language models like ChatGPT are trained on something close to the entire contents of the internet. Humans and other animals, in contrast, manage to learn just as effectively using much more minimal feedback, often requiring just one or a few exposures to the material to be learned. The successes achieved by deep-learning forms of technology provide no reason to doubt that actual minds are representational.

[4] Strikingly, not a single one of the empirical papers cited by Shapiro and Spaulding (2021) in their review of the field – said to be among those relied on by embodied-mind philosophers to support their proposed radical replacement for representation-involving cognitive science – actually provides any significant challenge to the latter at all. All admit of other interpretations.

A second point is that deep neural networks remain vulnerable to adversarial examples, not just in theory but in the real world (Goodfellow et al. 2015; Kurakin et al. 2018; Hendrycks et al. 2021), and there is reason to think that these failures are endemic (Ilyas et al. 2019; Shafahi et al. 2020). Adversarial examples are inputs that are adjusted in minor ways – so minor as to be undetectable to human observers – but which can lead a fully trained image-classifier to classify what is obviously a cat as a dog, or a dog as an ostrich, or (more worryingly) a stop-sign as a go-sign, for example. This, too, is powerful evidence that deep neural networks provide poor models of how human and animal cognition actually work. If our goal is to understand minds (and not just to make smart machines) then there is currently no viable alternative to representation-employing forms of cognitive science.

Chemero (2009) also appeals to dynamical-systems theory as a non-representational alternative to cognitive science. This attempts to model interactions between organisms and their environment using differential equations. Organism and environment are here thought of as co-equal partners, and no attempt is made to understand what may be going on inside the organism. Dynamical-systems approaches have been used to successfully describe some simple phenomena, such as coordinated finger-wagging, infant walking, and perseverative reaching behavior in infants (Thelen & Smith 1993; Kelso 1995; Thelen et al. 2001). But such models are merely descriptive and fail to causally explain the phenomena they describe (Spivey 2007). Moreover, there is no reason to think that they can "scale up" to more complex behavioral and cognitive phenomena. It seems fair to say that the dynamical-systems framework is not a viable alternative to the causal explanations that have been provided successfully for a wide range of cognitive and behavioral phenomena by cognitive scientists over the last few decades.[5]

1.7 Conclusion

This chapter has sketched the standard model of action and action-explanation that provides the main foil for the rest of the book. On this account, actions are caused and controlled by intentions, which in turn

[5] Indeed, consider Favela's (2020) favorable review of dynamical-systems theory, in which he proposes it as a replacement for representationalist forms of cognitive science. On examination, hardly any of the empirical papers cited in the review provide any real challenge or alternative to the latter. More than thirty years after it was first proposed, a dynamical-systems account of the mind still remains almost entirely aspirational. It is what philosophers of science refer to as a "degenerating research program."

result from decision-making in light of one's motivating reasons (one's beliefs and desires). The chapter has also explained and briefly sketched support for some key assumptions of the remainder of the book. These are that mental states are real (and not just an interpretative gloss on behavior), that mental states are physical, and that mental states are representational. All three assumptions are now shared by many philosophers, but are central to current cognitive science.

CHAPTER 2

Habits, Skills, and Know-How

This chapter is partly about how actions are executed and how the details of people's behavioral performance should be explained. But it also introduces some classes of action that find no place within the standard belief-desire model. These include habitual actions as well as speeded skilled actions, including many speech actions. To the extent that philosophers have addressed these kinds of action at all, their theories have run the gamut from complete mindlessness to full-blown intellectualism. The chapter critiques some influential accounts of the latter sort, after emphasizing that skilled actions are as distinctively human as are our rational capacities.

2.1 Habits

We begin with habitual actions, which are arguably ubiquitous in everyday life. But we first need to delineate the target phenomenon, since the term "habit" is used in a variety of ways, both in ordinary speech and among cognitive scientists. Indeed, almost any regularly repeated activity can be loosely described as a habit. One might say of a family that rents the same property for the same weeks every year for their summer vacation, for example, "They are creatures of habit: they always go back to the same house in Provence" or "They habitually rent the same place every year." But while comparatively less thought and planning might be involved, still multiple decisions need to be taken for the vacation to happen in the way that it does each year. Someone in the family needs to confirm the dates with the owners, arrange for the deposit to be paid – which requires finding out whether the price has changed – and then book the tickets for their trip. These are not things that can happen automatically, without conscious thought. However, the family might keep returning to the same place for vacation each year partly because it makes planning easier, and requires *less* thought: they already know how to get there, where the local shops are, which are the best local restaurants, and so on. The sense of "habit" I want to focus on, in contrast, concerns actions that are undertaken automatically, without prior decision-making.

People suffering from various kinds of addiction are also often described as having a habit. We talk of someone's drug habit, their gambling habit, their nicotine habit, and so on. And cognitive scientists often use the term "habit" in this way, too. But the actions in question are by no means automatic. They often require detailed planning – to secure access to the drug, to get to a casino, and so on. They can also involve powerful desires that can be hard to resist, and the object of one's addiction can seem extraordinarily attractive – in the language used in affective neuroscience, it is extremely "incentive salient" (Berridge & Kringelbach 2008; Olney et al. 2018). One's thoughts keep getting drawn back to the object of addiction, one feels a strong desire to engage with it, and there are apt to be action-urges involved that take some effort to suppress (Sripada 2022). In short, the object of addiction exerts a kind of magnet-like attractiveness.

The sort of habit that I want to focus on here, in contrast, involves stereotyped previously learned action sequences that are apt to be triggered by environmental cues without evaluation or decision-making. The verbal sequences involved in knowing one's times-tables, for example, are habitual in this sense. If someone says, "Seven sevens are … " one might automatically think "forty-nine." Similarly, the transitions involved in one's knowledge of the alphabet are habitual, with each letter in the sequence automatically cued by the previous one. Indeed, if asked what letter comes before "T," many of us might have to start from the beginning and run the sequence through, or begin with an earlier sub-sequence, like "L, M, N, O, P."

Habits in this sense are sequences of action that have become chained together by repetition-learning and are apt to be inflexible in their execution. It is effortful to repeat the alphabet while missing out all the vowels, or while saying only odd-numbered letters, for example. Yet they are not (as are addiction-habits) affectively laden (Miller et al. 2018, 2019). There is nothing "hot" or emotional about saying one's times-tables or repeating the alphabet. Habits in this sense often have triggering cues, but not always – one only repeats the alphabet when requested or when one needs to do so, for example, but the step from each letter to the next is nevertheless triggered automatically by the previous one, which is why it is hard to take things out of order or repeat the alphabet in reverse. The triggering cues characteristic of addiction-habits, in contrast – like a whiff of someone's second-hand smoke for someone trying to give up tobacco – are apt to trigger strong affective urges and desires.

Ordinary people tend to vastly underestimate the extent to which their daily lives are governed by habits (Wood & Rünger 2016) – just as do philosophers who embrace the standard belief-desire model. This is because in most cases one knows the goals in whose service the habit was formed, and so when one's attention is drawn to something one is doing or has just done, one's mentalizing system kicks in and readily interprets the action as goal-directed and purposive. In fact, people are subject to an illusion here that is not unlike the illusion of the richness of the visual field. As is now familiar to many people, one in fact only experiences a limited amount of detail at any one time.[1] People fail to be aware of this because they are ignorant of the fact that their eyes are continually in motion, making about three saccades each second outside of their awareness, picking up detail wherever they focus. Similarly, people are unaware that many of their actions are habitual, because whenever their attention is drawn to them they interpret them as goal-directed.

Consider someone who habitually sets about making coffee when they first enter the kitchen in the morning. In the early stages of habit-formation this requires thought and decision-making (and still does, when staying at a friend's house with an unfamiliar kitchen). But it no longer does. An initiating cue – stepping into the kitchen and turning on the light – automatically triggers the next stage in the process: taking down the coffee-pot from the shelf, then the coffee-grinder. If asked, "Why are you reaching for the coffee-pot?" one will reply, "Because I want to make coffee, of course." But in many such cases this is an error. While the making-morning-coffee habit ends with a cup of coffee, which is rewarding / enjoyed, there need have been no prior thoughts of coffee-drinking (either conscious or unconscious), nor was any decision taken to make coffee. Rather, the contextual cue initiated a well-rehearsed associative sequence, much like repeating the alphabet.

It is only when something goes awry that one realizes one has been acting out of mere habit. One finds oneself doing something inappropriate, like handing down a tea-pot instead of the coffee-pot because someone had left the tea-pot in the normal coffee-pot location on the shelf. Or having gone to the upstairs bathroom to collect some nail scissors on a gloomy afternoon one

[1] Dennett (1991a) provides a nice try-it-at-home demonstration: select a playing card at random without looking at it. Then with your eyes fixed straight ahead, hold the card at arm's length out to one side and slowly move your arm toward the center. Most people are amazed by how close the card has to get to the point of fixation before it is seen in enough detail to be recognized.

finds oneself in the middle of brushing one's teeth. Turning on the light when entering the bathroom had triggered the brush-teeth-before-bed habitual sequence, without one intending or deciding to brush them.

It should be stressed, however, that although habits are often *initiated* unconsciously by a cue of some sort, those cues themselves may be consciously perceived. And likewise, conscious experiences of the actions that constitute the habit will generally *accompany* those actions, even if they do not guide them. (See the sections of this chapter that follow.) Habitual action is quite unlike sleepwalking. It is generally accompanied by conscious experience and conscious thought. But it is not guided by those experiences, as we will see, and the only "decisions" involved are often low-level sensorimotor ones involving such things as one's precise grip-strength and hand orientation. (I have placed scare-quotes around the word "decision" here since this is obviously not an instance of deciding that commonsense psychology would recognize. More on this in due course.)

So, while people are well aware that they possess habits, and sometimes act habitually without any represented goal, it seems they greatly underestimate the extent to which the latter is the case. Indeed, by some estimates, almost half of daily human behaviors are habit-driven rather than intentional (Ji & Wood 2007; Neal et al. 2011, 2012; Wood & Rünger 2016). So, large swaths of human action are not best explained in terms of belief-desire pairings, in the way that philosophers generally assume. In fact, many of the actions that one performs frequently and regularly in the same or similar contexts are cued by features of the context and executed automatically, independently of one's goals. Thus, one did not reach for the coffee-pot because one wanted to make coffee and believed that retrieving the pot would help one achieve that goal. Rather, one reached for the pot because features of the context triggered a stereotyped action sequence.

It is worth noting in this connection that perception of features of the environment that afford or facilitate well-practiced actions can (and do) activate related motor plans directly, even though the action-tendencies in question generally get suppressed because inconsistent with one's current goals. There is extensive evidence from both monkeys and humans that perception of familiar tools, for example, will automatically activate the motor plans for grasping and using them. While these findings have been interpreted as supporting sensorimotor theories of tool-concepts (Barsalou 2009), in fact they are equally accepted by those who have argued for more abstract, amodal, accounts (Negri et al. 2007).

Such automatically activated tool-use motor plans need to be inhibited by top-down executive signals if they are not to be carried through to completion (Frith et al. 2000). As a result, people with certain forms of frontal lobe damage suffer from what is called "utilization syndrome." They have difficulty inhibiting themselves from grasping and using things in accordance with their familiar affordances even when instructed not to (Lhermitte 1983, 1986). Likewise, people who have damage to other parts of the frontal ("executive") lobes of the brain can suffer from so-called "alien-hand syndrome," in which one hand repeatedly responds to things that afford action – like undoing the buttons on one's shirt, or turning the pages of a book one is attempting to read – outside of the agent's control (Feinberg et al. 1992).

What these findings suggest is that habitual and well-practiced movements will get performed automatically unless there is an active goal of some sort that inhibits them. As a result, there are likely to be a couple of distinct ways in which habitual actions can get caused. One is where there is currently *no* active goal to compete with or suppress the automatically triggered motor plan. Thus one might stumble into the kitchen in the morning with no goal actively in mind (whether conscious or unconscious), reaching for the coffee-pot in consequence. But the other is where there *is* an active goal, but one that is consistent with the performance of the motor plan, and so one that doesn't suppress it. Thus, even in cases where one does actively aim at making coffee (whether consciously or not) the contribution of that goal to the act of reaching for the coffee-pot may be negative and indirect. One "decides" not to interfere with or suppress a motor instruction that is already in train, caused by an environmental cue of some sort.

2.2 Online Control of Action

The question of how actions, once cued or selected, are guided in their execution requires us to delve into the two-visual-systems hypothesis (Milner & Goodale 1995), which is now much more than a hypothesis. We have known on anatomical grounds for a long time that there are two distinct (albeit interacting) main pathways from the retina to visual cortex, populated by differing types of neuron – Magnocellular and Parvocellular (Van Essen et al. 1992). Both project to primary visual cortex (V1) via a subcortical structure known as the lateral geniculate nucleus, although importantly (as we will see) a Magnocellular pathway also projects directly to dorsal parietal cortex via another structure called the superior colliculus.

Magnocellular neurons are insensitive to color and have comparatively poor spatial discrimination, but are especially sensitive to motion (particularly fast motion); and they transmit information significantly quicker than do Parvocellular neurons (Edwards et al. 2021). Parvocellular neurons, in contrast, are specialized for representing colors and for fine-grained spatial discrimination.

While there is significant cross-talk between the two systems (especially in the early stages of processing), the Magnocellular pathway projects up through the back of the brain through parietal cortex, whereas the Parvocellular pathway projects forward along the sides of the brain through the lower (ventral) temporal cortices. The former has come to be known as "the dorsal stream" and the latter "the ventral stream." The dorsal stream is specialized for visual guidance of action, and only represents the locations and shapes of objects in a variety of body-centered and limb-centered coordinates. The ventral stream is specialized for object recognition and for conscious representation of the textures and colors of objects and their locations relative to one another in the environment. (For recent discussions see Goodale & Milner 2018; Ganel & Goodale 2019.)[2]

Strong evidence of the specific functions of the two visual streams comes (*inter alia*) from cases of neurological damage. People with damage to the dorsal stream can suffer from optic ataxia (Perenin & Vighetto 1988). They have no deficits in consciously perceiving the world, and can accurately identify objects, colors, and shapes, as well as the spatial positioning and orientation of objects, but they have severe deficits in visually guided reaching and grasping. They have difficulty orienting their hands correctly, have trouble reaching around obstacles, and tend either to reach too near or too far. Yet their difficulties are not ones of motor control as such (e.g. when their eyes are closed).

Bilateral damage to the ventral visual streams, in contrast, gives rise to the converse pattern of deficits. Famously, the patient D.F. studied by Milner and Goodale (1995) and Goodale and Milner (2018) suffered from visual form agnosia while being capable of normal reaching and grasping

[2] In fact the dorsal visual stream fractionates into three separate pathways, only one of which is specialized for the online visual guidance of movement (Kravitz et al. 2011). Another pathway projects to prefrontal cortex, where it underlies capacities for spatial working memory, and a third pathway projects to the inside surface of temporal cortex and the hippocampus, serving to link egocentric and allocentric spatial information to enable spatial navigation. In contrast with the sensorimotor ("how to") pathway, each of these second two dorsal pathways contributes to conscious experience. For simplicity, however, given our purposes here, I will continue to talk about "the two streams." See Ritchie et al. (2024) for a recent discussion showing why such talk is still warranted, despite the underlying complexity of the overall visual system.

behavior. She could not recognize objects, shapes, or their locations, and was at chance when attempting to describe them – although she still had some conscious experience of colors and textures utilizing spared components of the ventral pathway (but seemingly "unattached" to any object). Thus she performed no better than chance when attempting to distinguish among differently shaped and oriented blocks, and she was at chance when asked to indicate the orientation of a variously oriented letter-box-like slot. Yet when asked to reach and grasp an object (in fact a pencil held upright, say) she would reach normally to the correct position in limb-centered space with a normal finger-grip while insisting that she couldn't see where or what the object was. And when asked to post a letter through the varyingly oriented slot she was incapable of describing, she would orient her wrist and hand normally and in the correct position.

The dissociation between the two streams is also what explains the phenomenon of blindsight (Weiskrantz 1986, 1997). People with blindsight can have complete bilateral damage to primary visual cortex. In such cases they undergo no conscious visual experience. Exposed to a visual stimulus they say, truthfully, that they see nothing. But when asked to guess, they can distinguish an "X" from an "O," and they can trace with their arm the movement of a light across a screen. And at least one such person is able to avoid obstacles when walking across an unfamiliar cluttered room (de Gelder et al. 2008) – as could the surgically blindsighted chimpanzee Helen (Humphrey 1986). Although both the Magnocellular and Parvocellular pathways through primary visual cortex are equally damaged in such people, it seems that direct projections of Magnocellular neurons through the superior colliculus to the parietal cortex (mentioned earlier) are what explain their preserved abilities.

In summary, then, the ventral visual system is the one that issues in conscious visual experience. It utilizes a neural pathway from visual cortex forward through the lower portions of temporal cortex (along the sides of the brain), in the course of which it processes objects and their relations, issuing in object recognition, conceptualization, and a detailed representation of objects in allocentric space. When attended to, these representations are broadcast widely to prefrontal and other regions of cortex for reasoning, reporting, and action-planning, as well as for affective evaluation and the formation of long-term memories.

The dorsal (action-*guiding* or "how-to") system is significantly faster, traveling up the back of the brain toward motor cortex (which stretches in a band across the brain at the very back of the frontal cortex, just anterior to the central sulcus), as well as projecting directly to subcortical motor-control networks. It codes the positions and movements of objects in body-centered and limb-centered coordinates, and has a memory window of just a couple of seconds. It is the dorsal system that guides one's movements as one swings a bat at an oncoming ball, or as one reaches across the desk to pick up one's coffee cup; and it is the dorsal system that guides one's habitual actions, too, even when the latter are accompanied by conscious experience. The outputs of the dorsal system aren't themselves accessible to consciousness. Although it has been pointed out by philosophers before that conscious experiences can guide our decision-making and planning of actions, but not the details of the resulting movements themselves (Carruthers 2000; Clark 2001), it seems the message has still not been fully absorbed by the field; and in some cases it has been badly misunderstood.[3]

2.3 Fast Acting

When a baseball batter faces a fastball, the speed and direction of motion of the ball are processed swiftly by the dorsal stream, and a swing with a matching trajectory may be initiated. This happens significantly in advance of the batter becoming conscious of the motion of the ball. So when the batter says that he swung as he did because he saw that the pitch was a high fastball, he is mistaken. (Or at least, he is mistaken if by "saw" he means to imply "consciously," as he probably does.) For it takes about 350 milliseconds or more for a stimulus to become conscious (Dehaene 2014), which is almost as long as it takes a 96-mph fastball to travel from the pitcher's hand across the plate. His conscious experience played no role in his selection and initiation of the swing, in fact. But of course he is not aware that he initiated the swing before he consciously saw the ball. This is because time, like everything else, is represented in the brain, not given by the actual time of representing (Dennett & Kinsbourne 1992). So the first sight of the ball is represented / experienced as occurring shortly before proprioception represents the timing of action-initiation. There is thus

[3] For example, Briscoe and Schwenkler (2015) claim that the two-visual-systems view is inconsistent with the perspectival nature of conscious visual experience. This is on the grounds that Milner and Goodale (1995) describe the outputs of the ventral (conscious) stream as "allocentric" (or object-centered), whereas the outputs of the dorsal (action-guiding) one are said to be body-centered. But as Foley et al. (2015) point out in reply, the term "allocentric" is used here to emphasize that ventral vision represents the spatial relationships of perceived objects to one another (as well as to oneself), whereas the dorsal stream just codes locations in body-centered and limb-centered coordinates. The intention was never to deny that some objects are consciously seen as located in front of others (from one's own perspective), nor that others are positioned to one side of oneself rather than another.

nothing in one's conscious experience to challenge the illusion that such experiences guide one's actions.

Likewise, consider a professional tennis player receiving a serve from his opponent. A first serve from a male tennis player often travels at speeds in excess of 125 mph (>200 km/h). Since the tennis court is 78 feet long, this means that the ball will reach a receiver standing 12 feet behind the baseline in half a second. And since such serves are often returned, this means that the receiver must be able to identify the initial trajectory of the ball to select a forehand or backhand response, and then, while continuing to track the ball's trajectory and spin, generate and execute the movements of body, arm, and wrist necessary to bring the racket into contact with the ball – almost all of this happening prior to consciously experiencing the ball's motion. And just as this analysis would predict, a neurophysiological study of people engaged in a simple Go / No-go response-task found activity across sensorimotor systems corresponding to their decision whether or not to respond a mere 150 milliseconds following stimulus onset – well before the stimulus would have been consciously experienced (Ledberg et al. 2007; see also Wong et al. 2015).

Of course the tennis player himself (like the batter facing a fastball described earlier) is unaware that he is responding to unconscious visual information. On the contrary, proprioception of his own movements is integrated with the visual information being processed by the ventral stream and results in a conscious experience of himself seeing the initial trajectory of the ball shortly before he starts to move to set up his swing. For this is what enables sensory systems to make "best sense" of his overall experience. And that is the way he will describe what happened in retrospect. ("I saw the serve was coming to my forehand with heavy top-spin, so I went for a high forehand return stroke.") But if by "see" he means "consciously see" – as is almost certainly the case for most people, since most are ignorant of the existence of the unconscious "how-to" visual system – then his explanation is erroneous.

As noted earlier, however, conscious experience does guide action-planning on longer time-scales, of the sort that depends on the executive functions of prefrontal cortex. Such decision-making need not itself be conscious, but can be about implementing one's current goals in response to conscious experience of the situation. Under speeded conditions, in contrast, conscious experience isn't what guides or selects an action. Moreover, even in cases where one first reflects and then decides to do one thing rather than another, conscious experience isn't what guides the detailed execution of one's movements thereafter in an online fashion. When one decides one wants a second cup of coffee, for example, and reaches out and grasps the handle of the pot (which one consciously sees) to pour another, one's reaching and grasping themselves are *not* consciously guided.

In conclusion of this section, it should be stressed that the timing estimates relied upon above, for conscious experiences of the sort that can influence executive-level decision-making, are not themselves controversial. While there is debate about the timing of *phenomenal* consciousness, with some claiming that it happens more swiftly, identical to the contents of a fragile short-term memory system that figures earlier in the processing stream (Block 2007, 2011), it is *access* consciousness that matters for our purposes. Our interest, here, is just in the timing of whatever visual representations are available to frontal decision-making and reporting processes, not in identifying the neural correlates of phenomenal experience, nor in solving the so-called "hard problem" of consciousness. (On the latter, see Carruthers 2019.) And no one disputes that it takes between 350 and 500 milliseconds from the onset of visual stimulation to the "broadcasting" of the resulting visual information to downstream executive decision-making systems.

It is beginning to seem, then, that both philosophers and ordinary folk vastly over-extend the scope of the standard belief-desire model. That model is erroneously applied to a great many of our actions that are in fact initiated habitually, as well as to actions that respond swiftly to initiating cues. While in both cases the actions are generally *accompanied* by conscious experience, they are not caused by it; nor do the actions in question result from belief-desire decision-making.

2.4 Skilled Performance

While the acquisition of a skill generally requires conscious thought and careful attention to the results of one's practice attempts, some philosophers have described skilled performance itself as unintelligent, indeed "mindless" (Dreyfus 2002; Di Nucci 2013). This is, as others have pointed out, an error (Fridland 2017; Pacherie & Mylopoulos 2021). Skilled action, and indeed any well-practiced movement, involves a complex interplay of representational processes, in addition to being influenced in an online fashion by one's background goals. Moreover, it involves processes that have many of the functional properties of decision-making – although in this case happening within the sensorimotor system rather than consciously within frontal executive systems. But all this will take some unpacking.

Whenever a potential target for action is presented, the sensorimotor system constructs what is called an "inverse model" (so-called for reasons that will become clear shortly: it is the opposite of a "forward model"). This is an active representation of the motor-movements that could reach or accomplish the target. (Actually, multiple such models are constructed in parallel and compete with one another for selection; Cisek 2007.) The motor instructions involved in each of these inverse models creates a subsidiary signal (called an "efference copy" or "corollary discharge") that is used to create a sensory "forward model" of the expected sensory consequences of the movement – that is, what one's own movements should look like and what they should feel like proprioceptively. Once an action has been selected and initiated, if its forward model doesn't fully align with one's goals, the motor instructions can be swiftly updated, prior to receipt of any actual sensory feedback (Wolpert & Flanagan 2001; McNamee & Wolpert 2019). Forward models are then integrated with sensory feedback to fine-tune the action as it unfolds. As one's actions become more skilled, the initial inverse models become more precise, with closer to optimal selection among alternatives, and motor execution itself shows less variance or "noise," with lesser need for online corrections (Shmuelof et al. 2012).

As an action unfolds over time, the inverse and forward models are continually updated to achieve the goal of the action. The models themselves are nonconceptual motor and sensory representations, involving continuous – or analog-magnitude – representations of limb and body movements as well as of expected visual and proprioceptive feedback. Yet in one important sense the process is not an automatic one (*contra* Fridland 2017). For "choices" are made during execution to keep the action aligned with one's goals. Thus when a displacing force is applied to one's arm while reaching to grasp a peg, for example, one rapidly compensates to bring the movement back on track to complete the grasp; but when such a force is applied while one is reaching to grasp a horizontal bar, no compensation occurs – one simply grasps the bar further along its length in the direction that one's arm was displaced (Scott 2012). Here the sensorimotor system displays its sensitivity to one's background goals ("grasp the peg / grasp the bar"), demonstrating that its operations are not fully automatic.

It is widely agreed that the motor system is organized hierarchically (Jeannerod 2006; Merel et al. 2019). An action might begin with a goal or intention, which may (or may not – we will return to this issue in Chapter 5) have a conceptual / propositional content (e.g. *pick up that hammer*). This sets in train a cascade of increasingly low-level inverse and forward models of the action, bottoming out in instructions to tighten or relax specific muscle groups. Intentions and goals are stored in anterior prefrontal cortex (Volle et al. 2011; Mommenejad & Haynes 2013), and when activated create downstream activity in premotor and motor cortices. (As noted earlier, the latter are positioned in a band across frontal cortex just anterior to the central sulcus that divides frontal from parietal cortices.) But processing in motor cortices occurs in interaction with activity in the cerebellum (which is the corrugated "mini-brain" positioned underneath the visual cortices at the back of the brain). It is thought to be the cerebellum that is responsible for swiftly creating the inverse and forward models of the action that govern the latter's production alongside the evolving motor instructions and sensory feedback (Galea et al. 2011; Honda et al. 2018; Hull 2020).

One hallmark of skilled action is that it is generally composed of sub-components that are habit-like – that is, comprising associatively chained-together sub-sub-components (Diedrichsen & Kornysheva 2015). This is one reason why skilled performance can be so much faster than less-skilled actions, since fewer decisions need to be made during execution. Instead of selecting each individual movement in competition with others, one can just select a smaller number of habit-like "chunks." As we noted in Section 2.1, habit-sequences can be initiated by goals, as when one chooses to repeat the alphabet aloud, or counts the items in a set. But they can also form components of skilled actions, and can be selected and implemented in various different sequences depending on the circumstances. (Will one chop and fry the onions before cracking and beating the eggs when making an omelet, or vice versa?) Indeed, skill acquisition generally involves the "chunking together" and habitizing of component movements.

Another hallmark of truly skilled performance is its flexibility. A golfer whose ball has landed on the lip of a bunker may need to stand two feet below it and hold the club halfway along its length – something he may never have had to do before in quite that way. And a soccer player dribbling the ball up the pitch will continually be making adjustments of feet and ball as the situation changes (tacklers approach, her teammates become more or less open for a pass). Some of this flexibility may involve conscious decision-making and conscious mental rehearsal of possible variants of the action. (This is likely to be true of the golfer just described.) But often it occurs in an online fashion. This is very likely to be true of the soccer player; and similarly, a skilled dancer will need to respond continuously to variations in her partner's movements and swiftly recover from any errors that he makes.

A number of things help to explain the online flexibility of skilled action. One is that skilled agents can adopt general action-strategies suitable for the circumstances they find themselves in. A cricket batsman, for example, might adopt a general policy at a particular point in the game of playing defensively, thereafter limiting, in an online fashion, the range of actions that he selects among as the bowler releases the ball (Papineau 2013). Another factor is the continuous interplay of inverse and forward models in controlling performance, modulated by unexpected changes in incoming sensory information (e.g. one's dance-partner stumbles slightly). And yet another is that multiple inverse and forward models of alternative movements remain active in parallel. These continually compete with one another, and as circumstances change, some may become more dominant than others, shifting the control of one's overt behavior (Cisek & Kalaska 2010; Pezzulo & Cisek 2016). Moreover, as Fridland (2019) emphasizes, one effect of the chunking that takes place in skill acquisition is that those chunks remain independent and can be flexibly combined and recombined as needed.

Skilled action-sequences are thus composed of habit-like sub-components that are more or less strongly associatively chained together and with their triggering cues, and that can be flexibly combined according to the agent's goals and the affordances of the situation. It is likely, then, that even skilled sequences that happen at slow enough speeds that they could, in principle, result from conscious decision-making are actually guided by "choices" made within the sensorimotor system. But in these cases, too (as in the examples of speeded action discussed in Section 2.3), the agent will generally be blind to the fact that this is happening. As a result, people may offer retrospective interpretations using the common-sense belief-desire framework that are actually false. For example, an amateur tennis player in a fairly slow-moving game might say, "I saw that my opponent was behind the baseline, and believed that I could win the point with a drop-shot, so I decided to go for that"; but in fact the choice may have happened internally within the sensorimotor system.

It does appear that flexible action control involves sensorimotor *decisions* about which movement to execute next – or at least events that are functionally and computationally very similar to some of the kinds of unreflective decision-making that take place within executive (prefrontal) systems. Examples of the latter involve perceptual decision-making. Someone participating in an experiment involving random-dot stereograms may be required to judge swiftly on each trial whether the predominant movement of the dots is to the left or the right. This sort of decision-making has been successfully modeled in terms of neural accumulators that build their activity following stimulus onset (one corresponding to *left* and one for *right*), mutually inhibiting each other as they do so (Usher & McClelland 2001; Forstmann et al. 2016; van den Berg et al. 2016a). When one of them reaches a preset criterion-level of activity (set implicitly by the agent in light of the demands of a speed / accuracy trade-off), that constitutes a judgment of *left* or *right*, and the person responds accordingly.[4]

Indeed, decision-making of all sorts is likely to be realized in computationally similar neural accumulator processes (Murakami et al. 2014). Neural populations representing the options under consideration will build in activity in noisy, stochastic, and mutually inhibitory fashion, integrating the outputs of upstream populations that represent likelihoods, costs, and outcome values. When one of these populations dominates the others sufficiently to reach a criterion-level, set in the context by the urgency of the decision, then that *constitutes* a decision, either causing a representation of the action to be stored in prospective memory as an intention for the future or directly causing a cascading set of motor instructions to be issued.

Moreover, we know that the motor system is sensitive to a variety of factors of the sort that regularly enter into executive forms of decision-making. We have already seen that one's movements are influenced by one's goals (as when one does, or does not, adjust for a perturbed movement, depending on whether or not it impacts goal-achievement). But they are also influenced by biomechanical costs. It appears that one factor in action-selection and action-modification concerns estimates of the energetic costs involved (Cos et al. 2014). And as some background values become more salient (an opportunity of a different sort becomes available mid-action) that will influence one's movements too – perhaps bringing them to a stop, or taking them in a different direction (Pezzulo & Cisek 2016).

The differing forms of decision do figure at different positions in one's overall cognitive architecture, of course, and thus differ in their functional

[4] Models of the sort described here are variously known in the literature as "sequential sampling," "drift diffusion," or "leaky competitive accumulator" theories (Usher & McClelland 2001; Pleskac & Busermeyer 2010; Forstmann et al. 2016), and can take a variety of forms. Although there are some differences of detail among the various approaches, these need not concern us here. It is worth noting that recent findings suggest, however, that rather than the decision-criterion shifting with circumstances (as was originally assumed), there is a fixed criterion-level. What the need for speed adds is an independent neural "boost" to the various competing accumulators – driven by one's physiological arousal – so that they reach the fixed criterion more swiftly (Hanks & Summerfield 2017).

roles. A decision that is taken after conscious consideration and evaluation of the alternatives (whether deliberate and reflective or swift and intuitive) figures within executive systems of the brain. In contrast, a decision by a skilled tennis player or baseball batter among potential ways of responding to an oncoming ball involves swift evaluation of inverse and sensory forward models, with the comparisons involving activity in the dorsal visual pathway, motor cortex, and cerebellum in a manner that is simply inaccessible to consciousness. These differences in functional role do mark them out as distinct *kinds* of decision, at least. But is there any reason to prioritize executive forms of decision, insisting that sensorimotor forms are merely decision-*like*, rather than being decisions properly so called? Perhaps not, from a cognitive-science perspective. But I think nothing of scientific importance hangs on the question.

In summary of this section, we can conclude that skilled action is representational through-and-through. It is flexible, responding swiftly to changes in circumstances, costs, and opportunities. Indeed, it gives every appearance of at least a sort of low-level intelligence, utilizing processes within sensorimotor systems that closely resemble unreflective forms of decision-making. It is certainly not mindless (*contra* Di Nucci 2013), unless one equates "mind" with "conscious mind." But no one who takes cognitive science seriously does that. Yet most skilled actions fall outside the scope of the standard belief-desire model of action-explanation.

2.5 Speech as Skilled Action

Speech is a form of skilled action too, of course, and many of the same explanatory factors apply. (This will prove important in Chapter 4, when we come to discuss inner speech alongside other kinds of mental action.) It is often speeded and unreflective, as happens in quick-fire conversation or when arguing heatedly with an opponent. Indeed, speech production is extraordinarily flexible and skilled. And generally, when people speak, they succeed in communicating what they mean.

The traditional view has been that the production process begins with a *message to be communicated* (Levelt 1989). This would be a propositional content of some sort (a thought) that gets motorically encoded, first by selecting lexical items for an appropriate syntactic frame, and then using that to generate phonological plans and lower-level motor instructions. But this view is arguably too simple (even if it was once a useful idealization). In fact, speech production in general (like speech comprehension; Hickok & Poeppel 2007) seems to proceed in parallel (or at least interactively; Nozari et al. 2011), with decisions about *what* to say being taken while one is in the process of saying it (Dennett 1991a; Lind et al. 2014). If so, then one generally doesn't *first* formulate a determinate message *before* expressing it in speech; rather one often formulates messages *by* expressing them into speech (that is to say, in the course of doing so), perhaps involving competition among multiple possibilities.

One consideration supporting this idea comes from models of motor control quite generally. For forward-modeling accounts always make provision, not just for comparisons between sensory forward models and afferent feedback, but also for comparisons between forward and inverse models (or the goals of the action). This makes it possible to make motor adjustments in advance of afferent feedback in cases where the movements selected are in some way inadequate or suboptimal. But they also enable one to make adjustments to lower-level goals in the light of higher-level ones. In the case of complex actions that unfold over time (such as the production of a spoken sentence), one might expect that detailed goals (which words to select, in which order, with what tone of voice) would get chosen serially, involving continual interactions between one's goals at the most abstract level and the forward models produced as those goals are progressively implemented. And indeed, consistent with this suggestion, when people participating in introspection-sampling studies are "beeped" in the middle of saying something, they most commonly report that they don't know in any detail how the sentence in question would have finished up (Hurlburt & Schwitzgebel 2007).

Moreover, we know from decades of work in social psychology that there are generally multiple motivational factors at work, influencing how people answer questions and express themselves in speech (Schwarz 1999). There are dissonance effects and self-presentation effects, for example, and people may modify what they say when they anticipate disagreement from their audience. (See Carruthers 2011, 2015 for review and discussion.) Note that most of this literature concerns how people choose to answer a single determinate question, such as, "How opposed would you be to a rise in tuition-costs next semester?" We can assume that in free conversation there will be many more factors influencing what people choose to say in the moment (including a variety of communicative goals, memories or feelings evoked by the circumstances, estimates of what one's interlocutor already knows or believes, as well as factors in the immediately preceding conversation).

These suggestions are consistent with the data reported by Novick et al. (2010), that patients with damage to Broca's area (leading to a form of production aphasia) also show much wider deficits, especially in their capacity to inhibit prepotent actions. (For example, they perform quite poorly in the Stroop test.[5]) For the expressive difficulties experienced by some of these people emerge most clearly in cases where there are many competing things they could say. For example, when asked to generate verbs associated with a given noun, patients with damage to Broca's area may become paralyzed when prompted with "ball," since there are many related verbs to choose from ("throw," "kick," "bounce," "pass," "catch," and so on). But they may perform much better when prompted with "scissors," which is associated with just a single action ("cut"). Similarly, healthy people given the same test show increased activity in Broca's area when selecting a verb out of many alternatives, as well as during conflicting-action trials of the Stroop test. At the very least these findings establish that speech production involves competition among expressive *actions*, if not competition among intended messages.

The latter claim is supported, however, by findings from patients with Wernicke's aphasia, who often have severe speech-comprehension difficulties (Langland-Hassan 2016). For although the speech of such patients can be fluent, it is often garbled or completely unintelligible, containing misused words, non-words, and meaningless concatenations of the "Green ideas sleep furiously" variety (LaPointe 2005). Since Wernicke's aphasia is primarily a speech-comprehension deficit, we can infer that speech production normally proceeds in parallel with comprehension, evaluating the contents attaching to a range of potential speech actions while they are being constructed and implemented (Matsumoto et al. 2004; Aristei et al. 2011; Pickering & Garrod 2013). In fact, this may be the most common use of the forward-modeling networks mentioned earlier, with partially constructed motor plans generating sensory forward models that are semantically evaluated by the comprehension system and assessed against the abstract goals involved in the exchange. And in general the whole process will proceed unconsciously (as well as quite swiftly, given the speed with which normal speech can be generated).

To the extent that people are unaware of the multiple influences on their speech actions, their explanations for why they say the things that they do will be mistaken, or at best only partially correct. Moreover, not only are

[5] The Stroop test requires people to name the font-colors of a set of words as quickly and accurately as possible, under two conditions, in only one of which are the words themselves color-words that name colors that differ from their fonts. In the latter case one has to inhibit the habitual response, which is to read the word rather than name its font-color. The difference in reaction time between the two conditions is thought to provide a reliable measure of executive-function ability (MacLeod 1992).

the things that people say (sometimes) intelligent, but speech production itself displays all the flexibility and intelligence distinctive of other forms of skilled action. And like other forms of speeded and skilled action, many speech actions fall outside the scope of the standard belief-desire model.

2.6 Skills as Distinctively Human

We noted in Section 1.1, when presenting the standard belief-desire model, that one reason philosophers have given for their almost-exclusive focus on so-called "intentional action" is that these are the actions that are thought to reflect our distinctively human rational capacities. If this is the reason for their comparative neglect of speeded and skilled actions, then it is based on a mistake. For capacities for novel forms of skilled action are at least as distinctively human as are capacities for rational reasoning, enabled by uniquely extensive projections from human motor cortex to subcortical motor neurons in the medulla and spinal cord (Striedter 2005). Many animals are capable of fine degrees of physical control of a specialized sort, of course. Think of an elephant picking up a single peanut with its trunk, or a hummingbird that maintains its position in front of a nectar-bearing flower while being buffeted by a breeze. But no other animals are capable of learning anything like the range of precise physical skills that humans can acquire.

Other animals can be trained to execute specific skilled sequences of action, of course. (Think, here, of a seal trained to catch and balance a ball on its nose, or a dog trained to walk on its hind legs.) But even then they lack the capacity for flexible goal-directed use of those skills, in the way that a soccer player can decide to execute a pass at a particular point in the game, or a tennis player can opt for a specific cross-court top-spin backhand rather than a slice. And no other animal is similarly motivated to practice and rehearse physical skills in the way that humans do, seemingly taking their own skill acquisition as an intrinsic goal (Donald 2005). Indeed, without our distinctive capacity for skill learning, the basics of material culture could never have gotten started. There would have been no control of fire; no precision-made stone tools; no multi-part, finely constructed, specialized hunting weapons; no sewing of clothes; no weaving of cloth; and no pottery or basket making.

At least since Greek times, it has been common for philosophers to characterize what is distinctive about human nature in terms of reason and rationality. Humans, it is said, are rational animals. And if humans are rational creatures then it might make sense to focus almost exclusively on the kinds of action (intentional actions) that manifest our rational natures. But in fact it is more accurate to say that humans are *cultural* creatures (Boyd et al. 2011; Henrich 2016). It is culture and capacities for cultural learning that enabled premodern humans to adapt to every environment on the planet, from savannahs, to jungles, to mountains, to temperate forests, to deserts, and even to the frozen arctic. Moreover, although individual intelligence and innovation play some role in cultural adaptation, in fact chance and copying errors during imitative learning over extended periods of time are just as, if not more, important. Indeed, most cultural products and skills are actually opaque to their users, and have to be learned blindly.

Among hunter-gatherers (as well as in small-scale societies more generally), much of the extended childhood and adolescence that is distinctive of the genus *Homo* (and especially *Homo sapiens*) is devoted to acquiring the physical skills necessary to be a productive member of the group. These would include tool-manufacture out of stone, bone, antlers, or wood, as well as the motor skills needed to use those tools effectively – throwing, cutting, scraping, sewing, carving, weaving, cooking, building, and much more. An indication of how challenging the learning process can be is that hunter-gatherer children don't start to make a positive net contribution to their group's food production until their mid-to-late teens (Kaplan et al. 2000). In fact, it is capacities for accurate imitation and skill learning that lie at the heart of human distinctiveness, along with capacities to learn and internalize cultural values and norms (Chudek & Henrich 2011; Henrich 2016).

In addition, many of our rational capacities are themselves acquired through cultural imitation and (now) explicit forms of intellectual training (Henrich & Muthukrishna 2024). While some rational capacities appear to be innate, and are present in pre-linguistic infants (Cesana-Arlotti et al. 2018, 2020), at least some of these are shared with other animals (Ferrigno et al. 2021). But many others – especially so-called "System 2" reasoning capacities – are culturally acquired (Kahneman 2011). And even if Mercier and Sperber (2017) are right that there is an innately channeled adaptation for argumentation, this, too, will be grounded in our capacity for skill acquisition, since language-use is itself a skill, as we have seen.

If the philosophy of action is aimed at characterizing and explaining the forms of action that are distinctively human, then the standard belief-desire model needs to be abandoned, or at least severely restricted in scope. For even if most skilled sequences of action are goal-directed, the individual components of those sequences are not selected in light of one's beliefs and desires. Although a skilled agent might initiate action with the goal of knitting a sweater, or making an omelet, or winning a game of tennis, from that point on many of the actions in the subsequent performance of the skill are selected and guided seemingly automatically within the sensorimotor system, with no further deliberation or executive-level ("conscious") choice.

2.7 Philosophers on Know-How

Some philosophers have attempted to extend the standard model to behavioral skills and abilities (described as "know-how") by defending a strongly intellectualist account, claiming that these are actually kinds of knowledge or belief. On this view, know-how is really a kind of propositional knowledge (Stanley & Williamson 2001, 2017; Stanley 2011a, 2011b; Pavese 2017; Pavese & Beddor 2023). Knowing *how* to do something is said to be a mental state of the same general type as knowing *who* did something, knowing *when* something was done, knowing *where* something happened, and so on. In each case the knowledge involved is comprised of a proposition that answers a question ("who did it?" "when was it done?" "where was it done?"). In the case of knowing how, it is said to be comprised of one's propositional knowledge, of some way of acting, that acting in that way is an answer to the question, "how is it done?"

Some examples might help. If one knows *who* brought the donuts to the meeting, then one knows some proposition of the form, *N brought the donuts to the meeting*, for some *N* or *Ns*. Likewise, if one knows *when* the meeting ended, then one knows some proposition of the form, *T is the time the meeting finished*, for some specification of a time *T*. (This could be indexical – *a few moments ago* – or it could be descriptive – *when the last item was dealt with*, or perhaps, *as soon as it turned four p.m.*) And if one knows *where* to find donuts, then for some place or places *P*, one knows some proposition of the form, *P is a place where one can get donuts*. (Again, this knowledge could be indexical or descriptive.)

Similarly, then, if one knows *how* to navigate through the DC metro system, then one knows some proposition of the form, *W is a way of navigating the metro*. For example, what one knows might be this: first, locate your destination on the metro map; next, note the line-color of the metro-line it is on and the line-color of your present location (as well as the station-name where they intersect); then note the station-name located at the further end of the line you are on from your current position; finally, look for and follow that color and name on the signs as you proceed through the station. On this account, it seems that knowing *how* is somewhat like having knowledge of a recipe for doing something.

This account seems plausible enough for the example just described, and for many of the examples discussed by Stanley (2011b), such as knowing how to find coffee in New York City. But what of simple physical skills, like knowing how to crack eggs when making an omelet? This involves fine-grained movements and applications of force. If one had to specify what one knows in a proposition, one would have to do it demonstratively, saying, "Hold the egg like *so*, and then tap it on the edge of the bowl like *this*." Here important components of what one knows are repeatable action-types. So if knowing-how is propositional, then whatever underlies one's capacity for skilled action must also be propositional. The latter is exactly what Stanley and Williamson (2017) and Pavese and Beddor (2023) assert.

Stanley and Williamson claim that skills are *dispositions to form knowledge* of the sort needed to guide the action-types that manifest the skill. So the skill of cracking eggs (without breaking the yoke, and without breaking off pieces of shell into the bowl) is a disposition to form knowledge that an egg of *this* sort should be tapped on the side of a bowl of *that* sort like *so*. This doesn't appear to take us much further forward. For what is it to have knowledge of the action-type *like so*? How is that knowledge coded in propositional form such that it can then guide the action in question?

It is one thing to say that know-how and skills can be described in terms of sentences that attribute propositional knowledge. Up to a point, this is true. But it is quite another to say that know-how and skills are actually – really – constituted by such knowledge. Likewise, it is one thing to claim that our folk-psychology and/or our language *treats* know-how and skills as forms of knowledge-that. This, too, might well be true. (At least, I won't dispute it here.) But it is quite another matter to make a metaphysical claim about the real-world nature of know-how and skills (as Stanley and Williamson both do, it should be noted). For that, we need to turn to the science. Philosophical argument and analysis can't cut it, and common sense can be a misleading guide.[6,7]

[6] Note that implicit theories like folk-psychology and folk-physics are generally at least partly erroneous. This is because they only need to track the real structure of their domains closely enough to be useful for everyday purposes. And of course there are many additional pressures on linguistic structure besides truth-tracking, including ease-of-expression and ease-of-learning (Gibson et al. 2019). So philosophers who base metaphysical claims on linguistic analysis are even more likely to go wrong.

[7] In fairness, it should be noted that chapter 7 of Stanley (2011b) does purport to address the cognitive science of know-how. Much of the discussion is actually orthogonal to the main issues, however. For example, that chapter rebuts arguments from philosophers who claim that know-how can't be

Pavese and Beddor (2023) analyze skills in terms of propositional knowledge of a means of acting, but known under what they call a "practical mode of presentation." This in turn is said to be a matter of representing a means of acting in terms of one's basic practical abilities. Thus being skilled at chopping onions might be a matter of knowing a good way of chopping onions under a good (or sufficiently good) practical mode of presentation. And then to utilize that skill on a particular occasion is presumably a matter of calling to mind that knowledge and activating the practical abilities in question. But the latter are comprised of sets of motor instructions, which are quite un-concept-like. Moreover, when one activates the skill (grasping an onion and picking up the knife) the mental state in question has an imperative-like role, entirely different from the indicative, world-describing role characteristic of propositional knowledge.

I suppose it might be replied that when one activates the skill in a particular circumstance (chopping an onion) what one has knowledge of is the outcome – the fact that this onion has been chopped. But this would be to muddle prediction with causation. The activated skill isn't a predictive description of a future fact. It is rather a sequence of imperative-like motor instructions that are apt to cause or bring about such a fact. It is true, however, that one can call to mind one's knowledge of how to chop an onion by imaginatively representing the sequence of movements involved, and this might be what Pavese and Beddor (2023) mean by representing it "under a practical mode of presentation." But in fact one does this by activating the motor sequences in question, using them to create sensory forward models of what the resulting movements would look like and feel like while suppressing any actual movement, as we saw in Section 2.4. This is nothing remotely like knowledge of a proposition.

Moreover, skills and propositional knowledge implicate largely separate brain networks. Propositional knowledge is realized in networks centered on the hippocampus, medial temporal cortex, and/or the temporal poles, together with conceptual and sensory-like representations distributed across much of temporal and parietal cortices, as we will see in Chapter 7. Motor plans and skills, in contrast, are stored in premotor and motor regions of prefrontal cortex, and are learned, refined, and implemented in interactions between these regions, sensory systems, the hippocampus, and the cerebellum (Galea et al. 2011). It is obvious that we are dealing here with quite distinct mental kinds.

propositional because people can be unaware of it and can be unable to articulate it in speech, rather than actually examining the science of motor knowledge and motor control.

Consider an example of skilled action that is actually discussed by Stanley and Williamson (2017), drawing on the scientific findings of Yarrow et al. (2009). An expert cricket batter can estimate the likely trajectory and landing-spot of the ball from seeing the movements of the bowler's arm and wrist just moments prior to delivery. So here we have a disposition to form knowledge. But how is that knowledge coded? Almost certainly in nonconceptual sensory format. As a result of extensive prior experience of associations between bowling movements of various sorts and ball trajectory, perception of a specific instance of the former issues in a sensory prediction of the latter, representing speed, spin, trajectory, landing-place, and onward motion off the ground. If one had to represent this in the form of a proposition it would look something like this: *the ball will move at this speed, spinning at that rate, landing there, and bouncing thus*. But of course the actual representation that guides the batter's response need not (and almost certainly does not) deploy concepts like MOVE, SPEED, SPIN, and BOUNCE.

Indeed, since the representations picked out by "this [speed]," "that [rate]," "[landing] there," and "[bouncing] thus" must themselves be nonconceptual analog-magnitude ones, nothing is gained by insisting they must be embedded under concepts. It is simpler (and almost certainly correct) to suppose that the entire representation is an integrated set of analog-magnitude quasi-perceptual anticipations. The knowledge gained by the expert batter is not knowledge of a proposition, although it does depend upon implicit procedural knowledge of the relationships between arm movements and ball trajectories gained from previous experience. Indeed, as we saw in Section 2.2, perceptual guidance of action relies upon the dorsal visual stream, in which contents are coded in body-centered and limb-centered coordinates, and in which conceptual knowledge plays little or no role.

Having acquired knowledge of the future position and bounce of the ball (or more likely, *while* acquiring it – the processes overlap and interact in parallel), what is then involved in one's knowledge of the best way of responding / acting? This is nothing remotely like knowledge of the truth of a proposition. Rather, multiple motor plans are activated in parallel, issuing in sensory forward models of the resulting position and trajectory of one's bat, as well as forward models of the likely consequences for the ball when integrated with the incoming sensory prediction (which is updated by perception as the ball flies toward one). These are compared and evaluated (in part for the biomechanical costs involved; Cos et al. 2014), and the winning motor plan is implemented, interacting all the while with continually updated sensory information (Cisek & Kalaska 2010; McNamee & Wolpert 2019).

A sensory forward model is a representation in visual, proprioceptive, and sometimes auditory analog-magnitude codes of the likely sensory consequences of implementing a given motor plan (such as a step forward with a driving movement of the bat, or a step back and an upright blocking motion of the bat). This can be described in propositional terms, somewhat as follows: *if that action were implemented the result would be this position of the body and that movement of the bat there.* But of course the considerations discussed earlier give us every reason to think that this is an observer's gloss on what happens, not a representation that is actually deployed in the mind of the batter. Indeed, the use of sensory forward models to fine-tune and control action is of extremely ancient provenance, and can be found even in dragonflies (Mischiati et al. 2014), who almost certainly lack concepts like ACTION and BODY.

Now, what is the content of a motor plan itself? Is that constituted by knowledge of a proposition? Almost certainly not. To begin, a motor plan is more like an imperative, with world-to-mind direction of fit (it is designed to get the world to fit the plan), not a belief-like knowledge-state, which would have a mind-to-world direction of fit, constituting knowledge of how things are, or will be. It amounts to a set of instructions for coordinated movements of the body and limbs, initiating (if implemented) a cascade of ever more precise instructions ending with the constriction or relaxation of specific muscles or muscle groups (Mylopoulos & Pacherie 2017; Pacherie & Mylopoulos 2021). Moreover, not only are the representational format and content of motor plans quite un-belief-like and quite un-propositional-knowledge-like, but they also implicate largely separate brain networks, as we noted earlier. We are dealing here with quite distinct mental kinds.

Before concluding this section, we should consider De Brigard's (2019) science-based critique of anti-intellectualist arguments of the sort developed above. De Brigard devotes most of his discussion to undermining the so-called "standard model" of memory, according to which it involves multiple implicit and explicit dissociable systems. This had originally been motivated by neuropsychological studies of patients with damage to the hippocampus and surrounding medial temporal lobes, suggesting a double dissociation between explicit forms of memory (episodic memory in particular) and implicit kinds (including priming, affective conditioning, and motor-skill learning). De Brigard reviews more recent evidence supporting a much murkier picture that calls the standard model into serious doubt.

The only part of this discussion that is directly relevant for our purposes is De Brigard's review of evidence that hippocampal regions participate in motor-skill learning in addition to their better-known role in belief acquisition (episodic and semantic), and that damage to the hippocampal region equally undermines skill learning. In one way this is something one might have expected, given recent demonstrations that the hippocampus and surrounding areas are just as central to the representation of time and temporal intervals as they are for representations of space, in humans just as they are in animals (Eichenbaum 2017; Umbach et al. 2020). For most skill learning, too, requires representations of the sequential ordering and timing of events. And indeed, the evidence does implicate the hippocampal regions in skill acquisition (Gheysen et al. 2010; Jacobacci et al. 2020).

These findings do nothing to undermine the case against intellectualism about know-how and skills, however. First, this is because the findings relate to skill *acquisition* rather than skill *possession*. They fail to show that the hippocampus has any role in skills that have already been learned and consolidated. And in fact skills, once consolidated, no longer rely on the hippocampus, but involve networks linking motor cortices with subcortical networks in the striatum and the cerebellum (Doyon et al. 2009). Second, and more importantly, the networks implicated in skill acquisition, on the one hand, and in belief acquisition, on the other, are otherwise quite distinct. As we will see in Chapter 7, semantic memories are formed with hippocampal involvement, thereafter implicating a distributed set of representations across temporal and parietal cortices, but centered on abstract conceptual representations in the anterior temporal lobes. Episodic memories, in contrast, are centered on sparse temporal and spatial codes in hippocampal regions that link together both sensory and conceptual information across temporal and parietal cortices. Skill acquisition, on the other hand, involves a network linking hippocampal regions to premotor and motor cortices, together with the cerebellum.

The fact that motor skills and beliefs share a component (the hippocampus, but only at the acquisition stage) does nothing to undermine the sharp separation between the two argued for earlier, any more than the functional distinction between ventral and dorsal visual pathways is undermined by the fact that they both have origins in primary visual cortex (Ritchie et al. 2024). So De Brigard's (2019) critique of the anti-intellectualist case, although empirically informed, is argumentatively weak; indeed, it completely misses its mark.

2.8 Conclusion

We have noted a number of respects in which standard belief-desire explanations of action diverge from scientific ones. People are generally unaware that a large proportion of their daily actions are cue-triggered habits, and in consequence will offer erroneous belief-desire explanations of their performance. People are also mostly unaware that speeded online actions are guided in their execution by the unconscious outputs of the dorsal "how-to" visual system rather than their conscious experiences of the events (which actually lag significantly behind), again leading them to provide mistaken explanations. And to the extent that ordinary people and some philosophers think of skilled performance as "mindless" or a mere matter of "muscle memory," then they, too, are mistaken. On the contrary, skilled actions are flexibly guided by sophisticated representational processes involving forward and inverse models, which are sensitive to one's goals and involve a kind of sensorimotor decision-making; and they are just as distinctively human as are the actions covered by the standard belief-desire model. Likewise, if Stanley, Williamson, and others are right that a propositional – knowledge-like – account of know-how is implicit in our ordinary thought and speech, then those implicit assumptions are actually mistaken as well; as are philosophers who claim on other grounds that know-how and skill are forms of propositional knowledge (as does Pavese).

CHAPTER 3

Affect-Caused Action

Section 2.1 discussed one large class of actions that don't result from decision-making processes, and so in that sense aren't intentional – namely, habitual actions. The main focus of the present chapter is on another such class. These are actions that are directly caused by affective states (emotions, desires, and so on). Some of these actions are merely expressive, whereas others give the appearance of being instrumental, and are generally (but mistakenly) interpreted as goal-directed. But we begin with a review of some basic findings from affective science and neuroscience. (For more extended treatment, see Carruthers 2024.) This will help to set up the discussion in this and later chapters.

3.1 The Science of Affect: A Primer

All actions that aren't narrowly habitual (that haven't merely been activated associatively from previously learned cues, like saying "Q" after "P" when reciting the alphabet) are thought to be caused in part by affective states of one sort or another, directly or indirectly. Affective states constitute a broad class (including emotions, feelings of desire and revulsion, sensory and other forms of pleasure and displeasure, and even moods). They differ along a number of different dimensions. Some can take conceptual and/or propositional contents, as when one is afraid *that the bear will attack* or angry *that John insulted me*. Others can be wholly nonconceptual in nature, as are both sensory pain and nausea that results from food-poisoning. (But one can also be disgusted *that the Senator took a bribe* as well as terrified by a loud growl of unknown origin. Most kinds of affective state admit of both conceptual and nonconceptual types of content.) Some affective states have a discrete time-course, with sudden onset before dying away in seconds or minutes. (Emotions are often like this.) But others can build gradually and last for days or weeks, as do many moods, and as can chronic pain.

All affective states nevertheless share a common underlying structure. All begin with some form of evaluative appraisal involving core subcortical evaluative circuits (Rolls 1999; LeDoux 2012; Adolphs & Anderson 2018). These circuits evaluate the personal significance of the representational contents they receive as input, whether those representations are conscious sensations or perceptions, memories, or internally generated images or thoughts, as well as unconscious signals of these and other kinds. But evaluative appraisals are highly context-sensitive, generally responding to multiple cues simultaneously. An iced drink can seem quite attractive when one comes in from the sweltering August heat, but highly aversive as one shivers while waiting for a bus in January. A caress from one's partner can be pleasant, whereas the same sensation of touch felt in a crowded metro carriage can feel threatening. Even sensory pain can be experienced as pleasant in some contexts (Leknes et al. 2013), and the painfulness of pain sensations varies with signals of social support, expectations of recovery, and other factors (Ashar et al. 2017; Petrie & Rief 2019).

Note that my use of the term "appraisal" here is broader than is generally involved in so-called "appraisal theories" of emotion, where theorists often seem to have in mind only evaluations involving propositional judgments (Moors et al. 2013). As I am using the term, in contrast, an appraisal is any process (whether conscious or unconscious, associative or judgment-like) that evaluates a set of inputs (whether conceptual or nonconceptual) against one's stored values, issuing in an affective state as output. Some of these stored values are merely implicit in the "wiring" of the appraisal mechanisms, and constitute the innate initial settings of one's evaluative systems. (These are referred to in much of the literature as *primary* rewards and punishments.) Note, however, that this need not mean that they are unalterable; the initial innate settings can be modified through subsequent learning. Others are acquired via evaluative learning and conditioning of various sorts, as discussed below. (These are called *secondary* rewards and punishments in much of the literature: they are things that are associated with, or predictive of, primary rewards and punishments, but have acquired intrinsic value or disvalue of their own in consequence.)

Appraisals match stimuli to stored values, then. But what are values, in this context? They are dispositional properties of specialized neural circuits that respond to their inputs with a range of kinds of output (to be discussed below, including automatic motor activation, arousal processes, and positive or negative valence that gets used in both decision-making and evaluative learning). As already noted, the circuits in question are context-sensitive, adjusting their processing in response to properties of the environment (e.g. open versus enclosed spaces, in the case of fear) as well as properties of one's own body (e.g. calorie depletion or dehydration, in the case of desires to eat or drink something). What makes it appropriate to describe these dispositions as forms of value is that they have been honed through natural selection to enhance the individual's chances of survival and successful reproduction. LeDoux (2012) calls them "survival circuits," although it might be more appropriate to describe them as "inclusive fitness circuits." This is because they include dispositions that lead to successful mating and care of offspring, as well as (among humans) things that might enhance one's social standing or reputation.

The affective states that result from appraisal processes are comprised of three sorts of output, produced alongside one another in parallel. One of these outputs consists of automatic, directly activated, motor tendencies, which need to be inhibited if they are not to be carried through to completion. These can include expressive actions (the fear-face, the anger-face, the slumped lassitude characteristic of sadness), as well as both innate and previously learned seemingly instrumental actions (running away, in the case of fear; an urge to attack, in the case of anger; reaching for a desired food item; and so on). These motor outputs will be discussed in some detail in subsequent sections. They form the main topic of this chapter.

The second output of evaluative appraisal is some degree of bodily arousal or de-arousal. This can include increases or decreases in heart rate and breathing rate, pupil dilation, increased sweating, preparatory release of stress-related chemicals like cortisol and adrenaline into the bloodstream, and so on (Tiemann et al. 2018). Many of these changes are initiated before one even becomes conscious of the stimulus (Adolphs & Anderson 2018), and can also be caused subliminally, in the absence of conscious experience (Tamietto & de Gelder 2010; Van den Stock et al. 2011).

Some theorists have thought that distinctive patterns of arousal combined with automatic motor outputs constitute the very essence of emotion (James 1890; Prinz 2004) – wrongly, as we will see, since this omits the valence component of emotion altogether. Others have thought that it is arousal (specifically, signals from the body integrated together in the insula cortex) that plays the main role in affectively based decision-making (Damasio 1994). But this is now known to be wrong, too. Degrees of arousal signal the importance or urgency with which decisions need to be taken, and so can bias decision-making toward the more-urgent option; but it is the valence component of affect (anticipatory pleasure and displeasure, when conscious) that plays the main role in decision-making, as will be discussed in Chapter 5 (Storbeck & Clore 2008).

Patterns of arousal and de-arousal can nevertheless come to be valued or disvalued for their own sakes through evaluative learning (becoming positively or negatively valenced), and hence can be sought out or shunned in their own right. Some people have learned to love the relaxed bodily feeling that comes from sitting on the porch on a warm evening, for example, perhaps while enjoying a cold beer. And in contrast, sky-divers may pursue their sport in part because they have come to love the high-arousal effects of leaping from an airplane thousands of feet above the earth. ("I've never felt so alive," someone might say in retrospect.)

The third product of affective appraisal processes is valence (pleasure or displeasure when consciously experienced). This generally attaches to the appraised representation, or sometimes to a representation of the automatic motor output, or both. The valence attaching to future-directed representations (anticipatory valence) is received as input by decision-making systems that compare the degree of valence attaching to the current option alongside others, integrating it with estimates of likelihood and costs to issue in action-selection. The output of this process might include a decision to repress the initial action-urge, or to allow it to unfold, or to select some other action altogether. Valence attaching to a currently experienced or present-tensed representation (consummatory valence), on the other hand, is the main driver of evaluative learning, ratcheting upwards or downwards the value attaching to the type of represented object or event, as we will see. Valence will play a big role in Chapter 5, when we come to discuss decision-making, and again in Chapter 6, when we discuss the nature of pleasure and desire.

Emotions are well known to possess this sort of appraisal-based trivalent structure (Frijda 2010; LeDoux 2012; Adolphs & Anderson 2018). The same is true of bodily affective states like hunger, thirst, sexual pleasure, and sensory pain (Rolls 1999; Ashar et al. 2017). Even moods such as sadness and cheerfulness are thought by some scientists to reflect more-general appraisals of the opportunities afforded by the current environment, resulting in characteristic motor tendencies, arousal or de-arousal, and valence (Eldar et al. 2016, 2021). And positive or negative stimuli of any sort (e.g. angry or fearful faces; value-laden words) can bias decision-making on unrelated topics, even when subliminal (Winkielman et al. 2005; Marsh & Ambady 2007). But they also automatically activate approach or avoidance motor tendencies, as one can tell from reaction-time studies requiring forwards or backwards classification-movements (van Dantzig et al. 2008). Note, however, that it is the urge to get close to a positively valenced thing that is triggered automatically; the mode of action selected to bring about that effect can be flexible, while nevertheless being independent of one's intentions (Krieglmeyer et al. 2010).

As already noted, the stored positive and negative values against which all affective appraisals take place are of two basic kinds, either innate or acquired. Primary rewards and punishments are things or events that have acquired positive or negative value by increasing or decreasing organisms' inclusive fitness over evolutionary time. Primary rewards include such things as eating when hungry, drinking when thirsty, getting warmer when cold or cooler when hot, stroking touch, and (in humans, most likely) signs of approval or admiration from community members.

Secondary rewards and punishments are either learned through association with primary ones (see below), or can be inculcated through top-down expectations of value, resulting from a generalized kind of placebo or nocebo effect (Plassmann et al. 2008; Fernqvist & Ekelund 2014; Ashar et al. 2017; Schmidt et al. 2017). Indeed, the mere belief that something will be pleasurable or displeasurable is apt to make it so, provided the subsequent experience doesn't depart too far from one's expectations (Gneezy et al. 2014). Note that this means that being told, and coming to believe, that something is good or bad is apt to impact subcortical evaluative systems accordingly. This is one of the ways in which cultural values are acquired and sustained.

Mechanisms for associative learning of value are shared with other animals. One is "Pavlovian," and just requires an association between a predictive cue and an existing reward or punisher. With repeated experience the cue is apt to become positively or negatively valued for its own sake. If a retractable lighted bar becomes available to rats shortly before a food reward is provided in a nearby location, for example, then the rats will come to value the lighted bar itself (to greater or lesser degrees – there are individual differences here; Ahrens et al. 2016). They will hang out around it and try to play with it, even if that means getting less food; and they will work to make the bar appear, as well as coming to value and work to get yet other things that predict *its* appearance, even though it is no longer paired with food or when the food has become devalued through artificially induced nausea.

Another mechanism of evaluative learning operates on an actor / critic model. The actor selects an action in light of its anticipated reward value, predicted from appraisal against existing stored primary and secondary values. When the action is executed the critic tells the actor whether its prediction was too high or too low, and by how much (comparing it with the degree of consummatory valence experienced in the present). One's stored evaluation of the outcome event is then adjusted up or down by some increment accordingly.

Evaluative learning doesn't just take place through direct experience, but also through social observation. Thus rat pups will learn to fear what their mothers fear (Olsson et al. 2016), and some birds will learn to fear and mob anything feared and mobbed by another member of their species, even a bottle of laundry detergent (Gould & Gould 1994). It seems that one of the main mechanisms involved in social learning is emotional mirroring. Sensing their mother's fear, the rat pups experience fear in their own right, and the negative valence component of the latter then becomes associated with whatever cue predicts the mother's fear. The same process takes place among humans, of course, and is another way in which humans rapidly acquire a range of culture-specific values and disvalues.

We will return to discuss the role of valence in decision-making at greater length in Chapter 5, and then the nature of valence itself and its relationship to desire in Chapter 6. Here our focus will be on the automatic motor tendencies that are produced by all affective states (alongside arousal and valence).

3.2 Expressive Action

Famously, Darwin (1872) noted that multiple animal species (including humans) engage in what appear to be stereotyped – easily recognizable – behavioral expressions of emotion. While forms of expression vary across species, with some experience one can often tell whether an animal is surprised, fearful, enraged, or in pain. Almost as famously, Ekman (Ekman et al. 1969; Ekman 1980) proposed that there are universally recognizable facial expressions of emotion in humans across cultures, including anger, disgust, fear, surprise, enjoyment, and sadness. Although this view has been challenged (Russell 1994; Barrett 2017), a large meta-analysis of cross-cultural emotion-recognition studies found robust evidence of universality, together with a smaller own-group benefit that suggests some modulation by culture-specific learning (Elfenbein & Ambady 2002).[1] Moreover, facial expressions of distinct basic emotions are

[1] Barrett (2017) criticizes such studies on the grounds that they generally use a forced-choice method (e.g. requiring participants to choose from four alternative labels for a given facial expression). She points out that when participants can give free descriptions of the expressions in question the results are much less robust. This is probably because emotion-recognition is generally facilitated by

perceived as categorically different even in cultures that fail to draw any linguistic distinction between them, using the same term for both anger and disgust, for example (Sauter et al. 2011).

Emotions are not just expressed in the face, of course. They can often also be recognized from patterns of speech prosody, as well as from gestures and non-verbal sounds (such as cries or laughter). Sauter et al. (2010) found robust evidence of cross-cultural recognition of the latter, especially for negative emotions (anger, disgust, fear, sadness, and surprise, but also for amusement). And a recent meta-analysis found that people are actually capable of recognizing an even wider range of different emotions cross-culturally from both prosodic and non-verbal cues, while also, again, showing a smaller in-group advantage (Laukka & Elfenbein 2021). Moreover, whole-body expressions of sadness, anger, and fear are recognized across cultures, even in small-scale traditional societies that are quite isolated from the rest of the world (Witkower et al. 2021).

Pride and shame, too, are expressed in the body as a whole. The classic pride display includes an upright posture with backward head-tilt and smile, arms spread or raised, often with fists clenched, and with the chest expanded. Shame, on the other hand, is displayed through slumped shoulders with narrowed chest and a head-tilt downwards. These displays are found across widely separated cultures, and are recognized by children as young as four years of age (Keltner 1995; Tracy et al. 2005; Tracy & Robins 2008). Moreover, they are displayed in full by congenitally blind Olympic athletes from multiple cultures when winning or losing a competition, albeit with the shame display being significantly reduced among athletes from strongly individualist societies. (One can easily imagine a coach from a Western culture telling a blind athlete, "Stand tall; although you lost you did your best." But it is hard to imagine that anyone takes the time to describe and encourage the full-body expression of pride.) This is good evidence that the displays in question are innate (Tracy & Matsumoto 2008).

The universality of emotion-expressive behavior across cultures – in some studies cultures that have had little or no contact with one another – suggests

contextual and bodily cues of various sorts, and is quite hard in the absence of such supports. The four words presented in forced-choice methods may be playing the role of contextual cues that facilitate recognition. Note, however, that forced-choice emotion-recognition methods can have good psychometric properties and are widely used in measuring autistic-spectrum traits, correlating well with other measures (Fernández-Abascal et al. 2013; Vellante et al. 2013; Jones et al. 2018), and that people show above-chance accuracy even with very brief presentation times as short as 12.5 milliseconds (Schmidtmann et al. 2020).

that the behavior in question is not voluntarily produced (although it can be voluntarily inhibited and modified, of course). This implication is confirmed by the discovery of so-called "micro-expressions." These generally last for only 200 milliseconds or less starting soon after stimulus onset, and can betray a person's true feelings (e.g. of disgust that is rapidly covered up with a smile). These are especially likely to manifest when the emotion is more intense (Porter et al. 2012).

Micro-expressions can be remarkably hard to detect, however, at least in part because subtle changes around the eyes can be masked by accompanying or subsequent movements of the mouth (Iwasaki & Noguchi 2016). Nevertheless, it is claimed that some people can become better at detecting them with training (Ekman 2007). Since micro-expressions are potentially highly relevant for job interviewers, airport security screeners, and law enforcement officers (among others), there is now, as one might expect, a small industry attempting to develop AI systems for recognizing micro-expressions – with some success, albeit held back by the limited range of databases on which these systems can be trained (Xia et al. 2020; Zhao et al. 2023).

While the findings reviewed here may be interesting and perhaps surprising, there is little that presents any real challenge to common sense. People are well aware that they can simulate emotional expressions intentionally, such as pretending to smile in a friendly way at someone they dislike. And they are also aware that such *faux* emotional expressions have limited success. Moreover, it is part of common sense that emotional expressions can be hard to suppress. Think of familiar phrases like, "I couldn't stop laughing," "I tried to suppress my smile," or "I struggled to hide my disgust." So it is plain that the folk don't consider emotion-expressive actions as intentional or goal-directed. And they are right. Such actions are direct products of the affective appraisal process that issues in the emotion in question.

It is worth recalling the distinction drawn in Section 2.1 with respect to habitual actions, however, between those that proceed uninhibited when triggered because there are *no* current goals with which they conflict, and those that fail to be inhibited because *consistent with* or *permitted by* one's current goal. The same distinction can be drawn here. Often one allows oneself to smile or laugh naturally because there is no reason not to – there is nothing one is trying to achieve at the time that gives one cause to inhibit one's action. But there are some occasions when one might fail to inhibit an affect-caused smile, for example, because smiling is what one intended to do anyway. Consider someone entering a job interview who is vividly aware of their interview training: make sure you smile at your interviewer. But suppose the interviewer makes an amusing quip of some sort as the candidate enters the room. This might be a case where one's spontaneous smile fails to get inhibited because one already has the goal of smiling. It is a case of negative goal-directedness.

In contrast with goal-consistent habitual actions, however, I don't think the parallel case of goal-consistent affect-expressive actions is really very surprising. In the example described above, for example, the interviewee might quite naturally report, "Luckily, I didn't need to force my smile." One is unlikely to interpret one's spontaneous smile as voluntary. Matters are otherwise, however, with affect-caused actions that give the appearance of being instrumental. These will form the topic of Section 3.3.

3.3 Seemingly Instrumental Action

Section 3.1 noted that affective states can automatically produce two kinds of behavioral tendency: expressive and seemingly instrumental. But not all affective states produce both. All affective states produce motor dispositions of some sort, but not all produce tendencies that include both expressive and seemingly instrumental actions. Thus curiosity and interest dispose one to attend closely to the object of interest and to engage in innate or learned behavior sculpted to acquire information about the object (approaching closer, touching it, sniffing it, and so on). From such seemingly instrumental actions one can often recognize that the person or animal in question is interested or curious. But the behavior in question isn't *expressive* – it hasn't been designed to be recognized by others, in the way that the fear-face, anger-face, and disgust-face arguably have. Conversely, grief and sadness cause motor tendencies that are expressive (crying, slumped posture, the sad-face), but not ones that serve any instrumental purpose related to the object of one's sadness or grief. Indeed, sadness causes a sort of behavioral lassitude that can be thought of as a general inhibitor of instrumental action. Sad people are generally less motivated to do anything at all.

All affective states have been designed through evolution to be adaptive (or else they are socially constructed out of states designed to be adaptive). That explains why all produce motor dispositions of some sort, designed to help the organism deal with an adaptive threat or opportunity. But in some cases (e.g. sadness, grief) the adaptive problem results in a need for social support of some sort, and the automatic motor output may be purely expressive. In other cases (e.g. curiosity, interest) the adaptive problem is equally one that non-social creatures confront, such as gathering lifeway-relevant information, and the resulting motor tendencies are purely instrumental. But many emotions serve both signaling and instrumental functions. Thus fear alerts others to the presence of danger while also motivating one's own escape; disgust alerts others to the presence of a poison or contaminant while also motivating one's own withdrawal from it; and so on.

We can begin with a kind of affectively caused action that is purely instrumental: the case of curiosity. It is a constraint on theories of curiosity that they should make few if any conceptual demands on the creatures in question. This is because curiosity and interest are extremely widespread in the animal kingdom, perhaps even extending to insects. Almost all kinds of organism need to be motivated to acquire information that is relevant to their ecological niche and life-ways. Honey bees cluster around the dances of other bees, learning the location of nectar and other substances (and note that this is information that they may, or may not, choose to act upon; they don't act reflexively; Seeley 1995). Moreover, bumblebees can learn how to open a container successfully for themselves by observing other bees that have been trained to do it (Bridges et al. 2023). Information is a valuable commodity for almost all living creatures, and for the most part it needs to be sought out and attended to.

Common-sense explanations of curiosity-caused actions are metacognitive in nature, however. We say, "I walked over to have a look because I *wanted to know* what was going on." And indeed, curiosity is analyzed – rather unthinkingly, without supporting argument – as a *desire to know* (or a *desire for true belief*, or something similar) in most of the philosophical and psychological literature on the topic (Foley 1987; Goldman 1999; Williamson 2000; Litman 2005; Gruber et al. 2014; Sharot & Sunstein 2020). But it is quite unlikely that cats and rats (let alone bees) take their own states of knowledge as objects of desire.

The best account – which fits well with the science of affect in general, as well as satisfying the above constraint ("keep it simple") – is as follows.[2] Affective states of curiosity and interest are caused by appraisals of

[2] In addition to the common-sense metacognitive account, some philosophers have developed a questioning theory of curiosity (Whitcomb 2010; Friedman 2013a; Carruthers 2018, 2021). On this view, curiosity is a motivating attitude that takes a question rather than a proposition as its content. ("What is that?" "Who will win?" and so on.) This is more complex than the simpler motoric account developed here, requiring us to recognize a whole new type of mental content. And although it is less conceptually demanding than the metacognitive account, it still requires greater sophistication of curious creatures than does the motoric view.

nonconceptual signals representing the organism's (relevant) ignorance. Drawing on the noisy neural accumulator framework as background (Usher & McClelland 2001; Teodorescu & Usher 2013; Forstmann et al. 2016), Carruthers and Williams (2022) argue that failures of recognition and failures of prediction of the sort that give rise to curiosity (when appraised as relevant) are likely to be signaled by a population of neurons that has as its correctness-condition, *unknown*. But this can be an unconscious and purely nonconceptual metacognitive signal, one that can just as easily be ascribed to bees as to humans.

Carruthers and Williams (2022) suggest that when an unrecognized object appears in one's environment, or one fails to predict the outcome of an upcoming or ongoing event, a number of neural accumulators representing familiar types of object or possible outcomes for the event will become active, competing with one another and mutually inhibiting one another in a race to reach the criterion-level for judgment ("That is a fox," or "Joe will win the fight"). But general considerations of speed and reliability suggest that there should also be an accumulator that competes with and inhibits all the others and is apt to initiate curiosity-type behavior when it hits criterion-level first. Given its function, we can think of this accumulator as a symbol whose correctness-condition is *unknown*. But not all ignorance matters to the organism. There also has to be an appraisal of relevance or importance. This might be computed from what the unknown entity most resembles, perhaps (e.g. it appears to be some sort of unfamiliar predator), or from the importance to the organism of the outcome of the event (e.g. who wins the fight will impact one's own social status).

An appraisal of relevant ignorance will issue in automatic motor activation of innate or previously rewarded investigative actions (attending closely, walking over to touch, sniff, or observe from a different vantage point, and so on), depending on the nature of the situation and its affordances. When there is no competing goal to inhibit the execution of the motor instruction, curiosity behavior will manifest itself. But note that this is behavior without an explicitly represented goal. (Implicitly, one might say that the goal is to learn; for that is the behavior's adaptive function. But this is not a goal that the organism has.) It is automatically produced without any need for decision-making, and so in that sense can be said to be unintended.[3]

[3] In the language often used in philosophy, there is no *prior intention*. Note, however, that the organism's movements are not reflex-like, but are flexibly guided in their execution, utilizing sensorimotor decision-making of the sort discussed in Section 2.4.

How does curiosity itself enter into decision-making when it does, however? How does it compete with current goals and other affective states? The investigative motor tendencies caused by an appraisal of relevant ignorance will issue in sensory forward models of the action, of the sort discussed at some length in Section 2.4. These will be received by one's affective appraisal systems, which evaluate the action in light of its anticipated reward value, presumably calculated from the strength of the initial appraisal of relevance together with an estimate of the likelihood of the action resulting in learning, grounded in previous experience. So the investigative behavior itself becomes valenced in anticipation, and that degree of valence (the degree of anticipated reward) can then enter into computations of expected value in comparison with the other alternatives under consideration, in the manner to be discussed in Chapter 5.

Assume that this account is on the right track. (Although it lacks direct empirical support, it is the account that fits best with the entirety of the empirical evidence.) Then when one explains one's curiosity-manifesting behavior by saying something like, "I walked over because I wanted to see how it would turn out," or "I walked over because I wanted to know who would win," one's explanation is mistaken. Seeing, as such, was not an object of desire. Nor was knowledge. Rather, the motor instructions that would issue in seeing and learning were appraised positively enough to be chosen (or at least not inhibited). The only representations that actually figured in the causation of one's behavior (at least, downstream of the appraisal process that gave rise to one's curiosity) were motor representations and the valenced sensory forward models they created. There was no representation of seeing and no representation of knowing or learning.

The time-course of behavior motivated by curiosity is generally fairly slow (one's curiosity isn't often *urgent*), so it can be hard to distinguish behavior that is directly caused by one's affective state (and so in that sense isn't intentional) from behavior that gets selected in the light of downstream decision-making. And among humans the latter kinds of case might well involve thoughts about how much one wants to know something, thereafter selecting an action with that goal in mind. But many other types of emotion do often issue in immediate behavioral responses.

Consider disgust. Imagine that you are removing items from the kitchen cabinets so you can do a thorough cleaning. You are reaching toward something unidentified at the back of one of them when you realize it is the rotting corpse of a dead mouse. You withdraw your hand in disgust and step back. It would be natural for you to explain your actions by saying, "I saw that it was a dead mouse and didn't want to touch it." The explanation implies that your withdrawal of your hand was goal-directed, which is false. Rather, it was directly caused by an appraisal of the object you were about to touch as disgusting. True, the goal implicit in the design of the disgust system is to prevent contact with disgusting things (potential poisons and contaminants). But this is not a goal that you yourself had when pulling your hand back. Indeed, that action had no goal, and in that sense wasn't voluntarily produced. (Which is not to say that it was *in*voluntary, since this would suggest that you couldn't inhibit the action. That might sometimes be the case, but not generally.)

Now consider fear. Imagine that you are a young man living in an impoverished area of an inner city who is affiliated with one of the local gangs. You are on your way home, and turn down an alley to cut across to the next block. As you turn a corner you confront five members of a rival gang. They immediately draw knives and run toward you. Their intent is obvious, and you are terrified. You turn and race away as fast as you can. Explaining what you did afterwards you might say, "I could see that I was outnumbered and didn't want to get hurt, so I ran," or more simply, "I ran to save my life." Both explanations are false – or at least misleading – in suggesting that your action was goal-directed. But it was not. Rather, an appraisal of imminent danger produced intense fear, one component of which was automatically produced motor instructions for turning and running. You likely started to run before there was even time for thought or executively based decision-making (although as you ran you may well have taken a decision not to stop).

The account of fast-response fear sketched above has direct empirical support. There are distinct (albeit overlapping, and often interacting) neural circuits in the brain supporting fear behavior, depending on the imminence of the threat (Qi et al. 2018; Mobbs et al. 2020). When a threat is imminent, fear behavior (e.g. running away) is governed by a subcortical network in interaction with regions of motor cortex. When a threat is more distal, in contrast, behavioral selection depends on a wider network that implicates decision-making regions of the prefrontal cortex. This sort of division makes good adaptive sense. If there is no time to think or plan, and action is urgent, then you should rely on innate or previously learned motor plans. But when there is time, planning your response may lead to a more successful outcome.

Once again we find people offering explanations of affect-caused action that are mistaken. They treat such actions as goal-directed and explicable in the light of familiar belief-desire reasoning. ("I wanted to get away and saw that the only escape was to go back up the alley.") But in fact they are direct motor outputs of the affective appraisal process that issues in one's fear or one's disgust (albeit flexibly implemented through forms of sensorimotor decision-making).

3.4 Model-Based versus Model-Free Action

The directly affectively caused actions discussed in Section 3.3 are likely to belong among the innate outputs of the affective states in question (*approach* for curiosity, *withdraw* for disgust, and *run* for fear). But all affective states can come to be served by novel forms of behavior through processes of instrumental conditioning. Roughly, actions that lead to rewarding outcomes tend to be repeated in circumstances that afford those outcomes, and actions that issue in punishing outcomes are avoided. Note that although such actions are learned as a result of the benefits they are apt to bring about, this need not mean that their performance thereafter is goal-directed in the sense of having a represented goal. Quite the contrary.

Unfortunately, however, there isn't much in the extensive literature on instrumental conditioning and behavioral learning that speaks directly to our topic. What one would like to see is evidence demonstrating that forms of learned behavior can be produced directly by the appraisals that issue in affective states. But much of the literature is actually somewhat ambiguous. Explaining why will take us on a bit of a detour.

The main distinction drawn in the field is between model-based and model-free learning and behavior (Glüscher et al. 2010; Doll et al. 2012). Use of the term "model-based" to describe an animal's behavior suggests that it is pursuing a goal guided by beliefs about the state of the environment and the means available to pursue that goal (a "model"). Certainly there are many experiments in the field that fit this pattern. For example, Kheifets and Gallistel (2012) find that mice shift their choices between alcoves that deliver rewards of equal value when the probability of a reward changes among the alcoves at random intervals. At one time there might be a 20 percent chance of receiving a reward from one alcove and a 60 percent chance of getting one from the other, which then shifts to 50 percent from the first and 30 percent from the second. The animals track these changes in ways that are close to optimal. They are computing the current likelihood of receiving a reward from each alcove and choosing accordingly.

Many paradigms classify behavior as model-based, however, simply on the basis that responding ceases when rewards are no longer available or have been devalued, even when no choices need to be made among behavioral options. As a result, it is unclear whether the animal in pursuit of the reward selects a behavior expected to achieve it by constructing a simple plan ("if I do this I will get the food"), or whether prior conditioning leads to the activation of the instrumental motor plan directly from affective appraisal of reward availability. If the former, then the action would be genuinely instrumental: it would be selected *in order to achieve* the reward; if the latter, then this would be an instance of directly caused affectively based behavior. I am aware of no paradigms that have been designed to test for the latter kind of behavior, which would appear instrumental without actually being so.

In model-free learning, in contrast, actions that have been paired with reward are said to have acquired a "cached value," since they continue to be performed in the same circumstances even when rewards are no longer available or have been devalued. But there are two quite different things that can be meant by "cached value." One is that the action has become habitual, and is now a behavioral response initiated by the cue, independent of outcome. What has been "cached," on this reading, is the normal or previous instrumental value of the action. But the other thing that might be meant is that the action itself has acquired intrinsic (secondary) reward value. On this reading what has been "cached" or stored is a novel intrinsic (non-instrumental) value.

The habit interpretation of model-free responding is the one that is generally dominant in the literature (Balleine & O'Doherty 2010; Burton et al. 2015). Specifically, the claim is that a subcortical structure known as the ventral striatum codes for reward values, interacting with cortical regions to select and guide model-based behavior, whereas the dorsolateral striatum takes over control of behavior as the latter becomes habitual, becoming a matter of value-free stimulus-response. Hence when rewards are no longer available, the behavior is still performed nevertheless. But in fact, outcome-devaluation fails to discriminate between habitual behavior and behavior that has acquired secondary reward value (Miller et al. 2019). To test for this one needs to see whether the animal's behavior is flexible or stereotyped, and/or whether the animal will work for an opportunity to perform its cached-value action in the absence of any other reward (that is to say, whether the action in question can in turn be used as a secondary reinforcer, because valued in its own right).

DiFeliceantonio and Berridge (2016) tested for both of these properties in an experiment with rats, while pharmacologically stimulating the dorsolateral striatum. Having trained the rats to approach and manipulate a lighted bar prior to the delivery of food nearby, they then tested the animals in the absence of reward. They found that the rats would immediately approach the lighted bar even though it was placed in a new location (displaying flexibility rather than stereotyped responding), and they also found that the rats were willing to learn a new behavior (a nose-poke into a hole) in order to make the bar appear. Moreover, they did both of these things more reliably and vigorously when the dorsolateral striatum was artificially stimulated. The experimenters' conclusion is that, rather than coding for habitual responding, the dorsolateral striatum is centrally involved in what the authors call "incentive-salience," or the learning of secondary reward values.

Incentive-salience, like all other forms of affective state, is comprised of a number of components. One is a positive valuation of the incentive-salient object or event, with positive valence (anticipatory reward) attached to the representation of that object or event. And because of their positive valuation, incentive-salient objects and events tend to attract and hold one's attention – they become especially salient. But in addition, incentive-salience includes automatic motor activation, or a motoric urge to approach or acquire the incentive-salient object or event (Nguyen et al. 2021). In the animal-learning literature these actions will often be innate ones (approach, sniff, chew, and so on). But in humans, at least, they can be novel learned actions, as when drug paraphernalia and the actions involved in injecting a drug have become incentive-salient (intrinsically desirable) to a drug addict, even if the drug itself has ceased to provide any pleasure (Lewis 2015; Olney et al. 2018). So these cases, at least, provide instances of learned behavior that are directly caused by an affective state.

As we saw in Section 3.1, evaluative learning of secondary rewards and punishments can operate on an actor / critic model. Predictions of value (degrees of reward or punishment) for an upcoming action or outcome are compared with the consummatory value subsequently experienced, and the stored values associated with those actions or outcomes are ratcheted up or down by some increment accordingly. Instrumental learning has often been modeled using a similar framework, with any action one undertakes issuing in predictions of reward or punishment, and then with the outcomes teaching one to perform or inhibit those actions in the future. (These are so-called "temporal difference" models of instrumental learning; Sutton & Barto 1998.) But recent theoretical modeling combined with a raft of experimental work suggests that instrumental action-learning is best understood quite differently from secondary reward-learning, involving a retrospective search of memory of recent actions once a rewarding or punishing event has been experienced (Jeong et al. 2022). If this is right, then it implies that the two forms of learning are quite distinct. And indeed, Burke et al. (2008) demonstrate that they involve partially distinct brain networks that can be modulated independently, although both can be happening at the same time.

I conclude that it remains unknown whether all forms of model-based action involve executive decision-making, or whether in some cases a flexible learning-informed action-selection process is an immediate consequence of the initial affective appraisal. On the other hand, in at least some cases of model-free responding, we have seen that instrumentally learned (non-innate) actions can be caused directly out of an affective state of incentive-salience.

3.5 Instrumentally Learned Affect-Caused Action

Although the animal experimental literature is somewhat murky, there should be little doubt that learning can enable affective states to produce novel forms of automatically caused behavior – behavior that is set in train prior to and/or independently of executive forms of decision-making. Indeed, we already noted in Section 3.4 that drug addiction can involve learned behavioral urges of various kinds that are directly caused by affective desires for the drug.

For another sort of example, consider curiosity again. Assume that the account sketched in Section 3.3 is correct. That is, assume that the main product of appraisals of relevant ignorance (in addition to some degree of arousal) is a behavioral investigative urge. In that case it is obvious that the initial innate repertoire of curiosity-satisfying behaviors (perhaps attending, approaching, looking closer) gets enriched by learning during human development. Human infants soon learn to point and draw the attention of caregivers to things that puzzle them, and soon thereafter they learn to ask verbal questions. On the account sketched in Section 3.3, question-asking is a direct behavioral output (or impulse) resulting from an appraisal of relevant ignorance that issues in an affective state of curiosity.

This account is consistent with the familiar phenomenology of intense curiosity. Think of the way onlookers can be drawn to the site of a serious accident, for example. One of them might report, "Although it was awful to look at, I couldn't tear my eyes away." A curiosity-driven urge to look can be hard to resist. Although the motor urge to look is likely to be an innate behavioral output of curiosity, the same point applies to obviously learned curiosity-driven behavior. A parent whose teenager has returned from her first date, for example, and is (as we say) dying to know how it went, might report, "I had to bite my tongue to stop myself from asking." There can be a powerful behavioral urge to ask a question that can be hard to suppress.

I suggest, then, that many of the behaviors we perform, or feel an urge to perform, when in an affective state of any sort are likely to be immediate products of that state, caused by previous learning, but now performed automatically, with no goal in mind. This is especially likely to be true of affect-caused actions that are produced under time pressure, when there is little time for executive decision-making. When people explain actions taken in such cases by citing a goal, or in terms of a belief/desire pair, as they generally do, they are mistaken. But in everyday contexts it can be hard to know which these cases are. And there is something of a lacuna in the science here, as well. So we can be confident that folk-psychology and the standard belief-desire model issue in numerous errors of explanation, but we often lack the ability (at present) to identify which explanations are erroneous and which are not.

3.6 The Abstract Nature of Affective Action-Urges

We noted in Section 2.4 that the motor system is organized hierarchically. Motor instructions begin with an abstract representation of the outcome to be achieved, causing a cascade of increasingly concrete instructions for movements of body and limbs, bottoming out in instructions to tighten or relax specific muscle groups. There is no reason to think that directly caused affective actions should be any different. Indeed, in Section 3.1 we already cited evidence showing that they are not.

In one of the studies by Krieglmeyer et al. (2010), in particular, participants used a keyboard to move an avatar on the screen upwards or downwards. (They were told to imagine that they were the avatar in question.) The avatar could appear in the top or bottom portion of the screen, and on each trial a positive or negative word was displayed in the center. They were told to move the avatar in one direction if the word was a noun and in the other if it was an adjective. (The valence of the word was irrelevant to the task and was not mentioned by the experimenters.) Participants were faster to move the avatar toward a positive word or away from a negative one, no matter whether the avatar was moving upwards or downwards. It seems that the automatic and goal-independent motor instructions following an appraisal of positive or negative value are quite abstract – "get closer to that thing" versus "get away from that thing" – while the movements one actually performs to implement those instructions are very different (pressing one key rather than another to make the avatar move upwards or downwards).

Now consider the automatic motor outputs of anger. Anger causes an urge to damage the object of one's anger. In its basic (pre-hominin) form that likely meant *physical* damage, involving some sort of physical attack. But among social-living humans there are many additional forms of potential damage. One can also damage someone financially, or damage their property, or damage their social reputation, or damage their emotional state. Sometimes, of course, angry people can be slow to act. One stews in one's own anger until one decides how best to get back at the object of one's anger. But often one's anger-motivated response is speeded, almost immediate. These are the cases that interest us here.

I suggest that an appraisal of someone's action as having damaged oneself or something near-and-dear to oneself (e.g. one's family or one's property) automatically generates an abstract behavioral urge to hurt them back. (This is in addition to causing some degree of bodily arousal, as well as negative valence directed at the object of one's anger: what they did seems bad to one.) Then, just as with other speeded actions (see Section 2.4), multiple action-plans afforded by the circumstances will become active in parallel, competing with one another for implementation. Each generates forward models of their likely consequences, which are swiftly evaluated by one's affective appraisal systems, making them seem to some degree good or bad. One could strike the person; insult the person; point out the injustice of their action to bystanders; and so on. But each of these options is itself fairly abstract. There are many ways to physically attack someone; many forms and kinds of insult; many different things one could say to the audience in complaint. Yet one often responds within moments.

Suppose you are in a faculty or other form of committee meeting when someone you dislike says something that is deeply insulting to you. You are furious. You feel an impulse to strike back, and the sense of urgency created by your bodily arousal facilitates and encourages an immediate response. The options rapidly get narrowed down to a reputation-damaging verbal response (striking the person is ruled out in the circumstances, appealing to other members of the committee might seem like weakness). Multiple things one could say are processed in parallel, and the winning option is implemented moments later: one says acidly, "John, when was the last time you published anything?"

In many such cases, I suggest, there is no conscious goal, and no decision-making that involves one's executive systems. Rather, there is a competition among a variety of more-or-less concrete damage-causing motor instructions that gets rapidly resolved within the sensorimotor system, much as if one were a skilled soccer player "deciding" on the fly whether to pass to a team member or juke around a tackler. If one explains one's action in such cases by saying something like, "What he did made me really angry, so I wanted to get him back," then one's explanation is mistaken. A motoric urge that is apt to result in damage is not a desire to cause damage – that would require a positively valenced representation of damage that figures in executive ("personal-level") decision-making processes. If the person responds more slowly, of course, then there may well be such a desire. For then a conscious representation of the outcome of one's action may be positively appraised and become positively valenced. So in practical terms it can be hard to tell which desire-based explanations are true and which false; but if the person takes minutes to respond then one can assume the response is desire-based, whereas if their response is close-to-immediate, then one can assume it was produced by a motoric urge of some sort.

This section has been somewhat speculative. Generalizing from what is known about affect and motor control, it has suggested that many of our day-to-day actions that are motivated by affective states like anger, fear, or curiosity are actually direct products of the affective appraisals in question, bypassing any form of executive (or "person-level") decision-making. This is especially likely to be the case when one acts swiftly and without conscious reflection. In such cases one's actions will lack any represented goal. But it can be hard to distinguish these cases from actions that result from swiftly undertaken (unreflective) decision-making. So I suggest that many of our everyday explanations that cite the goals of our actions are false; but we often cannot know which ones these are.

3.7 Actions With and Without Intentions

We noted in Section 1.1 that almost all philosophical discussions of action have focused on so-called "intentional action." These are actions that are caused and/or rationalized by the agent's beliefs and desires, either directly or via the formation of an intention to act (Wilson & Shpall 2012; Piñeros Glasscock & Tenenbaum 2023). Yet over the course of this and the previous chapter we have seen that there are a number of forms of action that fall outside the scope of the standard model. Specifically, there are habitual actions, there are speeded and skilled actions, and there are directly affect-caused actions (both expressive and seemingly – but not really – instrumental / goal-directed). Taken together, these arguably constitute a very large proportion of our everyday actions. Part of the reason for this neglect is simple ignorance, no doubt. But there may also be deeper reasons. We critiqued one such reason in Section 2.6, which is the idea that only intentional actions supposedly reflect our distinctively human (rational) natures. Here we discuss another.

While many philosophers don't deny the existence of at least some of the alternative categories of action noted above, they may think of them as not truly emanating from the agent, person, or self. Personal actions are those that reflect the attitudes of the agent (the agent's beliefs and desires), whereas habitual actions, skilled actions, and affect-caused actions don't – they are caused automatically rather than intentionally. Indeed, Wu (2023) goes so far as to say that we are *passive* with respect to such actions. In a sense, they happen *to* us, he thinks, rather than being things that *we* (the agents) *do*. Intentional actions, in contrast, are things that we *will* ourselves to do – they reflect our (personal) choices and decisions.[4]

I conjecture that philosophers might attempt to justify their exclusive focus on intentional actions because they think of intentions as operating at the so-called "personal level" (the level of the agent, person, or self), whereas the motor instructions that guide habits, skills, and emotion-caused actions are *sub-personal*, and happen outside of personal control. But can the personal / sub-personal distinction bear this much weight? We have already had occasion to note in Section 2.4 that speeded and skilled actions depend on forms of sensorimotor decision-making (and are thus, in an important sense, not automatic); and that these are functionally and computationally much like executive kinds of decision-making. So in that respect the differences here are not deep, providing little reason for denying that all these forms of action are properly attributable to the agent, and are things that the agent actively does. Moreover, the personal / sub-personal distinction can be taken in at least a couple of different ways.

[4] Although Wu (2023) presents his book as a scientifically grounded theory of agency, it is largely disconnected from the scientific literature on affect and decision-making. The terms "affect" and "valence" don't even figure in the index; nor does "decision." There is a brief (two-page) discussion of reward and value, but described as just one among many biases on action, rather than its central motivator; and there are only a few pages devoted to emotion (again, described as a bias). More importantly for our purposes, there is nothing in the science that Wu cites that actually supports the idea that we are passive with respect to habitual, skilled, and affect-caused actions. That is his own gloss, no doubt because he views the data through the lens of the standard model.

One way in which people often interpret the personal / sub-personal distinction is to equate it with the conscious / unconscious distinction. Person-level mental states are conscious ones; sub-personal states are unconscious. Granted, habits and skills are not consciously guided in their execution. But then nor are most intentional actions guided in anything but the most abstract sense, assuming that the intention itself is conscious. And in addition, although we generally know about and can report our intentions, they are not themselves conscious events. Or so I claim, identifying, as I do, conscious states with global-workspace states (Carruthers 2019). For intentions don't figure among the contents of working memory, and are not "globally broadcast." Rather, they are among the executive processes that control entry into working memory, and that control and manipulate its contents (Carruthers 2015).[5]

An alternative way in which the personal / sub-personal distinction is often drawn is to say that person-level states and events are properties of the whole person, whereas sub-personal states and events are properties of a sub-system of the person. But all mental states and events are strictly properties of some or other sub-system. Conscious experiences are properties of the working-memory / global-broadcasting network, which interacts with many (but not all) other sub-systems of the person. Intentions are properties of the prefrontal executive system, just as skills are properties of the sensorimotor control system; and so on. Yet all of the kinds of process discussed in this and the previous chapter issue in *actions* that are attributable to the whole agent. It is *the soccer player* (the person or agent) who makes the pass, and *the tennis player* (the person) who returns the serve. And if philosophers insist that only intentions and intention-controlled actions are *properly* attributable to the agent as a whole (whereas habitual, skilled, and emotion-caused actions are not), then that just begs the question at issue.

I suspect that the weight philosophers are apt to place on the personal / sub-personal distinction may actually be driven by their intuitions about moral responsibility. Person-level decisions, actions, and other mental states are ones that we can hold the person fully responsible for, and that are subject to normative constraints; sub-personal ones are not. And

[5] Even if one endorses a higher-order theory of consciousness, and claims that conscious states are ones that we have non-interpretative knowledge of, the same conclusion follows; for our access to them is actually interpretative (Carruthers 2011). But if by "conscious" one just means "reportable," then intentions can qualify as conscious, since they are presumably available to control speech actions as well as motor-generating processes of other sorts (subject to the usual sorts of competing pressures on how one expresses oneself in speech, of course).

indeed, some have said that the rationale for emphasizing conscious decision-making in attributions of moral responsibility is that consciousness (or the "global workspace"; Dehaene 2014) enables all of a person's beliefs and values to contribute to the subsequent decision (Levy 2014). Hence there is a sense in which choices grounded in conscious deliberation reflect the beliefs and values of the person as a whole. Notice, however, that this would imply that speeded and skilled actions, for example, are ones that the agent can't really be held responsible for or given credit for. That would be a hard pill to swallow.

Moreover, the real contrast here is between decisions that are taken after extended conscious reflection and the remainder, including among the latter choices that are made unreflectively among consciously presented options. For there may be little difference between actions that are the direct output of affective appraisals and actions that result from immediate, swiftly taken decisions in response to consciously available information. In both cases a highly restricted range of beliefs and values will have become activated and contributed to the outcome. The real contrast is not between conscious decision-making and unconscious decisions taken within the sensorimotor system or underlying affect-caused actions, but rather between *reflective* – temporally extended and open-ended – decision-making and the rest. For it is only in the former case that large numbers of the person's beliefs and values can contribute to the outcome.

One natural suggestion in light of these points would be to say that moral responsibility for action is graded, ranging from full responsibility for actions taken after extensive thinking and planning, through more limited and briefer reflection, to executive decisions taken swiftly among consciously presented options. And standing on a par with the latter would be unconsciously initiated skilled and affect-caused actions. In all of these last three categories there will have been only limited activation of the agent's beliefs and values, and yet in each of these cases it can be true that the agent could have done otherwise had they decided to. There is no justification here for marking a categorical distinction of kind between intention-caused action and the rest.

More importantly, any attempt to argue from intuitions about moral responsibility would be methodologically unsound. Real distinctions of kind among states and actions are fixed by our best science, not by morality. Moral considerations should follow what is real; they don't fix what is real. And my own view is that the personal / sub-personal distinction finds no basis in the science of action-explanation, and needs to be abandoned.[6] It certainly can't be used to warrant the claim that people are passive with respect to their habitual, skilled, and emotion-caused actions.

3.8 Conclusion

All affective states produce automatic motor urges of one or another (or both) of two sorts – expressive and seemingly instrumental. Unless they get suppressed by executive decisions, these motor activations will issue in action. Common sense recognizes both kinds of urge. For example, one can be aware that it is hard to repress a smile or a look of disgust. And when confronted with a charging black bear (in which case one should stand one's ground and make oneself look big), one might report, "I found it hard to resist the impulse to turn-tail and run." Likewise, when angered by an insulting remark from one's boss one might later say, "I had to bite my tongue not to reply in kind." Nevertheless, we are also (mistakenly) apt to offer goal-based explanations of directly affect-caused actions. One might say, "I ran because I wanted to get away." And one might explain an insulting riposte by saying, "I was determined to hurt him back." A reasonable hypothesis to explain this apparent discrepancy (acknowledging the existence of motor urges while at the same time offering belief-desire explanations) is that people are apt to conflate motoric urges with the kinds of desire that figure in decision-making. And indeed, one popular philosophical theory of desire is that it is a disposition to bring about the desired state of affairs. This is a mistake, but an issue we revisit in Chapter 6.

[6] Unfortunately the distinction is sometimes made use of by cognitive scientists, too – generally while failing to keep separate the two possible meanings discussed earlier (conscious / unconscious versus property of the whole / property of a part). In my view this is one of a number of places where philosophers have had a bad influence on cognitive science (most notably alongside the so-called "hard problem" of consciousness).

CHAPTER 4

Mental Actions

This chapter considers what mental actions are, and how they are best explained. Mental actions, I will suggest, include mental rehearsals of action, prospective imagining, inner speech, attention, memory search, and (perhaps surprisingly) the spontaneous thoughts that occur to one while mind-wandering, as well as creative ideas that seemingly occur to one "out of the blue." The chapter will also discuss how controlled sequences of mental action can be explained, and will discuss events like judgments and decisions that armchair-philosophers have been apt to claim are mental actions, but really are not.

4.1 What Are Actions?

In order to address the question of mental action we need to know what physical actions are. For it is natural to think that, just as a physical action is a physical event of a particular sort, so a mental action should be a mental event of the same sort (since both are actions). As previously noted, the standard view among philosophers (although by no means universally endorsed) is that intentional actions are bodily movements that are both caused and controlled by intentions, where intentions in turn reflect some of the agent's desires and beliefs interacting in such a way as to issue in a decision to act (Piñeros Glasscock & Tenenbaum 2023). Such a view can naturally be extended into the mental realm by claiming that a mental action is a mental event that is caused and controlled by the agent's intentions – where the intention specifies the goal or success-condition that the mental action is intended to satisfy, and results from decision-making in light of the agent's beliefs and values (Peacocke 2021). Irving (2021) argues in addition that not just intentional causation but *guidance* of an unfolding event or series of events is a central feature of both physical and mental action.

Recall some of the variety of kinds of action discussed in earlier chapters, however. There are habitual actions that are triggered directly by contextual cues; there are speeded and skilled actions that are selected and implemented from within sensorimotor systems; there are affect-caused actions (both expressive and instrumental) produced directly by appraisal processes in a way that can bypass executive decision-making processes. Moreover, as we will discuss in Chapter 5 (and consistent with the standard model), there are actions that result immediately from reasoning-based or prospectively formed decisions for the here-and-now; and there are actions that result from activation of previously formed intentions that have been stored in prospective memory. The only thing that is common among all of these kinds of physical action is that they are physical movements that are cortically controlled by the motor system. So if one were to model mental actions on what all physical actions have in common (only transposed into the mental realm), then one would have to say that a mental action is a mental event of some sort that is cortically controlled by the motor system.

Not all of the types of action listed above are *intentional* actions as philosophers generally define them, of course. So we could choose to focus narrowly on the question of mental events that are caused and controlled by the agent's intentions. But in doing so we might miss important classes of mental action, just as a narrow focus on intentional physical actions would lead us to miss out on habitual, skilled, and affect-caused actions, which when taken together make up a large proportion of our everyday behavior. But equally, it seems overly restrictive to insist that mental actions must possess the one property that all physical actions share (i.e. control by the motor system). This might fit some kinds of what are, intuitively, mental actions. (It applies to mental rehearsals of action, for example, as we will see shortly.) However, there could well be other classes of mental action that more closely resemble intentional actions or affect-caused actions, but without involving the motor system, or which involve non-motoric forms of guidance and control.

I suggest that the most fruitful approach is to consider, for any putative case of mental action, the extent of its resemblance to one or more of the differing classes of physical action listed above. Any mental event that shares the same structure of causation and control as a physical action might reasonably be counted as a mental action. But in any case, for each putative kind of mental action – whether or not it is actually a species of action – we can ask how the events in question are best explained. That is the task we embark on in this chapter.

4.2 Mental Rehearsal and Inner Speech

The clearest, most straightforward, instances of mental action are provided by cases in which people mentally rehearse physical actions. It has been known for decades that mental rehearsal of the movements involved in a skill (such as putting in golf) can improve physical performance (Driskell et al. 1994; Jeannerod 2006; Toth et al. 2020); and also that it can help with the re-acquisition of skills following stroke damage (García Carrasco & Aboitiz Cantalapiedra 2016). This suggests that some of the same mechanisms are involved in each. Moreover, physical practice and mental practice appear to be structurally almost identical. Both can begin with an intention for the here-and-now to improve a particular skill, which guides subsequent performance and provides its success-condition. And both implicate similar motor-related brain regions, including premotor cortex and the cerebellum (Hardwick et al. 2018).

In seems that in each case what one does is initiate the high-level motor instructions for the intended movement. But in the case of physical practice those instructions then cascade down through the motor system to the point of completion (hence actually executing the action), with one thereafter perceiving and evaluating the results against one's target for the performance in question. In the case of mental practice, in contrast, one suppresses the later stages of the execution processes, and instead attends to the sensory forward model created by the initiating set of motor instructions. One thereby becomes aware of what it would have felt like and looked like had the action actually been executed, comparing this with one's target for the performance instead.[1]

There are more factors that one needs to appeal to when explaining a mentally rehearsed action than one does for the corresponding physical action. Both can involve intentional activation of a motor plan, and in both cases those motor plans will issue in sensory forward models of the expected sensory consequences of executing the physical movement in question. But then in the case of mentally rehearsed action alone, executive signals need to be generated to suppress or inhibit the later stages of the execution of the

[1] Interestingly, greater activity shows up in the dorsolateral prefrontal cortex in mentally rehearsed actions in contrast with overt actions (Hardwick et al. 2018). This is unlikely to reflect the demands of action-cancellation, since this is known to center on networks involving the ventrolateral regions of the prefrontal cortex (Zhang et al. 2017). Rather, since dorsolateral prefrontal cortex is especially involved in attentional tasks and working-memory tasks, the increased activity in this region associated with mental rehearsal may reflect the additional demands involved in focusing attention on a sensory forward model, as opposed to attending to an actual experience of action with a similar content.

motor plan, so that no movement actually takes place. In addition, attention needs to be directed to the sensory forward model, boosting it to the status of a conscious motor image that can then be evaluated against the target skill, or which can be used in other ways. Nevertheless, there is surely enough overlap between the two for both to qualify as forms of action – physical and mental respectively. For they share a common core of causation by an intention (which in turn is caused by a desire for improvement and the belief that mental practice will help) and subsequent control by the motor system.

Speech actions are among the physical actions that one can mentally rehearse, of course, giving rise to so-called "inner speech." Indeed, there is now broad agreement about how motor planning gives rise to inner speech. Motor plans are selected and activated, issuing in an efference copy (or "corollary discharge") of those instructions while downstream activation of the facial and throat musculature is suppressed. The efference copy then creates a sensory representation of what the speech act in question would have sounded like had it been carried through to completion (Tian & Poeppel 2010; Corley et al. 2011; Scott 2013).

We also know from work involving brain-scanning of various kinds that inner-speech production proceeds in two stages, with motor activations first creating a somatosensory representation of what the movements in question would feel like, which then creates an auditory representation of what the resulting speech would sound like (Tian & Poeppel 2013). The process begins with activity in Broca's area (the classic speech-production / speech-planning area), which then activates the relevant regions of primary motor cortex. That then causes activity in somatosensory regions of the parietal cortex, before activity is produced in abstract auditory regions of superior temporal cortex.

The representations that constitute the experience of inner speech can be more or less detailed and determinate, of course, just as can other forms of imagery. (One can visually imagine a reindeer on the roof without specifying whether or not it has horns, for example.) Inner speech can be confined to abstract phonological representations, in particular. For when people are asked to rehearse "tongue-twisters" in inner speech they rarely make errors, suggesting that (in these cases, at least) inner speech is confined to non-articulatory components of speech, omitting the level of motor activation that would issue in phonetic representations (Oppenheim & Dell 2008, 2010). But of course people *can* generate inner speech that includes details of accent, timbre, and pitch, as an actor might do when mentally rehearsing her lines for a performance.

I am suggesting that all inner speech is a form of mental action (provided that it isn't just an episodic memory of someone else's speech, of course). But then how are we to account for the robust finding from introspection-sampling studies that people frequently report a distinction between "inner speaking," which is active, and "inner hearing," which is not (Hurlburt et al. 2013)? The fact that people sometimes don't *experience* their inner speech as active simply has no bearing on the question whether it is actually produced by activating a motor plan, however. For the latter are always unconscious anyway. There is no such thing as conscious awareness of a motor plan as such. Rather, it may be that the distinction merely reflects the presence or absence of some degree of awareness of somatosensory activation in inner speech, where people take such awareness as a cue to self-produced activity. The experienced distinction between inner hearing and inner speaking may then merely result from subtle differences in the direction of attention (whether toward auditory sensory representations alone, or also to the somatosensory forward models implicated in production).

Mental rehearsals of action can be used for a variety of purposes. Like overt forms of practice they can be used to fine-tune one's performance, noticing errors and correcting one's motor planning accordingly. Thus a golfer might mentally rehearse a putting stroke to improve fine details of the movements involved, and an actor might mentally rehearse components of a speech in order to get the intonation just right. Perhaps more commonly, mentally rehearsed action can also be used for purposes of planning. One might mentally rehearse the different ways in which one could pick up an awkwardly shaped heavy object, for example, selecting the one that seems easiest and safest. Or one might use mentally rehearsed speech to evaluate a variety of ways in which one could ask someone out on a date, trying to decide which might create the best impression and maximize the chances of acceptance.

In fact, mental rehearsals of action constitute one of the ways in which prospective reasoning can be implemented, of the sort to be discussed in Chapter 5. Sometimes we mentally rehearse a variety of actions in order to evaluate and select among them as such, as in the example of lifting the awkwardly shaped object. But more often we rehearse actions in order to predict and evaluate their likely consequences, as one does when rehearsing various ways of asking someone out. How do these latter kinds of case work? When the sensory forward model produced by each action-rehearsal is attended to and becomes conscious, it is received as input by a range of implicit and explicit memory systems (including a physics emulator, bodies of implicit statistical knowledge, and the mentalizing system) which create a representation of the likely outcomes. These are then attended to in turn, and are received and appraised within one's affective / evaluative systems. The resulting degrees of positive or negative valence can then figure in one's decision-making alongside degrees of likelihood.

Notice that although mental rehearsals surely qualify as (mental) actions, in most cases they fail to conform to the standard belief-desire model. Admittedly, sometimes they do. A golfer might mentally rehearse a particular chip-shot because she wants to execute it successfully and believes that mental rehearsal will help her to do so, subsequently forming the intention to rehearse. But more commonly, mental rehearsal is something one does spontaneously, without requiring any support from a mediating belief and without forming any prior intention. Someone confronting a heavy awkwardly shaped object may mentally rehearse different modes of lifting it out of habit, or as a conditioned behavior. And inner speech will generally result from unconscious affective appraisal processes of the sort to be discussed in Section 4.4. One doesn't have to *believe* that mentally rehearsing various ways of asking someone on a date will lead to success. Rather, most inner speech (even inner speech that is goal-directed, as here) will result from appraisals of relevance that take place spontaneously within the sensorimotor system, as with other forms of skilled action. So there are vast numbers of actions in addition to those discussed in Chapters 2 and 3 (namely, most cases of mental rehearsal of action) that don't conform to the standard belief-desire model employed by armchair-philosophers.

4.3 Imagination, Memory Search, and Attention

While mental rehearsals of action are often used predictively to estimate and evaluate their likely outcomes, sometimes we just imagine and evaluate outcomes themselves. One can imaginatively suppose that something is the case, or imagine what would have happened had something happened differently in the past, responding affectively to each. How does imagining that is *not* a product of action-rehearsal work, and is imagining of this sort also a kind of mental action?

Sometimes the outcomes one imagines and evaluates are presented to one from outside, as when participants in a neuroeconomics experiment are given a binary choice on each trial. ("A 10% chance of receiving a cookie or a sure-thing viewing of a beautiful face.") On other occasions the outcomes are self-generated as possible or salient implementations of a more abstract goal. ("A local restaurant for dinner this Saturday.") One uses the conceptual information embedded in the goal as a probe to activate and elaborate knowledge stored in memory (e.g. of particular restaurants, their noisiness, their menus, their distances away, and so on). The resulting conceptualized images are attended to, become conscious, and are received as input by affective systems for evaluative appraisal. Indeed, Shea (2022) goes so far as to suggest that concepts themselves can be regarded as "plug and play" devices. Concepts and combinations of concepts (thoughts) are used as top-down probes to construct mental simulations of outcomes and events, drawing on stored knowledge (both implicit and explicit) to do so.

Is intentional imagining of outcomes a form of mental action? Although it need not involve motor-system activation, it otherwise shares many of the features of physical action. It is a mental process that is caused and controlled by the agent's goals (such as determining which restaurant to choose). It is initiated by a goal that is used to probe memory systems to create rich representations of sensory details as well as simulated events and outcomes. And often, the process involves intentional shifting of the conceptual probes in such a way as to construct additional elaborations for evaluation. ("Which restaurants have outside seating?") In this respect, also, it resembles physical forms of action, which often require shifts and adjustments in the course of their execution. But here too (as with mental rehearsals of action discussed in Section 4.2) most individual acts of imagining fail to conform to the standard model. One doesn't imagine a particular outcome because one believes that doing so will help one to reach a good decision. Rather, one imagines it as part of a skilled sequence, resulting from appraisal of unconsciously activated options that compete with one another to be brought to (conscious) mind. (Section 4.4 will discuss the mechanisms involved.)

Simple searches of memory, too, appear action-like. Given a goal of driving to the grocery store, but not seeing the car keys in their usual place, one might generate a series of probes of memory ("where did I last have them?" "what did I do with them?" and so on). Likewise, a hungry scrub-jay might probe its memory for the location of a food cache. If animal memory searches work in the way that human memory search does, the bird uses a conceptual or concept-like goal representation of some sort to activate stored representations in long-term memory. And as with human memory search, partial results (such as an image of a knot-hole in a tree, but without the location of the tree yet specified) will encourage continued probing ("in the forest?" "on the edge of the meadow?" and so on). So a goal (to obtain the car keys, or to obtain food) is used to initiate a mental process, controlling the execution of that process thereafter to flexibly retrieve the information necessary to achieve the goal. This, too, looks structurally very similar to the kinds of physical action discussed in Chapter 2.

Next, consider *attention*. As is now familiar to many, this can be either overt or covert. Overt visual attention involves movements of the eyes and head. Some instances of it are definitely forms of physical action, and can be fully under intentional control. One can decide to keep one's eyes fixed on a traffic light, knowing that the driver next in line will become irritated if one does not move off immediately when it changes; and if one becomes distracted by a passing ambulance, one's goal can motivate returning one's gaze to the lights once again. Moreover, overt visual attention can be a direct behavioral product of affective systems, too, as when one has to struggle to look away from the scene of a gruesome accident. Indeed, it seems that overt attention admits of some of the same varieties as do other forms of physical action, discussed in Chapters 2 and 3.

Eye-saccades are more ambiguous as instances of physical action, however. On the one hand, sensorimotor decisions about where, in detail, to look are taken two or three times each second. It seems that the ways in which one's eyes saccade across a scene, it particular, are dependent on previous patterns of reward as well as on learned strategies for maximizing information-gain in specific types of context (Chukoskie et al. 2013; Yang et al. 2016). In this respect saccades resemble cases of speeded and skilled action, discussed in Sections 2.3 and 2.4. But on the other hand, saccades are not *controlled* movements; they are ballistic (Optician & Pretegiani 2017). In this respect they are more like reflexes such as an eye-blink or a knee-jerk. Some would claim that this is sufficient to prevent them from qualifying as actions.[2] In accordance with the open-minded strategy adopted in this chapter, however, we don't need to attempt to settle the question. We can simply note that controlled production is a feature of almost all forms of physical action, but is absent here.

Now consider covert forms of attention. This is involved in both imagination and memory search (as well as in mental rehearsals of action). It has been heavily studied. Covert *visual* attention often operates in parallel with overt attention, shifting to the target of the next eye-saccade

[2] Indeed, Strawson (2003) denies that mind-wandering is comprised of mental actions on just such grounds, claiming that the thoughts in question are produced ballistically, in ways that are not under control. In this he is mistaken, as we will see in Section 4.5.

some milliseconds before any overt movement, preparing the target region to process the resulting input. It is comprised of neural signals that impact mid-level regions of visual cortex, boosting and helping to organize neural activity of the targets while suppressing non-targets (Carrasco & McElree 2001; Jensen et al. 2007; Bisley 2011). Targeting by covert attention is a necessary condition for visual representations to become conscious (entering working memory and becoming globally accessible), and it is sufficient for consciousness provided those representations have enough intrinsic baseline activation (Dehaene 2014; Carruthers 2015).

Covert attention appears to be a single domain-general resource that can operate across all sensory modalities. In addition to attending to visual stimuli, one can attend to a sound, to a taste, to a smell, to a touch, to one's own felt movements, and so on. And when one divides attention across modalities the same overall signature limits apply. (Entry into working memory is limited to roughly three or four items at a time, and the limits on working memory abilities derive in part from limits on attentional capacities themselves; Cowan 2001; Shipstead et al. 2012; Tsukahara et al. 2020.) Moreover, covert attention operates in the same basic way within each modality: boosting, organizing, and suppressing, as well as (normally) issuing in conscious awareness of the attended contents.

Covert attention, like overt visual attention, quite closely resembles a number of different kinds of physical action. It can be intentionally controlled and guided, as when one focuses attention on the periphery of one's visual field to detect brief flashes of light during an eye-exam (Vuilleumier 2015; Jiang 2018). It can be habitual, shifting among components of a stimulus in a way that reflects previous learning (Anderson 2016; Jiang 2018). Or it can be an automatic or semi-automatic output of affective appraisal processes that seemingly grab one's attention (Vuilleumier 2015).

Importantly for our purposes later in this chapter, covert attention (hereafter "attention") is controlled by a number of interacting cortical and subcortical networks (Petersen & Posner 2012). In particular, there is a top-down network that controls and directs attention itself, which is centered on the frontal eye-fields (a region in dorsal motor cortex) and the intraparietal sulcus (in the superior parietal lobes). One component of this network is externally directed, whereas another is internally directed (Chun et al. 2011). And then there is a bottom-up network, located mostly in the right hemisphere. (This is sometimes called the "salience network," sometimes the "ventral attentional network"; although there may be two separate but overlapping systems involved; Fiebelkorn & Kastner 2020.)

The network involves ventral regions of the right parietal lobe, ventrolateral prefrontal cortex in the right hemisphere, and the anterior insula, interacting with affective subcortical networks (Corbetta et al. 2008; Uddin 2015). The bottom-up system monitors unattended but active representations (whether sensory or mnemonic), evaluating them for salience and relevance, and competes for control of the top-down system for entry of the representations in question into consciousness.

In addition to mental rehearsals of action, then, it seems that imagining situations or events, controlled memory search, and covert attention can all qualify as kinds of mental action. Each is similar enough structurally to one or more of the forms of action identified in previous chapters to count as instances of the same (or at least a similar) kind. But in most cases they fail to conform to the standard belief-desire model. One doesn't generally engage in mental action because one believes that doing so will help one to achieve one's goals.

4.4 Controlled Thinking

Physical actions can be complex, hierarchically organized, and extend over significant periods of time. Traveling to New York City is an action, and generally requires planning. It breaks down into actions that are themselves complex (get to the station; purchase a ticket; get on the train; get off the train), each of which is in turn composed of yet simpler actions (insert a credit-card into the ticket machine; walk onto the platform), and so on. Such extended actions rely on a number of different factors: explicit knowledge of facts (New York City has a train station); know-how of various sorts (how to look up timetables, how to purchase a ticket); and skills (walking, avoiding other pedestrians, inserting a card into a slot). What holds them all together is the hierarchical plan that is designed to achieve a specific goal. And in the course of executing the action one has to keep track of where one is in the process and call up prospective memories of the next stages of the plan, making flexible adjustments when necessary.

To what extent are sequences of controlled thinking – thinking that is directed at a particular goal – similar to such temporally extended and hierarchically organized physical actions? There are certainly important differences. The main one is that controlled thinking is always or generally conducted in the service of decision-making. And since planning is itself an instance of controlled thinking, there can't be an already existing mapped-out sequence of mental actions intended to get one to a decision – one can't have decided which thoughts to think in advance of thinking them, in the way that one can have decided in advance on a sequence of physical actions. So there can't be a plan for an upcoming sequence of thought directed at reaching a decision that has the sort of determinacy that a plan to get to New York City can have.

Perhaps a sequence of controlled thinking is more like the sort of physical-action goal-pursuit in which one has little idea how to achieve the goal in advance. When one goes on a first date with someone one does have an overall goal: to make a good impression and perhaps to begin a relationship if it turns out that you like one another enough. Some people might well attempt to plan out the evening roughly in advance. But many will just "wing it," seeing where the conversation goes and developing the evening from there, albeit with some very general ideas about the kinds of things one might say, discuss, and do.

Trying to decide whether to accept a job offer may be a bit like that, too. One's thinking is organized under a single goal (to decide yes or no). One might have some idea in advance of the relevant parameters for the decision (salary, location, colleagues, opportunities for one's spouse, children's education, and so on), but little idea how to weigh them and prioritize them. One's thoughts will range back and forth, adding new considerations as they occur to one ("what about housing costs?" "what about places for running and hiking?"), elaborating and responding affectively to their contents as they do. Note that each one of the sub-components in such sequences of thinking either is or results from a mental action, however. Some occur in inner speech, some involve active imagining, and some result from probes of memory ("what is the place like in winter?").

Some episodes of controlled thinking can be a bit more organized than this. For example, a philosopher whose goal is to construct a counterexample to a thesis that she disagrees with may have a pretty clear idea of how to proceed: first, deduce and lay out the main entailments of the thesis; then probe each one, trying to think of situations that might falsify it. Notice that the latter stage can't be planned in advance, however. Rather, although she can actively probe memory, and can actively construct related scenarios in imagination, at some point, inevitably, she just has to rely on ideas to occur to her, seemingly passively. How that happens is something we will return to shortly.

People have a variety of resources that can enable them to structure, or partially structure, sequences of controlled thinking. Some might be innate. These might include some innate logical abilities, and perhaps also an innate "adaptation for argumentation" (Mercier & Sperber 2017).

The latter is said to have evolved initially to protect against persuasion by others as well as to enable persuasion of others in social contexts, but can perhaps be deployed inwardly to constrain sequences of inner speech. Some additional resources might be implicit norms acquired from observing others, as surely happens in various kinds of intellectual apprenticeship. And some might be explicit norms acquired through both informal and formal teaching. And then some will be strategies and heuristics acquired through instrumental conditioning. Finally, sequences of thought can also be habitual, of course, resulting either from training (as with the basic sequences involved in mental arithmetic) or from simple repetition.

In many cases, then, there need be no mystery about how one thought causes another, provided that the thoughts themselves are mental actions. The sequence in question can be a habitual one, or can have been instrumentally conditioned. Or the thought might be activated automatically from an affective appraisal of what needs to happen next in the context (where the source of appraisal is an implicit or explicit norm). Alternatively, the "adaptation for argumentation" might issue in a particular continuation of the sequence of thoughts, making it seem good and right.

Controlled sequences of thinking can be more or less hierarchically organized, then, albeit never approaching the level of advance-specification that extended sequences of physical action can have. And although some of the thought-transitions that occur during such thinking can be habitual, or can be caused by appraisals of normative commitment, and so on, on many occasions one is reduced to just trying things out in thought. One often has to engage in what one might call "exploratory thinking," albeit directed at achieving a specific goal or decision. In prospective decision-making, for example, it is often the case that the alternatives are not given to one in advance. On the contrary, they can be open-ended, as when one spends one's coffee-break thinking (in a goal-directed manner) about what one might do for one's next summer vacation. Where, in such cases, do the ideas come from? How are they generated?

The answer lies with the salience network and/or ventral attentional network, mentioned briefly in Section 4.3 (Menon & D'Esposito 2022). These networks continually monitor unattended stimuli, as well as unattended memories and motor plans that have been activated associatively and in parallel by aspects of the internal or external environment. These are evaluated for relevance against both stored values and current goals, integrating information from multiple sources. (The core of this network appears to be the anterior insula, hidden in the fold behind anterior temporal cortex; Sridharan et al. 2008; Molnar-Szakacs & Uddin 2022.) This system then interacts with the top-down attentional network via the dorsal region of anterior cingulate cortex (just above the frontal portion of the corpus collosum), competing to redirect the focus of attention from its current target. Hence one will notice anything unusual happening in the environment, and ideas that are deemed relevant enough to one's goals and values will be apt to break through into working memory, thereby becoming conscious.

When one has a specific cognitive goal (to find a counter-example to thesis *P* or to decide where to go on vacation) the concepts implicated in the goal can function as probes of one's memory systems, activating related contents. These will then compete with one another in mutually inhibitory fashion and for relevance to the goal. When one of them hits the criterion for a switch of attention, it becomes highlighted by top-down attention and enters consciousness (being broadcast widely to multiple systems) where it can be held in place long enough to be evaluated more fully. Here the switch and maintenance of attention constitute forms of mental action, of course, as we saw in Section 4.3. But what of the contents that emerge into consciousness themselves? Are they, too, mental actions?

Often a goal-directed search for ideas will issue in a phrase or sentence in inner speech. That, as we have seen, is itself a mental action, motivated by its relevance to the goal (to find a counter-example to *P*, perhaps). Other times what emerges might be imagery, or imagery tied to a word or phrase (such as "Martinique"). Again, this qualifies as a mental action. It is a mental event caused and sustained by a goal (to decide on a vacation destination).

In conclusion, although episodes of controlled goal-directed thinking are unlike some temporally extended physical actions in that they cannot be fully planned in advance, they are like others (such as aiming to make a good impression on a first date) in containing a sequence of mental actions that are selected and executed as one goes along, but in the service of an overall goal.

4.5 Mind-Wandering and Creative Thought

Mind-wandering is the opposite of goal-directed thought. It is not a coherent hierarchically organized action in its own right. So it is not at all like the action of traveling to New York City. Nor is it even like trying to make a good impression on a first date, since this at least organizes action in light of a single goal. But mind-wandering has no goal. It is a sequence of undirected thoughts. But that need not mean that it is passive, as Irving (2021) claims, any more than someone who is wandering aimlessly round an unfamiliar city is passive. A physical wanderer is someone whose movements have no overall goal. Rather, one might decide now to go this way, now to go that, influenced by the whims of the moment. But physical wandering is still active, of course; it is just not *an* action. So the same might be true of mind-wandering. It can be comprised of an undirected sequence of mental actions. Indeed, we have already seen enough in this chapter to know that it is.

When one mind-wanders the salience / ventral-attentional systems are dominant; there is no overarching goal that directs and organizes top-down attention. Associatively activated ideas and motor plans are appraised for relevance to one's affective values and easily accessible standing goals, competing with one another for the resources of top-down attention and entry into working memory. If the selection process works in the same basic way as it does in perceptual decision-making, then the associatively activated representations will compete with one another in mutually inhibitory fashion within the ventral attention system, and the neural population that reaches criterion first will cause a switch in the direction of top-down attention. In effect, one takes a decision to attend to the contents of the winning representation. The resulting mental event (an idea, an image, or a phrase in inner speech) results from a decision and is sustained and elaborated while targeted by an ongoing intention-to-attend until the next idea defeats it and takes over.

The component events in mind-wandering appear to be caused and sustained in ways that are quite similar to the kinds of sensorimotor actions involved in skills and/or affect-caused actions. The events in question are not intentional in the strong sense of resulting from decision-making processes that involve practical reasoning involving one's beliefs and desires. (But then nor are the events in goal-directed thought intentional in that sense, as we noted in Section 4.4.) Consider affect-caused physical actions first. Recall from Section 3.5 how anger can result directly in a verbal insult. There need be no beliefs involved. Rather, one's anger directly causes an urge to damage the source of one's anger. A variety of action-types (either innate or acquired from previous instrumental learning) become activated in parallel. Their immediate consequences are predicted and affectively evaluated in mutually inhibitory fashion, and the winning representation is then implemented (provided one doesn't take an executive decision to inhibit it).

Likewise in many cases of mind-wandering: various associatively activated mutually inhibiting representations are appraised for their relevance to one's standing values and goals, and the winning representation causes a switch in the direction of top-down attention, thereby becoming conscious. There is no practical reasoning involved, and no beliefs need be implicated. Nor is any decision taken in the light of an already active goal or intention. Rather, the resulting conscious imagery or phrases of inner speech can be thought of as the results of an affectively caused decision-to-attend. They are active in the same kind of way that an anger-caused insult is active (except that not all of the mental actions that figure in mind-wandering need implicate the motor system, in the way that both overt and inner speech do). Mind-wandering actions can be directly affectively caused in a way that bypasses executive decision-making processes, just as anger-caused actions can.

Now recall from Section 2.4 how skilled actions can be independent of one's beliefs, too, directly caused within well-trained sensorimotor systems. Recall the soccer player deciding to pass rather than to juke around an opponent. There need be no beliefs involved. Nor are executive decision-making / practical-reasoning systems implicated. Rather, a pair of mutually inhibitory competing motor plans are appraised for success given the perceived affordances of the situation, resulting in a decision to implement one rather than the other. But here (unlike the case of affect-caused action) there is an overarching goal or intention (to advance down the pitch) which provides the success-criterion against which the motor representations in question are evaluated. The motor representation that is appraised as more likely to advance the ball successfully is the one that wins the competition and is implemented.

Sometimes the ideas that occur to us when mind-wandering are caused in a way that resembles this, in that the appraisal of relevance isn't to one's standing affective values but rather to some goal or intention that one has. But skilled physical actions are selected by appraisal against active goals one is currently pursuing (such as to advance the ball down the pitch), whereas in mind-wandering the goals in question can be "dormant," albeit easily accessible. Thus knowing that one will soon be required to list all fifty US states while one is currently engaged in meditation-like focusing on one's breath, one's mind will be more likely to wander to images of US maps or to US state-names (Morsella et al. 2010). In such a case the word "Nebraska" may intrude into consciousness because its relevance to an upcoming task causes it to attract top-down attention.

Mind-wandering can also implicate active goals, however, albeit ones that are easily displaced by others because none are deemed urgent or important enough to warrant sustained attention. Someone wandering around a city may well pursue temporary goals, too, such as walking up one street to look at a striking shop-sign and down another to see a building with unusual architecture. Likewise when mind-wandering, one might spend a few minutes thinking about what to cook for dinner (without resolving the issue) before switching to think about one's upcoming summer vacation, before switching again to attend to a car going past, and so on. In some cases one's thoughts are affectively salient (a noisy or brightly colored car), in some they are deemed relevant to a goal that has just become reactivated (such as deciding on a dinner menu).

I have been arguing that individual mental episodes during mind-wandering are mental actions. This is obviously so whenever the episode in question is a phrase or sentence in inner speech, or involves some other form of mental rehearsal of action. But even when it is just an idea, such as an image of an object or event, it results from an online decision to direct and sustain attention. This is quite similar to the sorts of decision-making and subsequent guidance that are involved in sensorimotor skills or in affect-caused actions.

If mind-wandering is comprised of mental actions, however, then why does it feel passive, in a way that wandering around an unfamiliar city does not? Why doesn't mind-wandering *feel* active, if it actually *is* active? Ultimately the answer lies in the limitations of common-sense psychology; but this will take a little unpacking.

When one wanders around a city one is fully aware that the component events are actions, of course. Walking is an action, and so is turning one way rather than another when one reaches a corner; and everyone knows this. In contrast, folk-psychology doesn't clearly recognize events of wondering, remembering, or imagining as forms of (mental) action. Indeed, as we noted earlier, even inner speech is sometimes experienced as a form of passive "inner hearing" as opposed to active inner speaking. But it is still active for all that.

Moreover, when physically wandering one generally has some awareness of the factors that induce one to turn in one direction rather than another, including things on the walk that happen to catch one's attention. ("I turned up that street because I was curious to see what the sign above the shop said." "I turned down that one because I was struck by the design of one of the buildings." And so on.) When mind-wandering, in contrast, one generally lacks such awareness. For the decision-making happens among unconsciously activated representations in the ventral attentional network. And even when one can guess at the reason why one's mind wandered to a particular topic ("I suppose I thought of Nebraska because I was soon going to be tested on US states"; Irving 2021), this is not something one was aware of at the time in the way that one was aware of the shop-sign or the interesting piece of architecture. Rather, it is a bit of retrospective self-interpretation.

Now consider creative thought, which strikes most people as passive. As is familiar to many, mind-wandering can facilitate creating thinking (Baird et al. 2012). One may have reached an impasse in some task or problem (how to avoid what seems like imminent check-mate in an online game of chess; how to finish a poem or complete an article or story; and so on). Then while one is in the shower, or is half awake in the middle of the night, or is strolling through the woods, a solution (or apparent solution) can leap suddenly into one's conscious mind. The process is paradigmatically passive-seeming. Indeed, the ancient Greeks thought that the sources of creative ideas lay outside of one's own mind entirely, whispered into one's ears by the gods known as the Muses. But on the account outlined here, the process is actually active.

Creative insight depends, in part, on the way memory can get restructured during an interval, especially when one sleeps (Wagner et al. 2004; Diekelmann et al. 2009), but something still has to pull an aspect of the restructured information into consciousness. Here is how it can work. One has some cognitive goal that one can't currently achieve. One turns one's mind to other things, and the goal is no longer active, but is still readily accessible. One is then engaged in something that is not attentionally demanding (making one prone to mind-wander) or one is actually already mind-wandering. Features of the perceived environment (such as a snatch of a nearby conversation, or an advertisement on a passing metrobus) or of one's own current thought processes will continually be associatively activating a range of concepts, memories, and motor plans. These are evaluated for relevance to affective values and to one's accessible goals. When an idea is appraised as relevant enough to the unsolved problem one had set aside, it wins the competition for top-down attention and emerges into consciousness.

The only part of this process one is aware of is the last: one finds oneself with a potential solution in mind, which one can then set about evaluating more systematically. But while the novel idea results from a process that isn't itself an action (associative activation), the idea's entry into consciousness *is* an action, resulting from a decision to switch and sustain the direction of attention given the idea's relevance to the goal.[3]

I have argued here that both common-sense psychology and philosophers who have relied on common-sense intuitions are deeply mistaken about the supposedly passive nature of the creative thoughts that occur to us "out of the blue," as well as of the thoughts that occur to us when mind-wandering. On the contrary, both are active in ways similar to sensorimotor skilled actions and/or affect-caused actions, of the sorts discussed in Sections 2.4 and 3.5. They result from motivated decisions to switch and sustain attention to the contents in question (where switching is an action, or at least action-like), and many of the mental events attended to are themselves active in nature (as are inner speech and mental rehearsals of action, among others).

4.6 Judgments and Decisions Are Not Actions

It is widely agreed among philosophers that judgments are a form of mental action (Peacocke 2008; Dorsch 2009; Sosa 2015; Peacocke 2021). But some, plainly, are not. Consider perceptual judgments. One is tasked by an experimenter with judging on each trial whether the dominant motion in a random-dot stereogram is toward the left or the right (van den Berg et al. 2016a). Activity in two neural populations – representing leftward motion and rightward motion respectively – builds in response to the stimulus in mutually inhibitory fashion until the activity in one of them hits criterion-level, and one then responds accordingly. When the leftward-motion population reaches criterion first, that *constitutes* a judgment that the dominant motion is to the left. But there is nothing remotely action-like about this event. It is not caused and controlled by a prior intention, nor does it express an affective appraisal of the stimulus. And although the event does take place in the context of one's goal of complying with the experimenter's instructions, there is nothing analogous to a sensorimotor appraisal of an affordance-to-succeed of the sort that

[3] Consistent with the account of creative idea-generation sketched here, Zabelina et al. (2015, 2016) find that measures of real-world creative achievement correlate with what they call "leaky attention." For example, creative people find it harder to ignore elements in a stimulus-array that are irrelevant to the task. This makes sense, given the account of creativity provided above. For it is a matter of chance whether the ideas that are activated associatively by one's current circumstances or aspects of one's current thoughts really provide (the germ of) a successful solution to the backgrounded problem for which one requires a novel answer. So, other things being equal, the more often such ideas break through and intrude into consciousness, the more likely it is that one will end up developing a creative solution.

happens in skilled action (although moving the joystick to the left as a result of one's judgment can itself qualify as a skilled action, of course).

I conjecture that all forms of unreflective judgment are like this. Someone tells one something, for example, and one judges (unreflectively, unconsciously) that they are trustworthy, and accepts what they say, thereby coming to believe it. Here multiple sources of information will get integrated, including the person's demeanor and tone of voice, their past history of reliability, their in-group status, their knowledgeability about the subject matter of the assertion, and so on. As with a perceptual judgment, one can assume that all these sources feed into a neural accumulator representing *believable*, which competes in mutually inhibitory fashion with one representing *untrustworthy*. And again as with perceptual judgment, when the former neural population reaches criterion-level that constitutes a judgment that the statement can be trusted. (It will at the same time be accompanied by an analog-magnitude representation of likelihood, computed from the differing rates of gain of the two populations.) There is nothing action-like here, either.

Reflectively formed judgments, in contrast, are another matter. (And in fairness to the philosophers cited above, these constitute paradigmatic instances of the sorts of judgment-making that philosophers generally have in mind.) And these are, indeed, a form of mental action. When one makes up one's mind about some matter of fact, that is an action, motivated by one's assessment of the evidence combined with a desire to reach a decision, and to do so now rather than later. A juror will review the evidence presented in the trial, finally making up her mind that the accused is guilty (say). That mental event of making-up-of-mind is an action.

As we will see in Chapter 7, however, in many cases an act of making up one's mind is really a *commitment* to think, reason, and act in the future on the assumption that the proposition in question is true. It is a mental action because making a commitment is an action, just as promising is. It is not really a judgment at all, if we assume that judgments are attitudes with mind-to-world direction of fit. On the contrary, the act of making up one's mind has a world-to-mind direction of fit – one undertakes to constrain one's thoughts and behavior in the future in such a way as to honor, or satisfy, one's commitment.

There is good reason to think, then, that unreflective judgments are not actions, whereas reflective "judgments" are genuinely action-like, but are perhaps not really judgments at all – they are, rather, commitment-making mental actions. But what, then, of decisions? These, too, are commonly thought by philosophers to be a form of mental action

(McCall 1987; Mele 2000, 2021; Peacocke 2008; Peacocke 2021). They can be caused by the agent's beliefs, desires, and practical decision-making processes, just as any resulting intentions and actions can be. And reflectively formed decisions can be a kind of making-up-of-mind, just as reflectively formed judgments are.[4]

A reflective decision can be constituted by an active commitment to do something, expressed in outer or inner speech, for example. ("I'll cut the grass after lunch.") But the action that constitutes making a commitment here is not itself a decision, but is rather a speech action. There is a decision in the background, but it is a decision to say one thing rather than another, following affective appraisal of the alternatives and their anticipated consequences in light of one's practical reasoning. Yet having made the commitment, it thereafter functions in a manner similar to an intention, as we will see in Chapter 7. One might recall having made up one's mind and feel obliged to act accordingly.

Reflective decisions are not really decisions then (or at least many of them aren't), any more than reflective judgments are really judgments. But what about the decisions that underlie making a commitment, such as the decision to say, "I'll cut the grass after lunch"? These, too, can be caused by the agent's beliefs, desires, and practical reasoning. But they are not caused by intentions, of course, in the way that intentional physical actions are; rather, they are the causes of those intentions. So in this respect they are unlike paradigmatic intentional actions. But more importantly, they are not controlled events, in the way that all physical actions are (or almost all, depending on how one comes down on the question of the active status of eye-saccades). Indeed, decisions are momentary events, with minimal temporal extension; there is no ongoing process to control. One possible speech action from among those competing for implementation hits criterion first, issuing in the action. It is the criterion-crossing that constitutes the decision.

All genuine decisions, then (whether unreflective or underlying reflective commitments), are quite unlike intentional actions in two central respects. They are not caused by intentions, and they are not controlled temporally extended events. But do they perhaps resemble skilled actions or affect-caused actions? Neither of these types of action is caused by a prior executively formed intention either, of course. But they *are*

[4] Indeed, Mele (2000, 2021) argues that decisions can be actions of *executive assent* to the content of an action-plan, where the act of assenting is modeled on what one does when assenting to someone else's proposal for what one should do. By agreeing to do it, one has thereby committed oneself to doing it.

temporally extended controlled events, nevertheless. The action of kicking the ball in the way necessary to get it to one's team-mate through a gap in the defenders takes time, and it has to be precisely controlled (albeit by a well-trained sensorimotor system). And actions motivated directly by anger, likewise, need to be controlled and guided in their execution. So decisions fail to resemble skilled and affect-caused actions in this central respect as well.

How are decisions to be explained, then? Probably in terms of computations of expected value of the sort to be discussed in Chapter 5, realized in interactions among the kinds of competitive neural accumulators discussed at various points in this book. Presented with a choice of some sort, accumulators representing the values of the alternatives and the likelihoods of achieving them start to build in activity, mutually inhibiting one another until one of them reaches criterion. (Or if the process goes on too long, one might decide to flip a coin or to move on to something else.) The event of the accumulator representing option A hitting criterion *is* the event of one deciding to pursue it. That event causes the formation of an intention to go for A, which then guides subsequent performance. Nothing about the decision here looks action-like, except that it is a downstream effect of one's beliefs and desires. And although it issues in an action-controlling intention, the decision itself has little or no extension in time and is not itself a guiding event. I conclude that decisions, like judgments, are not sufficiently action-like to qualify as mental actions to any significant degree.

4.7 Conclusion

We have once again found numerous respects in which both commonsense beliefs and philosophers' theories about actions and their explanation are in error. While the active natures of mental rehearsal, imagination, memory search, and controlled attention are perhaps not so surprising, in most cases they fail to conform to the standard belief-desire model. And both the folk and most philosophers are mistaken in thinking that mind-wandering and creative inspiration are passive in nature. As has been repeatedly observed throughout this book, armchair-philosophers who rely mostly on their intuitions, with insufficient attention paid to the sciences of the mind, are apt to go badly wrong as a result – as they do in maintaining the active nature of judging and deciding.

CHAPTER 5

Decision-Making and Goals

Previous chapters have examined forms of action that the standard model ignores. This chapter starts to dig deeper into the standard model itself. It is about how decisions get made (especially decisions that are commonly described as conscious ones), and about how those decisions subsequently give rise to actions. It draws on the scientific literature on prospection and on what is often called "neuroeconomics" to argue that valence (pleasure and displeasure when conscious, as we will see in Chapter 6) is the common currency of all decision-making. It also argues that the goals and intentions that result from decision-making are real, and distinct from beliefs and affective forms of desire.[1] When cued into activity, intentions can issue directly in actions in a manner somewhat similar to the habits discussed in Section 2.1. The chapter begins by showing that the ordinary notion of desire conflates two very different kinds of mental state, however, and it concludes by discussing how intentions and affective desires interact when they conflict.

5.1 The Fragmentation of Desire

Consider, first, the ordinary distinction between standing – or stored – desires and currently activated ones (such as might figure in one's ongoing practical reasoning and decision-making). One might truly be able to say of someone who is asleep that she wants to get into medical school, for example, but one can't rightly say that she is now *desiring* to get into medical school; that only happens when she reactivates, or calls to mind, her desire to go to medical school when awake. This distinction is real, and is something that folk-psychology gets right. Indeed, it mirrors a similar

[1] I propose to use the terms "goal" and "intention" interchangeably throughout. Note that a plan is just a hierarchically organized chained sequence of intentions; it doesn't require separate discussion (beyond that of Section 4.4).

distinction that can be drawn for most kinds of mental state. Thus knowledge of all kinds can exist in a stored state (e.g. in episodic or semantic memory) and can correctly be attributed to people when asleep; or that knowledge can become active and be "brought to mind" on particular occasions. Likewise, all forms of skill and "know-how" exist in a stored state until one has occasion to activate and make use of those skills.

The ordinary notion of a standing or stored desire encompasses at least two quite different kinds of mental state, however. Compare someone who wants his children to flourish with someone who wants to go to medical school. Both have standing motivational states that can correctly be attributed to them even while asleep. But the former description likely picks out a stored set of values in the affective system while the latter is more intention-like. Many of the values that one might ordinarily characterize as cares or concerns are of the first sort (Jaworska 2007). But they can equally be described as things that one *wants*. They are among the stored values (innate or acquired) appraisal against which is apt to issue in a variety of more concrete affective states (such as disappointment when one's child does poorly in an exam, or hope that the child gets into the swim team and joy when she succeeds).

Wanting to go to medical school might sometimes be of this sort, albeit perhaps comprising a convergence of multiple stored values. That is, someone might experience a sort of affective yearning whenever she considers the possibility of medical school, even though she may never take a related decision and never does anything about it (perhaps because it is so unlikely, given her grades). In contrast, the desire to go to medical school might be a stored goal or intention, a product of earlier prospective reasoning and resulting from a decision. This is a very different kind of motivational state, quite differently realized in the brain, as we will see shortly. No affective feelings need now be involved. Whenever she reaches a related choice-point ("party with friends or work on my paper?") she recalls the goal of getting the perfect grades necessary for medical school, and is motivated to take an instrumental decision accordingly. The goal of getting into medical school constrains and helps organize her thinking and planning without her needing to revisit the affective evaluation that led her to adopt that goal in the first place. So it has the distinctive functional profile of an intention (Bratman 1987, 1999). Nevertheless, from a common-sense perspective one might naturally say, "She declined to go to the party because she wants to get into medical school."

The same distinction between affective and intention-like desires also applies to active desires – that is, to things that one is currently desiring.

These can be incentive-salient affective states, as when one looks longingly at a desired slice of chocolate cake. But they can also be activated memories of the products of previous decision-making – that is, active intentions. A student receiving an invitation to a party, for example, might recall her desire to go to medical school ("remember, I need the grades to get into med school") before declining. In doing so, she is taking what she thinks is a necessary step to fulfill her desire. But there need be nothing affect-like about what folk-psychology here describes as a desire; there may be no current feeling of longing or attraction. The active state is, rather, an abstract goal, here playing the role of an intention and activated from what cognitive scientists call the prospective-memory system, not from evaluative / affective ones.

Prospective memory is memory for what one is going to do, or memory for what one intends. It comes in two activated forms: actively sustained and evoked (McDaniel et al. 2013). In the sustained case, one continually monitors the environment for the cues indicating that one should act. ("When the lights turn green I will move off.") Evoked intentions, in contrast, are activated from storage in a distinctive long-term memory system by contextual and/or temporal cues. If one had previously formed an intention like, "When the sun comes out I will cut the grass," then awareness that the sun has begun to shine may be sufficient for one to recall the intention, which then leads one to act by default (unless one changes one's mind). The brain networks underlying stored goals and intentions implicate prefrontal regions that overlap hardly at all with those underlying affective states of desire, as we will see.

As one might expect given the engagement of the prefrontal cortex in working-memory tasks and executive-function tasks generally, actively sustained forms of prospective remembering exhibit activity in many of the same prefrontal regions, including the dorsolateral prefrontal cortex (just forward of dorsal premotor cortex). For keeping actively in mind a task to be performed while searching the environment for the initiating cues-for-action bears a close resemblance to many working-memory tasks, in which one has to keep information actively in mind while waiting to respond. But uniquely in the case of prospective memory, its contents during both sustained-activity *and* cued delayed-intention tasks can be decoded from a region of rostrolateral prefrontal cortex, which is almost at the front of the brain on its outside surface, but set away from the mid-line (Momennejad & Haynes 2013). Moreover, damage to this area differentially impacts prospective-memory performance of both sorts (Volle et al. 2011). This is a region that is located slightly forward of dorsolateral prefrontal cortex, which is the region that regularly shows up as a critical node in working-memory tasks, as noted above (Barbey et al. 2013).

As we have said, prospective memories (intentions) can be stored in a form of long-term memory and then evoked into activity by temporal or contextual cues, or they can be held actively in mind while one monitors the environment for the cues for their implementation. In this respect they resemble episodic memories, which can be evoked in bottom-up fashion or can be actively searched for. Indeed, it is worth noticing that evoked forms of prospective memory, like episodic memory, are dependent upon the hippocampus. (Episodic memory, however, is realized in networks linking the hippocampus to medial temporal cortex, as well as representations distributed across temporal and parietal cortices, rather than to rostrolateral prefrontal cortex, as we will see in Chapter 7.)

Prospective-memory retrieval is associated with hippocampal activity (Martin et al. 2007; Poppenk et al. 2010; McDaniel et al. 2013). And prospective-memory ability is known to deteriorate progressively in Alzheimer's disease (Farina et al. 2013; Lecouvey et al. 2019), which in turn is associated with deterioration in the integrity and connectivity of the hippocampus (de Leon et al. 1993; Allen et al. 2007). This makes sense. For in order to store an intention for the future, one has to associate it with appropriate contextual or temporal cues which, when activated, will serve to retrieve and reactivate the intention, in something like the way that contextual or temporal cues can evoke an episodic memory. Likewise, some forms of prospective memory deteriorate in semantic dementia. This, too, makes sense. For the tasks in question are especially ones that would benefit from semantic / conceptual encoding of the retrieval cues, such as remembering to buy a crossword puzzle when passing a news-stand (La Corte et al. 2021).

The brain networks that underlie affective forms of desire, in contrast, have no overlap with those just described. Positive (attractant) desires are realized in a network that involves regions of the subcortical ventral striatum, regions of the orbitofrontal cortex (on the lower horizontal surface underneath the prefrontal cortex just behind the eyes), and the ventromedial prefrontal cortex (which is on the lower inside surface of prefrontal cortex). Negative (repulsive) desires involve distinct regions of the ventral striatum and orbitofrontal cortex together with regions of the anterior insula (which is on the outside lower surface of prefrontal cortex, hidden behind the fold of temporal cortex).

In addition to centering on a distinct brain hub, the functional role of prospective memory is very different from that of affective kinds of desire.

The main motivational role of the latter is indirect – affective desires figure upstream of, and as input to, decision-making processes. They need to be combined together with beliefs about means and likelihoods to compute an expected value, and are always in competition with other values (if only the value of inertia, or inaction). Once decisions are made they give rise to intentions and goals, which can then either be acted upon immediately or stored for future use in prospective memory.

Prospective memories, in contrast, issue immediately in action when triggered, unless inhibited by other considerations. Their motivational force is immediate, and not dependent on decision-making processes. For instance, having formed the intention of cutting the grass as soon as lunch is over, the act of putting away the lunch things can cue the intention into activity in such a way that one immediately heads down to the garage to collect the mower, with no further thought. Indeed, intentions can usefully be thought of as abstract motor plans that sit at the very top of the motor-control hierarchy. When activated, they initiate the cascade of increasingly lower-level motor instructions that will normally issue in an intentional action.[2]

Given these differences in functional role, together with the distinctness of the brain networks involved, it seems certain that intentions and affective desires belong to distinct psychological kinds. In which case common sense draws too few distinctions among kinds of desire (just as we will see in Chapter 7 that it may fail to distinguish adequately among kinds of belief). So if common-sense psychology is committed to desires constituting a unitary mental kind (albeit sometimes active, sometimes inactive), then it is mistaken. In fact there should now be no doubt that goals and intentions are distinct kinds of state from affective ("felt") desires. They are realized in distinct brain networks and have quite different functional roles. While on a coarse level of description one can say that they both motivate actions, intentions do so directly whereas affective desires mainly do so indirectly, via the decision-making processes into which they enter.

5.2 Irreducible Intentions

The distinction between affective and intention-like desires drawn in Section 5.1 has resulted in the claim that these belong to distinct psychological kinds. That claim will be defended further here against the

[2] In this respect intentions – especially conditional intentions like, "when lunch is over I will . . ." – are a bit like habits. They can issue in action directly without affect or decision-making.

arguments of some armchair-philosophers, who have claimed that intentions are just a special kind of desire (Davidson 1963; Audi 1973; Sinhababu 2013), or who claim that intentions are just a special sort of belief (Marušić & Schwenkler 2018).

Consider, first, the processes that control ongoing action. Philosophers generally refer to these as "intentions *in* action" (Searle 1983). There is now an extensive body of knowledge about motor control, and its location in the brain, as we discussed in Section 2.2. Once an action is initiated (from a *prior* intention, such as might result from a decision to have a sip of one's morning coffee) a cascade of increasingly precise motor instructions gets generated, influenced by perceptions of the affordances of the environment (the position of the mug and the orientation of its handle) as well as competition among, and evaluation of, alternative ways of implementing the intention – reaching with this hand rather than that, selecting the speed and precise trajectory of one's reach, selecting the precise grip-positioning and force of one's hand, and so on (Jeannerod 2006; Cisek & Kalaska 2010; McNamee & Wolpert 2019).

The representational contents involved in motor control are exclusively low-level nonconceptual ones, of a sort shared with virtually all mobile creatures. Moreover, in humans they are realized especially in processes that take place in interactions between premotor and motor cortices (on the upper surface of frontal cortex just anterior to the central sulcus that divides it from parietal cortex) and the cerebellum, with projections then to subcortical way-stations and then on to the spinal cord and limbs. The brain networks underlying intentions-in-action distinguish them sharply from beliefs (realized in hippocampal, temporal lobe, and parietal lobe circuits) and also from affective desires (realized in interactions between subcortical regions with insular, orbitofrontal, and ventromedial prefrontal cortices).

It is clear that intentions-in-action are a different kind of psychological state from either beliefs or affective desires. But it remains possible that *prior* intentions should belong to one or other of those psychological categories. For such intentions often have propositional contents (but not always), and they can interact with one's beliefs to motivate actions – thus seemingly having a desire-like role. And indeed, Sinhababu (2013) claims that intentions are really just a distinctive kind of desire (following Davidson 1963 and Audi 1973). In contrast, cognitive science has studied the nature of prior intentions under the guise of prospective memory, which is the sort of memory that is required for recalling and/or keeping actively in mind what one is going to do and when, or in what context. And as we saw in Section 5.1, the upshot is that intentions are regarded as distinct mental kinds from affective forms of desire.

Sinhababu (2013) says that intentions are just desires that, when paired with a belief that doing something will bring about the object of desire (or at least render it more likely), automatically (without further reasoning of any sort) produce the motivational force needed to initiate the action. Notice that this accurately describes the functional role of prospective memory, as described in Section 5.1. For example, intending to buy a crossword book on the walk home, and being reminded by the sight of a news-stand that they stock them, this leads directly to the intention-in-action of stopping to make the purchase. But this does nothing to show that prospective memories belong to the same psychological kind as affective desires. For the latter only lead to action following affective appraisals of the value of a thing or event, and always involve computations of expected value and comparisons with the expected value of alternative actions (counting inaction as one such alternative). Indeed, Sinhababu's (2013) account just reiterates the common-sense view that these are both instances of the same kind of mental state (wanting). But as we have seen, common sense is in error on this matter.

Admittedly, affective desires do issue in automatic motor activation, either innate (like the urge to attend to an unfamiliar object motivated by curiosity, or the urge to flee from an advancing grizzly bear) or learned (like the urge to ask a question when curious), as we saw in Sections 3.3 and 3.4. So in this respect they resemble activated intentions. But the latter are always a product of previous decision-making processes, whereas the automatic motor-activation components of affective desires result from appraisals of things or events against stored values. The etiology of the two types of motor activation is quite different. And of course affective desires *also* comprise arousal and anticipatory-valence components that are lacking in active intentions. There is no doubt that these are distinct kinds of state.

Prospective memories (intentions) are quite distinct from affective forms of desire, then. But they are sometimes described in terms suggestive of belief. For example, one might ask oneself, "What was I going to do?" One then recalls, "I know, I was going to cut the grass." Here it seems that one's prospective memory is comprised of a belief-like state, one's knowledge that one is going to cut the grass. And just as some philosophers have claimed that skills and practical abilities are a kind of belief (as we saw in Section 2.7), so some have argued that intentions, too, are a kind of belief. That view will be considered here.

Marušić and Schwenkler (2018), in particular, argue that the difference between intentions and other forms of belief lies just in their etiology. Regular beliefs about the future are formed in the light of evidence about the future, whereas intentions are beliefs about the future that are formed as a result of practical reasoning and decision-making. In the latter case, we come to have a belief about the future by deciding to make the embedded proposition true. However, Marušić and Schwenkler have nothing whatever to say about why this differing etiology should mean that one type of belief is apt to lead directly to action (independent of any other intention or affective form of desire) whereas the other does not. How does the difference in etiology confer on them such different causal roles, if both are really of the same psychological kind (belief)? They provide no answer. And indeed, one might think that such a large difference in functional role (differing in both their distinctive causes and their distinctive effects) is just what it means to say that these are states belonging to distinct psychological kinds (especially given the differences in the brain networks involved).

Here is a likely hypothesis for how Marušić and Schwenkler (2018) manage to go so badly wrong. In the course of their discussion they say that to have a regular (non-practical) belief in something is to be committed to it being true. And then intentions, they say, are of the same general sort, except that here the commitment is to *make* the content of the belief true. So what beliefs and intentions have in common (allegedly constituting them as the same mental-state kind) is that both are commitments to truth.

In claiming that (non-practical) beliefs are commitments to truth, Marušić and Schwenkler may well have in mind what seems to be a paradigmatic sort of belief (at least for armchair-philosophers, if not for regular folk), which are what result from a making-up-of-mind (Frankish 2004, 2009). When philosophers think of beliefs they are apt to have in mind people who consider the evidence and the considerations that count in favor of and against the truth of a proposition, and who then *decide* one way or the other (or remain agnostic and uncommitted). But as we will see in more detail in Chapter 7, commitments to truth of this sort aren't really kinds of belief at all (or not kinds of belief with the right content, at any rate). Rather, in some cases they are comprised of an *intention* to think, reason, and act in the future on the assumption that the proposition is true (where the intention gets created by the act of committing oneself to the truth of the proposition). And in other cases, while they do comprise a form of belief, it is a higher-order belief that one possesses the relevant first-order belief. Aware that one has committed oneself to the truth of

P (for instance, having heard oneself say so in outer or inner speech), one forms the belief that one believes that *P*. But this is a belief that only motivates the actions appropriate for a *P*-believer via interaction with one's affective systems and subsequent decision-making. Thus one might recall making the commitment and then feel obliged to act in accordance with it, perhaps motivated by the positive value one assigns to self-consistency.

There is, of course, a much weaker sense in which a commitment to truth is implicit in the normal functional role of episodic and semantic memories (i.e. regular beliefs). For when one *expresses* a belief of either kind one thereby becomes committed to its truth (one can be held responsible for what one has asserted, for example). And when one acts on the assumption of what one believes, one's action then relies on – and is in that sense implicitly committed to – the truth of the belief. Someone who believes that the café on the corner sells donuts, for example, will be apt to assert when asked, "The café on the corner sells donuts," thereby committing to the truth of the proposition expressed. (They can be held responsible for having said it thereafter, and can be taken to task if it turns out that there is no café on the corner, or no donuts for sale.) And likewise, someone with that belief who is in search of a box of donuts to take to a meeting will be apt to head for the café on the corner to purchase them, committing themselves via action to the truth of the proposition. For the act will fail if the belief is false. In such cases a commitment to truth is downstream of the belief itself, however – being part of its normal functional role, rather than constitutive of believing as such. The person thinks, reasons, and acts as if the proposition were true that the corner café sells donuts *because they believe it*, rather than believing it in virtue of thinking, reasoning, and acting appropriately.

Similar points apply to episodic memories, or first-person experiential beliefs about the past. When one first forms an episodic memory there is no commitment made, except for a weak kind of "taking-to-be-true" that is implicit in all perception. One simply observes an event taking place, and if the event is salient enough its components get linked together and stored in long-term memory where it is later consolidated. There is nothing commitment-like here, except that when the event is recalled it strikes one as having really happened. But when one articulates what one remembers one thereby becomes committed to its truth, and one can be criticized if one's statement is erroneous. Likewise when one forms the semantic memory that the café on the corner sells donuts, this might result from an overlay of numerous experiences of seeing (and smelling) donuts when one visits (Renoult et al. 2019). The belief is an automatic product of those merging and consolidation processes, without anything appropriately described as a "making-up-of-mind."

So Marušić and Schwenkler (2018) get things exactly backwards. It is not that intentions are a kind of belief, but rather that the kind of state they designate as "belief" (a making-up-of-mind grounded in evidence, which is really a commitment to think, reason, and act as if the proposition in question were true) is actually an intention, and not a belief. Either that, or it gives rise to a higher-order belief (either the belief that one has made a commitment to truth, or the belief that one has come to believe the proposition one committed oneself to), which only leads to action when interacting with values like a desire for self-consistency. We will return to this point when discussing (alleged) kinds of belief in Chapter 7.

There is nothing here to challenge our earlier conclusion that prior intentions (prospective memories) and affective forms of desire belong to distinct psychological kinds. Folk-psychology is in error, then, when referring to them both as forms of wanting or desiring. So are philosophers who work with an undifferentiated notion of desire. But it should be said that the philosophers discussed in this section are to some degree outliers. Within the philosophical community as a whole it is widely accepted that intentions are distinct from, and differ in functional role from, both beliefs and desires. Bratman's work (1987, 1999), in particular, has been especially influential in helping people to see how intentions help organize planning and can issue in action in the absence of further affective appraisal or decision-making.

5.3 Prospection

Intentions and goals are thus distinct from beliefs (episodic and semantic memories) and from (affective forms of) desire – hereafter just "desire." And intentions themselves result from decision-making processes involving one's beliefs and desires. But what does the decision-making process itself look like? How are the decisions that create intentions arrived at?

There is now a widespread acceptance in the field that reflective forms of decision-making – the sorts of decision-making that are sometimes described as involving "System 2" – depend upon prospection of the future (Gilbert & Wilson 2007, 2009; Seligman et al. 2013, 2016; Benoit et al. 2014). When one reflects on a choice of any sort one mentally rehearses the actions one is considering, or one imagines their outcomes, or both. These representations are received as input by one's affective-evaluation systems, which respond with some degree of positive or negative valence attaching to the contents of those representations. Valence comprises two fully comparable analog-magnitude scales of value, enabling properties of very different kinds to be evaluatively compared. These evaluations are then integrated with beliefs about likelihood, and the option with the highest expected value is generally chosen.

In most instances of decision-making, people are interested in the consequences of their actions, rather than just the actions themselves, and prediction of those outcomes depends upon additional resources, as we will see shortly. But sometimes it is actions as such that are chosen. When people choose prospectively among two actions they mentally rehearse each – activating the motor instructions for performance of each action while suppressing its actual execution, and attending to the sensory forward model produced by those instructions, resulting in an imagined experience as-of performance of the action. A choreographer might decide among two different hand-gestures to be made at a particular point in a dance, for example, by mentally rehearsing each. This creates models of what each gesture would feel like and look like, which can then be affectively evaluated (for elegance, perhaps, or just ease of performance), issuing in a decision.

On other occasions one mentally rehearses an action or sequence of actions in order to anticipate their likely consequences, and it is the latter that are affectively appraised in the first instance. (All actions are always appraised for their energetic and other costs, both online – in the course of acting – and in anticipation; Cos et al. 2014.) But sometimes known or potential outcomes are imagined and evaluated directly. In both cases one is imagining the future (or a potential future). Recent research has uncovered the constitutive role that the episodic memory system plays in future imagining (especially networks involving the hippocampus and medial temporal cortex; Buckner 2010; Benoit & Schacter 2015). Information stored in memory is used to construct and elaborate the most likely future events and outcomes. The same brain networks regularly show up in both remembering and future imagining, and people suffering from amnesia are equivalently poor at each. Indeed, some cognitive scientists go so far as to claim that what the episodic memory system is *for* is to enable rich and generally accurate representations of future outcomes to be used in decision-making (Schacter & Addis 2007; Schacter 2019). This is an idea that we will return to in Chapter 7.

Strikingly, Seligman et al. (2016) entitle their book, "*Homo Prospectus*," presumably because prospection plays such a ubiquitous and central role in human decision-making. But there is no reason to think that the *capacity* for prospection is uniquely human. On the contrary, there is evidence that both apes and corvids can engage in future-planning, and do so in ways that suggest they are imagining potential future consequences of the actions open to them, selecting the ones that will achieve the best outcomes (Bird & Emery 2009; Taylor et al. 2010; Hanus et al. 2011; Gruber et al. 2019). But in their everyday lives even these animals don't appear to engage in prospection very often.

Humans, in contrast, use prospection not only when there is some imminent task or problem they need to solve, but also for much of the time when off-task, when mind-wandering. When we mind-wander we are frequently imagining future scenarios of various sorts, from the mundane (what to cook for dinner) to the life-transforming (whether to pursue one sort of career path rather than another, or whether to have a child). Responding emotionally to the things we imagine can help us to make up our minds later, if and when there is an opportunity to choose. But mind-wandering can also focus on the past, and on counterfactual scenarios. One revisits an argument one had with one's partner, or reimagines an embarrassing faux pas at a faculty meeting; and one imagines what would have happened had one acted differently, or what one's life would have been like had things turned out differently – all the while affectively appraising and evaluating the contents of what one imagines.

Sometimes humans face choices whose ramifications cannot all be grasped at once. In one famous example, someone might spend days or weeks trying to decide whether to pursue a career as a lawyer or as a professional clarinetist (Raz 1986). Depending on the stage of training at which the question arises (e.g. having completed a music-performance BA with the grades necessary to get into law school versus someone who has already qualified as a lawyer whose musical skills are good enough to go professional) one will rehearse and imagine various aspects of the choice. One will consider the costs and onerousness of law school, perhaps, or whether earnings as a professional clarinetist would be sufficient to enable one to pay off one's law school tuition debt. One will imagine a potentially and at least partly itinerant life-style as a musician (which can seem attractive or not depending on one's family status and attitude toward travel), comparing that with the mundane day-to-day activities of much work as a lawyer.

Philosophers have commonly claimed that decisions of this sort are hard because they involve incommensurable values (home life versus travel; social contribution versus aesthetic pleasure, and so on; Hsieh & Andersson 2021). And it is true that the stored values, appraisal against which issues in one's varying affective responses as one considers aspects of these scenarios, are very different from one another. But that is entirely consistent with the claim that one of the outputs of those appraisal processes – and the output that plays a central role in decision-making – is a common currency of valence. The reason why such cases are so hard is not because there is no common currency of value to enable comparison (there is: it is the valence produced by appraisals against the differing stored values), but rather because they are so multi-faceted (*contra* Walasek & Brown 2024). One cannot entertain all the relevant properties and outcomes in working memory at once in such a way as to provide them as input for affective appraisal. One has to proceed piecemeal, with no obvious way of summing the outputs of one appraisal with the outputs of later ones. As a result, one may have to resort to some kind of decision-making heuristic to settle the matter (Gigerenzer & Gaissmaier 2011).

How does one select among heuristics themselves, however? How does one decide when, and which, heuristic to employ? Sometimes the outcome might be a context-sensitive habit-like selection learned through repetition, resulting from previously rewarded choices. ("When choosing among multiple fairly trivial alternatives, choose at random.") But most often the selection will result from a kind of cost–benefit analysis of engaging in further reflection. It is now well established that focused thinking is experienced as effortful and aversive by default, and recent models of decision-making routinely take into account the estimated costs of cognitive control (Kurzban et al. 2013; Shenhav et al. 2014, 2017; Inzlicht et al. 2018). So as one reflects on a difficult multi-faceted choice one will be weighing the expected benefit of continuing (including an estimate of the likelihood of reaching a resolution) against the felt costs.

In some such cases reflection can be brought to an end by relying on any one of a variety of previously used and rewarded stopping-rules, some of which can be habit-like, while others resemble standing intentions. ("Whenever I face a choice between similarly valuable, fairly trivial options, I'll just toss a coin.") Some of these will have been learned through trial and error, some through observational learning, and some through explicit instruction. ("Why don't you just to toss a coin?") But others may be innately channeled "ecologically rational" decision-rules, that are adapted for specific kinds of choice-context (Todd & Gigerenzer 2012). Some of the latter might be explicitly represented, while others are evolved biases influencing one's appraisal of the anticipated costs of continuing search. For example, consider the heuristic, "when choosing among an open-ended set of sequentially presented items of differing value, estimate the value of the first few and then choose the next one that is better than any of those previously evaluated" (Gigerenzer et al. 2000). This might be realized initially in hope for something better weighed against increasing anxiety about failing altogether, followed by an appraisal of rightness attaching to the item chosen. In any case, there is nothing in all this to challenge the claim that valence is the common currency of decision-making.

5.4 Neuroeconomics

Most day-to-day decisions are taken unreflectively, of course. When one is presented with a choice of some kind one might pause for only a moment or two, and when one of them seems better than the other, one chooses that. Unreflective decision-making of this sort has been extensively investigated in the lab using sequences of pairwise choices among a variety of goods with varying odds of delivery (sometimes while lying in an fMRI brain-scanner). Thus one might be asked to trade off electric shocks of some particular likelihood against a chance of some amount of monetary compensation; or one might trade shocks against money combined with a sip of juice, or electric shocks against a chance to see beautiful faces or to avoid social exclusion, and so on. People respond in apparently coherent ways, and modeling of the ensuing decisions suggests that they result from integrating together odds and anticipated outcome values to issue in a measure of expected value, which in turn determines choice (Huys et al. 2011; Orsini et al. 2015; O'Doherty et al. 2017). It is generally assumed in this literature, too, that there is a shared common currency of value across all the varied kinds of choices that humans and other animals can make (Levy & Glimcher 2012; Chikazoe et al. 2014; Ruff & Fehr 2014; Sescousse et al. 2015).

The idea of a common currency of value is further confirmed by the finding that there are neurons in the brains of monkeys (in the subcortical ventral striatum) that fire not only on receipt of a liquid reward, but also when the monkey receives the information that a reward is upcoming (Bromberg-Martin & Hikosaka 2009) – attesting to the reward value of information, it should be noted. Indeed, the same neurons also fire when the monkey is *expecting* a reward (having received the information that a reward is coming) or when the monkey is merely expecting information about a reward. (For broadly similar work with humans, see Kobayashi & Hsu 2019.) And the negative evaluation of cognitive forms of effort, too, is represented in the same domain-general network that computes all other forms of value and disvalue (Westbrook et al. 2019).

As we will see in Chapter 6, the common currency in question comprises degrees of pleasure and displeasure (at least when conscious). It is perhaps no surprise, then, that some in the field have assumed that this should lead us to endorse motivational hedonism (Gilbert & Wilson 2007, 2009; Miloyan & Suddendorf 2015), which is the doctrine that everything one does is aimed at achieving pleasure and avoiding displeasure. But whether or not this is so depends upon the best account of what pleasure *is*, in fact. I argue at length in Carruthers (2024), and again more briefly in Chapter 6, that pleasure is an analog-magnitude (nonconceptual) representation of value. So in decision-making one is selecting among the odds of achieving differing degrees of value, not among good or bad (pleasurable or displeasurable) experiences as such.

Value is computed in interactions between subcortical structures (especially the ventral striatum) and prefrontal cortex. It is thought that orbitofrontal cortex (on the underneath surface of prefrontal cortex just behind the eyes) codes for outcome values alone, binding valence representations computed in interaction with subcortical structures with incoming sensory or imagistic representations (Grabenhorst & Rolls 2011; Yarkoni et al. 2011; Chikazoe et al. 2014). Nearby regions of ventromedial and medial prefrontal cortex (on the lower inside surface of prefrontal cortex, located in the gap between the two hemispheres) are thought to integrate valence with likelihood and energetic costs to provide representations of overall expected value (Levy & Glimcher 2012; Ruff & Fehr 2014). And then competition among options and with existing goals is resolved through interactions between anterior cingulate cortex (just above medial prefrontal cortex on the inside surface of the brain, immediately above the corpus callosum) and dorsolateral prefrontal cortex (where current goals and intentions are actively realized), issuing in decisions to act (Wallis 2007; Shenhav et al. 2014, 2018).

The experiments discussed above have generally involved decision-making for the here-and-now or for the imminent future. What happens, though, when one has to decide between present and future goods? The same decision-making procedures are followed – evaluative appraisal of the options combined with estimates of likelihood, issuing in an expected value for each alternative. But choices for the future are automatically discounted in value, and in a hyperbolic manner – more steeply in the short term, being discounted less steeply as the option under consideration recedes further into the future.

It should be emphasized that discounting of future goods (and harms) is built into the functioning of the decision-making system, and is independent of representations of likelihood. It is true, though, that imagining of future events becomes less rich and vivid the more remote in time those events are anticipated to be (Peters & Büchel 2011). This means that one's affective responding to those images is likely to be less strong, too. And indeed, one method for decreasing the extent of temporal discounting is to encourage people to imagine the future option in greater detail (Peters & Büchel 2011; Benoit et al. 2014). But this is by no means a complete explanation of the phenomenon of temporal discounting of future goods.

All species that have ever been tested discount the future, and discount hyperbolically, albeit with differing rates of discounting across species. Species-specific discount rates correlate with body-mass, which in turn correlates with both metabolic rate and longevity (Stevens & Mühlhoff 2012). This makes sense, since if you burn energy fast and/or will only live for a short time, near-term goods are more likely to be adaptive than distant ones. But there are also differences among species that are best explained by ecological factors. For example, lemurs and capuchins have similar body-mass, but the discount rate for lemurs is three times as large as for capuchins. Why? Probably because lemurs are leaf-eaters, whereas capuchins get a significant amount of their food from nuts, which they have to crack open using stones that they often carry around with them (Vanderveldt et al. 2016). The latter kind of life-style requires patience, whereas the former does not.

Automatic temporal discounting in decision-making makes adaptive sense in general, since all sorts of factors can intervene during a longer interval to prevent acquisition of any given future good. It seems that species-specific discount rates are evolution's best guess at the riskiness of relying on deferred satisfaction given the ecological niche in which the species has evolved. Among humans, however, most of the focus has been on individual differences in discount rates, with shallower rates of temporal discounting correlating with a wide variety of successful outcomes, including educational attainment, health, wealth, and more (Mischel et al. 2011; Moffitt et al. 2011). This might seem paradoxical ("if willingness-to-wait is good, how can temporal discounting be adaptive?"), but it is not. For human-specific discount rates were set by evolution over extended periods of time, during most of which the future was much less predictable and much more dangerous than it is in contemporary societies. For instance, although many now bemoan the fact that people don't save enough for retirement, in ancestral conditions few people would actually have lived that long.

There is also an extensive literature on so-called "risk preference" and "risk aversion," in which people (and other animals) can reliably fail to choose the option with the greatest expected value because they select a higher-risk alternative with a more-valued outcome, or a lower-risk alternative with a less-valued outcome instead (Kahneman 2011; De Petrillo & Rosati 2021). These preferences vary across species and across contexts, as well as being trait-like properties of individuals. The variations are best explained by a biologically grounded "risk-sensitivity theory," which assumes a common currency of value that goes proxy for adaptive value / inclusive fitness (Mishra 2014).

Species differences in risk sensitivity can be explained by many of the same factors involved in variations in temporal discounting rates, including body size and diet reliability (such as leaf-eating versus fruit-eating). In addition, state differences involve such factors as current energetic state and time of day or year. For example, larger-bodied animals are likely to engage in more risk-prone hunting at times when they otherwise have plenty to eat, whereas the opposite pattern is found in small-bodied animals who may need to take the risk in order to survive (Gilby & Wrangham 2007). Finally, trait differences in risk preference are partly genetic, but also partly an adaptive response to childhood trauma and adversity (Kim et al. 2013; Mishra 2014; Barch et al. 2020). For if one's life chances don't look promising, one may need to take more risks in order to be successful.

How might risk preferences/aversions be realized computationally, however? One possibility is that there are variations in the ways in which likelihood estimates are integrated with outcome values to issue in an expected value. Thus in some species or in some circumstances risk aversion might be effected by shifting further downwards the impact that a given degree of low likelihood has when integrated with a given outcome value. For example, instead of multiplying the two measures together, the combination procedure might be systematically biased upwards for high likelihoods and downwards for low likelihoods (with these biases reversing in cases of risk preference).

Another possibility, however (suggested by the terms "risk preference" and "risk aversion" themselves), is that all or most creatures have a distinctive evaluation process targeted at the output of likelihood processing, with species-specific initial innate settings. This would appraise the likelihood component of expected-value computations (which integrate outcome values with likelihoods), adjusting the resulting expected values up or down by adding a boost of positive or negative valence, with the appraisals in question varying with the circumstances and the degree of likelihood involved.

Although I am unaware of evidence that directly discriminates between these possibilities, the second hypothesis strikes me as more plausible. It is consistent with the familiar fact that high-risk options often make people (and other animals) experience anxiety or fear. And it is consistent with the finding that incidentally induced happiness or anger, on the one hand, or sadness or fear, on the other, can cause people to become more risk-seeking or risk-avoiding respectively (Lerner & Keltner 2000; Lerner et al. 2003; Ferrer et al. 2017). Indeed, even honey bees that have been put into an anxious state (by shaking them in a box, simulating a predatorial attack on their hive) are less likely to take the risk of approaching an ambiguous stimulus that might result in a noxious taste (Bateson et al. 2011).

5.5 Verbal Decision-Making

It is beginning to seem, then, that all decisions of the sort that issue in intentions (whether reflective or unreflective) involve a common currency of value (positive and negative valence). These values are integrated with estimates of likelihood, with the option delivering the highest expected value generally being selected (albeit modulated by temporal delay and attitudes toward risk). This is consistent with (modified versions of) decision-theoretic forms of a standard philosophical model of action-explanation, which understand all choice as involving calculations of expected utility or value (Joyce 1999). What of decision-making that is undertaken verbally, in inner or outer speech, however? This is perhaps the paradigm of what decision-making looks like to many philosophers. One articulates the reasons for and against each option, generally selecting the one that is favored by the balance of the reasons.[3]

It is doubtful that the mechanisms here are fundamentally different. First, this is because words and sentences are rapidly elaborated into related forms of imagery (Zwaan et al. 2004; Zwaan & Taylor 2006; Bedny & Caramazza 2011), which are then received as input by evaluative affective systems, leading to affective evaluation of the content of any sentence one

[3] It should be said that in the domain of moral decision-making, at any rate, the evidence suggests a very limited role for explicit consideration of reasons (Haidt 2001, 2007; Stanley et al. 2018). But this leaves open that reasoning might issue in decisions in contexts that are less affectively loaded.

entertains. And second, it is because sentence-formation is itself an action, as we saw in Section 2.5, and results from affectively influenced decision-making just as other forms of action do. So as one reasons verbally about what to do, one will be formulating sentences in inner or outer speech that result from value-based decision-making, influenced by what one takes to be warranted by previously entertained sentences and by one's affective responses to them. Reasoning will conclude with a decision-like sentence, expressed in inner or outer speech, which will often take the form, "I will do X."

Some transitions among sentences are likely to be governed by both innate and acquired norms, evaluative appraisal against which favors the production of one sentence over another, as well as being one factor in the acceptance of those sentences once produced (alongside consistency with existing beliefs and many other influences). As noted previously, Mercier and Sperber (2017) make a compelling case for what they call "an adaptation for argumentation," in particular. This is an evolved faculty for evaluating statements and arguments produced by other people, as well as for generating successful arguments for oneself. In consequence, some sequences of sentences will strike one as more acceptable than others. Formal education, too, may lead to the acquisition of additional norms of reasoning, either explicitly learned or acquired via imitation and example. Yet other transitions among sentences will be governed by heuristics, or "rules of thumb" (Gigerenzer et al. 2000). These can be thought of as habit-like sequences of sentence-types, acquired through forms of instrumental conditioning and/or observational learning from others.

How does concluding that one will do something get one to (be disposed to) do it, however? How does saying that one has decided lead to an intention? (In cases where one's statement expresses an already formed intention this issue doesn't arise, of course.) One possibility is that it might do so directly. Hearing oneself say, "I will do X" may directly cause an intention-in-action that guides the doing of X when the time for action is now, or it may cause a prior intention to do X to be stored in prospective memory for later implementation. But it is unclear what the mechanism could be that underlies such a transition. More plausibly, hearing oneself say, "I will do X" may cause one to *believe* that one has decided to do X. Then this belief will interact subsequently with the value one attaches to steadfast or strong-willed agency to issue in an intention to do X. I am not aware of any scientific research that attempts to tease apart these two options.

We will revisit some of these issues in Chapter 7. For the moment we can safely conclude that many or most decisions, at least, result from affectively grounded decision-making and computations involving degrees of valence – including those that result from verbally based consideration of reasons.

5.6 How Intentions and Desires Interact

Reflective decision-making involving prospection of the future and affective responding to anticipated outcomes makes decision-making of this sort "hot" or affect-involving. But how does prospection interact with existing goals and intentions? How does one integrate and/or decide among existing goals and newly prospected affectively laden options? What happens, in particular, when one is prospecting among options, and responding positively to them, only to realize that they conflict with the outcome of previous decision-making (an intention)? Does one then have to reactivate all of the affective values that initially went into that decision in order to compare the valence produced (the seeming-goodness) with the valence attached to one's currently considered alternatives? That would rather defeat the organizing role that intentions are supposed to have.

Sometimes such reconsideration does happen, however, and happens appropriately. One might realize, for example, that the options one is currently prospecting among had not been envisaged when the intention was formed (perhaps because circumstances have changed). Trying to decide between reading a novel and doing some advance preparation for dinner on a wet afternoon, one might recall one's earlier decision to cut the grass in the yard that afternoon – but at that point one hadn't anticipated that it would be raining.

Indeed, given that goals aren't themselves value-representations, this is one of the ways in which people sometimes decide whether or not to reconsider their goals rather than pursue them. Prospective memories are somewhat like episodic memories in that they come embedded within a framework of circumstances and background conditions that one expected to be in place when the goal was formed. Indications that those have significantly changed signal that it might be appropriate to reconsider one's goal. Thus when one formed the intention of cutting the grass immediately after lunch, one might have envisaged that the weather would be dry while tacitly assuming there would be no emergency call from a relative who is being taken to hospital. But if it is raining, or one gets such a call just as lunch ends, then all bets are off.

Two factors mean that existing intentions (when recalled) are likely to rule out further consideration of alternatives by default, however. One is that, realizing one had already made up one's mind to do something, the value that one attaches to being steadfast or strong-willed can kick in, somewhat in the way that a conflict between alternatives one is currently prospecting over and something one had *promised* to do will rule out the former by default. But the other is that intentions and goals do interact with affective systems, in any case, in a "top-down" manner. Indications of progress toward a goal are appraised positively, issuing in positive affect, whereas obstacles or things that might frustrate a goal are appraised negatively (Juechems & Summerfield 2019). Moreover, achievement of a goal is generally experienced as rewarding (pleasant). So when one notices that an alternative one is currently prospecting would prevent one from realizing an existing goal or intention, that will produce significant negative affect, serving to inhibit further consideration of the prospected option.

Moreover, when recalling a goal one might also recall the extent to which one takes that goal to *matter*, forming or bringing to mind a metacognitive belief about its overall importance. For instance, if one had formed the belief that getting the grass cut this afternoon is especially urgent (with persistent rain on the way, perhaps, or with the local housing association representatives threatening legal action over its length) then that can issue in a positive affective evaluation of completing the goal in the same kind of top-down manner that expectations and beliefs can alter affective experience generally (as in the placebo and nocebo effects discussed in Section 3.1). Believing that cutting the grass is important will produce some additional positive affective valuation of goal completion without requiring one to revisit the original considerations that led to the decision.

Do goal-achievement and indications of progress toward goal-achievement carry a direct (non-metacognitive) "imprint" of the importance of the values that led one to form that intention in the first place, however? This seems unlikely, when one recalls how easily frequent signals of progress toward a goal can get one locked into pursuits one actually regards as trivial. (Think, here, of deciding to play another game of patience – "just one more" – having come close to completing previous rounds, or how people can find it hard to pull themselves out of playing a video game by the constant gains they make in the course of play.) Rather, it seems likely that goal-achievement of any sort has a default reward value, which can then be modulated upwards or downwards in specific contexts or for different types of goal through reward-based learning. As a result, one can become increasingly good at steadfastly pursuing particular types of goal – in extreme cases achieving a state of "flow" in which one effortlessly pursues a task while making continued progress toward completing it (Nakamura & Csikszentmihalyi 2002).

A number of factors further buffer actively pursued goals against distraction or interruption. One is that it is active intentions that drive the direction of both top-down attention and memory search, pursuing and accessing information that is relevant to the execution of the goal. And one of the fundamental facts about top-down attention (whether externally or internally directed) is not just that it selects, organizes, and boosts the activity of targeted neural populations, but that it actively suppresses competitors (Gazzaley et al. 2005; Chun et al. 2011). So to some degree, then, attentional focus is self-sustaining.

The same thing is true of motor selection: any activated motor plan not only selects and boosts lower-level motor instructions, but at the same time suppresses any competing motor activation (Cheney et al. 1985; Duque & Ivry 2009). So what one might call the "actional-focus" of intentional activity is apt to be self-sustaining also. Once a high-level motor plan (an intention) has become activated, competing motor plans will be to some degree suppressed; with the same thing cascading down through the motor hierarchy as more detailed implementational choices are made among options: each choice, once made, suppresses its competitors (Griffin & Strick 2020).

There are thus two layers of protection that serve to buffer current goals against interference. One is that goal-directed attention and goal-activated motor plans will actively inhibit competing stimuli and motor tendencies, rendering it significantly less likely that they should even intrude into consciousness for consideration. The second is that when alternatives do break through, they will be appraised negatively as interfering with the present goal, making them seem considerably less attractive and choiceworthy than they otherwise would. Moreover, when alternatives to the current goal become salient, that will lead to a positive appraisal of continued goal-pursuit, making the current goal seem more attractive in comparison. As a result, in many such cases one immediately returns attention to pursuit of the current goal without further thought or reflection. Only more rarely does one reflectively revisit the importance of the current goal, comparing it with the attractiveness of the alternatives.

5.7 Conclusion

This chapter has argued that our ordinary talk about what people desire or want encompasses two quite distinct kinds of psychological state. One is comprised of goals and intentions, which are products of previous decision-making processes and are apt to issue in action directly by default, without further thought or evaluation. The other is constituted by affective states of incentive-salience, which are produced by appraising the options against stored values, resulting in positive or negative valence that attaches to the representation of each. It is these valenced representations that play a major role in all forms of decision-making (along with beliefs about means and estimates of likelihood). As for decision-making itself, this comprises a number of different varieties, all of which integrate valence with likelihood, and all of which issue in decisions and subsequent intentions (either for the here-and-now, or to be stored in prospective memory).

Anyone who is committed to thinking that what are referred to as "desires" or "wants" in ordinary speech constitute a single psychological kind is mistaken, therefore. (This may be true of folk-psychology generally, and is true of some of the philosophers who embrace the standard model.) On the contrary, intentions and goals are very different in kind from affective forms of desire.

CHAPTER 6

Pleasure and (Affective Forms of) Desire

Recall from Section 1.1 that the standard philosophical model of intentional action-explanation appeals to states of belief and desire to do the explaining. This chapter and the one following evaluate what philosophers have had to say about the nature of these states. In Section 5.1 we saw that the ordinary notion of desire encompasses two very different kinds of mental state: goals and intentions, on the one hand, and affective or emotion-like forms of desire, on the other. Our focus here is mostly on the latter. The chapter shows that desires of this sort always incorporate anticipatory pleasure, and that pleasure itself is an analog-magnitude representation of value. The chapter begins with what the science can tell us about the respective natures of pleasure and desire, before comparing the results with claims made by armchair-philosophers. Many of the latter are false, albeit sometimes containing partial insights.

6.1 The Nature of Pleasure

As we noted in Section 3.1, one of the automatic outputs of affective appraisal processes is valence, either positive or negative. Although valence can figure in unconscious processes of various sorts, when conscious it can (and should) be equated with pleasure and displeasure. But valence can be generated by two different kinds of appraisal: future-directed and present-tensed. Valence can be *anticipatory*, or it can be *consummatory*. Our focus in this section will mostly be on consummatory pleasure and displeasure, returning to discuss anticipatory varieties further in Section 6.2. But it is a constraint on theories of the nature of pleasure that they should be capable of explaining both roles. This is because evaluative learning takes place when anticipatory valence is compared with the valence actually experienced, resulting in an error signal that drives value change.

Consummatory pleasure is rewarding (as is consummatory positive valence more generally), and consummatory displeasure is punishing.

Both play essential roles in evaluative learning, as we saw in Section 3.1. When the pleasure one experiences is higher than one tacitly expects, the stored value attaching to events of that kind is ratcheted upwards by some increment, whereas if it is lower than expected, the stored value is ratcheted downwards. Likewise, *mutatis mutandis*, for displeasure. At the same time, events that were associated with or predictive of the arrival of reward can acquire secondary value through processes of Pavlovian learning; and actions that preceded the rewarding experience are more likely to be repeated in similar circumstances in the future. In this way new values (and disvalues) are acquired, and new affect-caused motor tendencies are learned.

Note, however, that the values against which consummatory experiences are appraised must be distinct from those that created the expectations of value with which they are compared. Consider, for example, what happens when children are conditioned to like the bitter taste of broccoli by dipping it in sugar or peanut butter (Havermans & Yansen 2007; Yeomans et al. 2008). (Bitterness is a primary punisher; sugar and fat are primary rewards.) There is an initial expectation of negative value created in light of the stored evaluation of bitter broccoli. But when the broccoli is consumed, it is much more pleasant than expected, because some of the negative valence of bitterness is overridden by positive valence created by fat and/or sugar. As a result, the value attached to broccoli (and its component tastes) is ratcheted up by some increment. After a while the sugar can be removed, and broccoli is now positively evaluated in its own right. The compound taste (and sight) of bitter broccoli is now a secondary reinforcer.

Consummatory pleasure results from a current stimulus or event being appraised positively against stored values, modulated by context (such as one's own current state of calorie depletion or dehydration, in the case of pleasure experienced from eating or drinking). Likewise for displeasure. So pleasure carries information about the current positive value attaching to the event, and displeasure carries information about current disvalue, or current badness. And that they carry such information explains how their roles in evaluative and behavioral learning have become stabilized. Stored values are incrementally altered in light of greater-than-expected or lesser-than-expected pleasure because of the information that pleasure carries about the current value of the stimulus. This enables one to track changing values in one's environment (such as the increasing nutrient value of fruit with the onset of Fall), and/or to learn finer discriminations of value (e.g. that red tomatoes generally taste better than green ones). Moreover, events associated with pleasure acquire value because they are predictive of things or events of value; and actions that issue in pleasure are reinforced because they are apt to issue in valued things.

As we noted in Section 1.5, most naturalistic accounts of the nature of representation (especially as the notion is deployed for explanatory purposes in cognitive science) center around the idea of the *information* carried by an event, where (roughly speaking) one event carries information about another if it is reliably enough caused by it. Some say that the content of a representational state is the subset of information it carries that it is the *function* of the state to carry information about (Millikan 1984, 1989; Papineau 1987; Neander 2017). On such accounts it follows that pleasure represents current value because its function is to carry information about current value. Others stress that the content of a state is what, from among the information that it carries, explains how the role of the state has become stabilized, either by evolution, or by learning, or both (Dretske 1995; Rupert 2018; Shea 2018). On such accounts, too, pleasure represents current value and displeasure represents current disvalue. On most if not all naturalistic accounts of representation, then, consummatory pleasure is a representation of current value, and consummatory displeasure is a representation of current disvalue. Accordingly, that is what we should accept.

Pleasure and displeasure admit of degrees, of course; they have magnitudes. And if pleasure and displeasure are representations of value and disvalue, then they qualify as analog-magnitude representations of those values. They are graded nonconceptual representations of value, in fact – which is as it should be, since affective learning and conditioning are exhibited by almost all living creatures, including ants and snails (Kobayashi et al. 1998; Cammaerts 2004), which may well lack concepts altogether. Moreover, when acknowledged as representations of value their role in decision-making is explained in a way that can apply to animals as well as humans. Indeed, even bumblebees can adaptively trade off high concentrations of sucrose solution against noxious heat (Gibbons et al. 2022). Decision-making systems in all organisms can use degrees of pleasure and displeasure as their common currency, integrating anticipatory pleasures and displeasures with likelihoods to compute expected values, thereby selecting which action to take.[1]

[1] If one wants to insist that pleasure and displeasure are conscious states, and also to avoid begging any questions about consciousness in animals, then strictly speaking one should say that it is analog-magnitude *valence* signals in animals that represent value and enable decision-making through computations of expected value. We will return to the question of consciousness in Section 6.4.

A natural worry to have about the idea that pleasure and displeasure represent degrees of value and disvalue is that values aren't the kind of thing that our minds can track or carry information about, in the way that they can track colors, shapes, movements, and other properties in the world that admit of degrees. Surely, one might think, values aren't out there in the world, existing independently of us in such a way that our affective systems can track them. While the worry is real, the answer is straightforward – albeit surprising to common sense. This is that the values in question are *adaptive* ones, comprising things that advance one's inclusive fitness or unfitness. There are objective facts about what things and actions have advanced organisms' fitness over evolutionary time. Those facts admit of degrees – something can be more or less adaptive. Moreover, these are just the properties that one would expect organisms to be sensitive to in their decision-making. Indeed, cognitive scientists, when advancing the idea of a cross-species common currency of decision-making (valence), have often made the point that the currency ultimately boils down to degrees of inclusive fitness (McNamara & Houston 1986; Montague & Berns 2002; Mishra 2014).[2]

As we noted in Section 3.1, primary rewards and punishments are innately specified, with the initial settings of appraisal systems fixed by default in advance of further evaluative learning. These are things that have promoted or inhibited individual survival and reproductive success over evolutionary time. So the output of an appraisal of a primary reward (issuing in primary pleasure) carries information about adaptive value, and that it does so explains the role that it has in learning and decision-making. And likewise, the affective learning mechanisms that create secondary rewards and punishments on the basis of primary ones have been selected for their adaptive value, often enough getting organisms to intrinsically value events that predict or lead to things that already have adaptive value.

Pleasure and displeasure don't represent adaptive value and disvalue *as such*, of course; and organisms that make decisions on the basis of expected value need have no idea that they are (probably) advancing their own inclusive fitness. Rather, what is accessible to the organism are just a pair of analog-magnitude signals that make events seem good or bad when current, and which when attached to future options make those options seem

[2] For illustration, consider this quote from Shizgal and Conover (1996, p. 37): "The relative utility of two different goal objects will depend not only on their abundance but also on the physiological state of the consumer and the ecological context in which the goal objects are embedded. In effect, we treat utility as a subjective estimate of the potential contribution of a goal object to fitness."

attractive (incentive-salient) or aversive (disincentive-salient). In this respect valence is not unlike analog-magnitude representations of color and other sensory qualities. Color experiences carry information about (and represent) the reflective properties of surfaces, while what is accessible to the perceiver are just a set of analog-magnitude properties that are located within a space of other more-or-less similar properties (as is often depicted by vision scientists in the color / brightness cone; Rosenthal 2010; Lau et al. 2022).

Consummatory pleasure and displeasure in general should be seen as representations of degrees of adaptive value or disvalue of the current stimulus or event, then. They are representations of inclusive fitness or unfitness. For this is what makes best sense of the design of systems for affective learning and decision-making. But for purposes of predicting or explaining the behavior of individual people on particular occasions, it will be most useful to think of the pleasure or displeasure that they feel as representing what *they* value in the circumstances. This is because each individual's values vary with accidents of culture and cultural learning, as well as with their own unique life experiences. The results can be extremely varied, in ways that make it almost impossible to make individualized judgments of the extent to which those values are tracking inclusive fitness. Granted, the pleasure that an individual takes in something as a result of evaluative learning can be thought of as their individualized estimate of the adaptive value of the thing. But it is the value *they* attach to it that explains their individual behavior, not the inclusive fitness that it may, or may not, promote. In short, adaptive value is what cognitive science needs to appeal to in explaining why affect and affective learning in general are organized as they are, whereas it is individual values that are more useful for purposes of explanation targeted at individuals.

6.2 The Nature of Desire

As we have seen, consummatory pleasure and displeasure (and consummatory valence more generally) are analog-magnitude signals that attach to a currently experienced action or event, representing the degree of value or disvalue of that action or event. The contents of current experiences are appraised against stored values (both positive and negative), modulated by a variety of contextual factors, resulting in a representation of their degrees of value or disvalue.

Desires and aversions, in contrast, are forward-looking: they are about future actions or events.[3] They result from an appraisal of the significance of those actions or events for one's stored values (again, modulated by contextual factors like calorie depletion). The output of the appraisal process is comprised of three components, produced in parallel, mirroring the outputs of affective appraisal generally. As we saw in Section 3.1, these are an automatically produced set of motor tendencies (e.g. to approach or avoid the thing or event appraised as good or bad), some degree of bodily arousal or de-arousal, and some extent of positive or negative valence attaching to the represented future action or event, making the latter seem attractive or aversive.

For example, a desire for a slice of the chocolate cake displayed on the dessert trolley in a restaurant will comprise an urge to acquire it (to reach for it, to ask the waiter for it, and so on), together with some accompanying bodily arousal (one's mouth may be watering in anticipation), and the act of consuming the cake will be seeming good to one in anticipation – it is positively valenced. As has long been recognized in the literature on prospective reasoning and decision-making, representations of future options are appraised in the same kind of way as those that are current, with one's affective systems responding with some extent of pleasure or displeasure (positive or negative valence) that is then attached to the represented future option (Gilbert & Wilson 2007, 2009). When pleasure is bound into the content of a future-directed representation it becomes, in effect, future-directed itself: one is representing a pleasant future event. And since pleasure is itself a representation of value, one is thereby representing the future event as (nonconceptually) good. (See Carruthers 2024 for a lengthier discussion of this point.)

Desires have been studied extensively in affective neuroscience under the guise of *incentive-salience* or "wanting" (Berridge & Kringelbach 2008; Olney et al. 2018) – where the quote-marks around "wanting" are intended to bracket any concerns about conscious status. (In contrast, I am not aware of any literature that uses the language of "disincentive-salience" for negative desires or repulsions, although the basic structure of repulsion is quite similar: motoric avoidance-urges combined with negative valence bound into the represented object of repulsion.) Incentive-salient objects or events produce a motoric urge to approach, acquire, or consume them;

[3] Given a broad enough understanding of the term "desire" it might be more accurate to say that desires are *distally* directed rather than future-directed. (Likewise for aversions.) If wishes are desires, for example, then one can desire (wish) that something had not happened in the past. And if regrets are a kind of aversion, then one can be averse to (regret) what one has done.

they produce some matching extent of excitement or arousal; and they seem good and attractive in anticipation, exerting a "magnet-like" force on both attention and decision-making.

It should be emphasized that the anticipatory-pleasure component of incentive-salience is not at all the same as – and need not require – *believing* that the future event will be pleasurable. Long-time drug addicts, for example, may know full well that taking the drug is no longer experienced as pleasurable. And if the addiction in question is to a drug like cocaine that often fails to produce physiological withdrawal symptoms, being without the drug might not be experienced as physically painful, either. But still the addict may be fascinated by and attracted to drug paraphernalia, may find it hard to stop thinking about taking the drug, will feel a motoric urge to acquire and use the drug if it is available, and will find the thought of consuming the drug extremely attractive (Sripada 2022) – where the correct gloss on the latter is that the addict is experiencing anticipatory pleasure bound into the content of the thought of consuming.

Notice that the value-representing account of valence (and of pleasure and displeasure) enables desires and repulsions to fit smoothly into the neuroeconomics framework discussed in Section 5.4. Decision-making among desired (and repulsive) options integrates the degree of anticipatory value attaching to each with the estimated likelihood of acquiring it (as well as the costs or degree of badness attaching to the means of acquiring it) to compute an overall expected value for each option. The alternative with the highest expected value is then generally chosen. The computations underlying human and animal decision-making thus utilize analog-magnitude representations of likelihood together with analog-magnitude representations of value and disvalue to compute an (approximate) overall expected value. Since the representations involved are analog-magnitude / nonconceptual ones, this means that the basic neuroeconomics framework for decision-making should be available to any creatures that are capable of representation at all (including bumblebees; Gibbons et al. 2022).

Setting aside the arousal component of desires and repulsions for the moment, I conclude that desires are comprised of an acquisitive motor urge of some sort together with (and in parallel with) the nonconceptually represented goodness of the object of desire. Likewise, repulsions are comprised of avoidance motor urges combined with the seeming-badness of the objects of repulsion. We can now explore to what extent this scientifically grounded account of desire conflicts with views espoused by armchair-philosophers.

6.3 Desires Are Not Propositional Attitudes

Philosophers are almost universally agreed that desires are propositional attitudes. I will argue otherwise. Their contents are said to be possible states of affairs that can be described through the application of a propositional that-clause. So when Mary wants to go to graduate school, the content of her desire is said to be *that she goes to graduate school.* Although desires are sometimes also described in such a way as to suggest that their content is an object – as in "Mary wants an apple" – it is generally thought that such descriptions are elliptical. For Mary, in wanting an apple, might want to eat it, or stew it, or plant its seeds, or throw it for the dog to chase, and so on. In any particular case the desire will be for some such event or state of affairs.

As for what it is to take an attitude of *desiring* to a proposition (rather than believing, say, or wondering), most think that it is comprised of a disposition to make the proposition true, or to bring about the state of affairs in question. On this view, in wanting to eat an apple, Mary is disposed to make it the case that she eats an apple (subject to the availability of apples and the absence of competition from other desires). We will leave the nature of the attitude for discussion in Section 6.6 (and again in Chapter 8). Here our focus is on the content(s) of (affective forms of) desire.[4]

The upshot of Section 5.1 is that there two different kinds of affective state-type to consider, whose contents might well differ from one another: standing values (cares or concerns) and activated values (incentive-salience). We will consider them in turn.

Standing (or stored) values are complex dispositional states of appraisal mechanisms. They take a variety of types of input, both conscious and unconscious, as well as conceptual and nonconceptual. When the inputs are present-tensed and consummatory (tasting the cake, feeling the cold draught from an open window, and so on) the output is some degree of pleasure or displeasure. When the inputs to stored values concern events that are distal in time or space, then they are apt to produce the three types of output described in Section 6.2: motor urges, arousal or de-arousal, and valence (positive or negative). Some inputs are deeply unconscious and

[4] Recall from Sections 5.1 and 5.2 that intentions and goals are often (mis-)classified as desires and that these are, indeed, dispositions to bring about specified states of affairs. And in many cases – albeit not all (recall the dancer who intends to execute a particular sort of fine-grained movement at a particular point in her dance) – the content of an intention is a propositional representation of the state of affairs that it is apt to bring about.

nonconceptual, as are the signals of sugar and fat received from the gut. Others are nonconceptual sensory representations, like the sensory component of pain. And yet others are conceptual or thought-like, such as a belief that one's boss is about to issue one with a negative performance review.

Typically the appraisal processes integrate a number of different inputs to produce their suite of outputs in highly context-sensitive ways. Thus how one responds to the sight of the last piece of chocolate cake in the fridge might depend on one's current state of hunger, whether or not one is currently sated on chocolate even if one is still hungry, one's knowledge that one's partner will be angry (or alternatively, pleased) if one eats it; and so on. It is plain that the stored values against which all affective appraisals take place are not propositional attitudes, even though they can sometimes receive propositional representations as inputs.

Now consider the output of evaluative appraisals of distal events: incentive-salience.[5] The arousal or de-arousal component lacks content altogether. Increased heart rate, for example, doesn't represent anything, and lacks a correctness-condition. The other two components do have contents, but of very different kinds. The motor urges produced (e.g. to reach out for the positively appraised slice of cake) are nonconceptual sets of high-level motor instructions (as discussed in Section 3.5). They have an imperative-like role, and will normally issue in action unless inhibited. They represent those actions in motoric code, not in a propositional one. While one can choose to inhibit these motor urges, they themselves do not result from anything resembling decision-making. So they are quite unlike the sorts of actions that philosophers normally think of as being the dispositional outputs of desires. For the latter are said to be actions one is disposed to take in light of one's beliefs and other desires, not caused directly, as here.

Alongside the expressive and/or instrumental motor-urge component of incentive-salience will also be a representation of the outcome action or event. These outcomes are represented (nonconceptually) as good or bad. When looking with longing at the last piece of cake, the thought of eating it seems attractive and good (positively valenced). The outcome

[5] Note that past and counterfactual events can be objects of evaluative appraisal, too, and can give rise to desire-like affective states. Although nothing of importance hangs on it for the discussion that follows, it does seem that an affective state of wishing that something hadn't happened, for example, is similar enough to regular affective desires in etiology and output to be described as such. This is a problem for disposition-to-bring-things-about theories of desire, of course, since one can't be disposed to change the past.

representations in question can be purely conceptual, purely nonconceptual, or mixed. When one finds the thought of getting one's paper accepted by a top journal attractive, the representation of the outcome might be purely conceptual (although conceptual thoughts tend to be rapidly elaborated in sensory imagination). But even here, the positive valence that attaches to it is graded and nonconceptual. When one envisages eating a piece of cake, in contrast, this might be a purely sensory-like representation produced by mentally rehearsing the action. And then of course there can be mixed cases, such as when one envisages *hearing* that one's paper has been accepted, or imagines the accolades of one's colleagues.

Notice that the valence component of incentive-salience – in contrast with the motor-urge component – is neither imperative-like nor directly motivating in nature.[6] On the contrary, it is comprised of two belief-like / perception-like components with correctness conditions rather than satisfaction conditions. One is a representation of a future action or outcome (eating the cake). The other is a nonconceptual representation of the value of that action or outcome (its degree of goodness or badness). If one attempts to capture the content of such representations using conceptualized language, one has to say something like this: one is representing that eating the cake would be to-such-and-such-a-degree good. This utilizes a propositional that-clause to describe the desire, but in doing so distorts its true content (to some greater or lesser extent).

The valence component of incentive-salience is one of the main inputs for decision-making processes, as we noted in Section 6.2, where it is integrated with estimates of likelihood, as well as estimates of the costs or effort of acting. These are combined to compute an overall expected value which can be compared with the expected values of the alternatives. Notice that although the motor-urge component of incentive-salience is not directly involved in those decision-related computations, indirectly it can be. This is because the urge will need to be inhibited if that option isn't chosen, and inhibition can be more or less effortful and aversive. The degree of difficulty involved in resisting or repressing the urge to grab the slice of cake can be one of the factors in one's decision.

The contents of the incentive-salience kind of affective desire are always at least partly nonconceptual, then. When we describe what someone wants (whether affective or intention-like) in language, we have little

[6] Some claim otherwise (Martínez 2011, 2015; Barlassina & Hayward 2019a, 2019b; Barlassina 2020). See Section 6.5 for a brief rebuttal, and Carruthers (2024) for more extended discussion. It turns out that this is another instance where philosophers have worked mostly from intuitive examples while being insufficiently attentive to the science.

option but to employ a propositional that-clause, of course. This is, no doubt, why there is such widespread agreement among philosophers that desires are propositional attitudes. But as we have seen here, such claims are only partly correct. Some states of a kind that philosophers are apt to describe as desires (goal-like desires) have propositional contents, while many of them do not. And although affective – felt – desires are sometimes partly propositional (e.g. embedding the proposition, *that I eat that slice of cake*), they are always at least partially nonconceptual, since the anticipatory-valence component is a nonconceptual representation of value.

6.4 Philosophers on Pleasure (1): Intrinsic Feeling

How close have armchair-philosophers come to accurately describing the nature of pleasure? And to what extent have they managed to capture the relationship between pleasure and affective forms of desire? These are the questions to be discussed in this section and the one following.

Some philosophers have maintained that pleasure is a distinctive sort of intrinsic feeling that attaches to our experiences, providing them with a sort of "hedonic gloss" that makes those experiences seem attractive and choice-worthy (Moore 1903; Mendola 2006; Smuts 2011; Labukt 2012). Moreover, Morillo (1995) not only endorses an intrinsic-feeling account of pleasure and displeasure, but uses it to ground a form of motivational hedonism. She claims that all decision-making is about maximizing positive feelings and minimizing negative ones.

An initial worry about intrinsic-feeling accounts of pleasure and displeasure is how to render them consistent with the cognitive science of reward and punishment. For this maintains that rewarding and punishing events can be unconscious. The best response for intrinsic-feeling theorists to make, in my view, is to postulate that the causal and functional roles of pleasure and displeasure are carried by analog-magnitude tags of some sort that can be attached to perceptual and other representations generally, whether conscious or not. When those representations occur in whatever way renders them unconscious, the tags still play the role of conditioning behavioral change and adjusting stored values. But when those representations figure in the "global workspace" (Dehaene 2014) – or in whatever manner renders experiences conscious – then the tags in question are consciously felt, adding a hedonic gloss to the experiences in which they are embedded.

Once unconscious forms of reward and punishment are acknowledged, however, then how should the terms "pleasure" and "displeasure" be used thereafter? One option is to insist that "pleasure" is the name of what a rewarding event feels like when conscious (likewise *mutatis mutandis* for "displeasure"). The other option is to allow that there can be unconscious forms of pleasure and displeasure. I propose to adopt the latter alternative. For our goal is to get at and refer to the real psychological kinds in question, not to capture common-sense intuitions that are grounded in introspection. As a result, one should describe the unconscious conditioning of sugary and fatty foods caused by signals received from receptors in the gut as depending on unconscious pleasure, even though such signals are deeply unconscious (Small & DiFeliceantonio 2019; Li et al. 2022). And one should describe the adjustments that one makes to one's posture during the day without awareness as resulting from unconscious discomfort, or unconscious bodily displeasure.

Other philosophers have objected against these intrinsic-feeling theories that (conscious) pleasures and displeasures are too heterogeneous to have anything in common phenomenologically (Korsgaard 1996; Feldman 1997). They claim that there is no such thing as the "hedonic gloss" that can be felt in common between the pleasure of slaking one's thirst, enjoying a massage, experiencing an orgasm, enjoying a run, admiring a sunset, and enjoying a game of chess or a conversation – to mention just a few of the many disparate types of experience that it can be pleasant to undergo. (Similar points can be made about the heterogeneity of displeasures, of course.) What ties all these things together, they claim, is just that one wants to experience them. This is the desire-theory of pleasure, to be discussed in Section 6.5.

While the representational nature of pleasure and displeasure defended in Section 6.1 need not stand or fall with the claim that conscious pleasures and displeasures have a distinctive phenomenological profile, I actually think that they do (as argued in Carruthers 2024). But it is a phenomenology that is much less noticeable than sensory phenomenology, in part because it is amodal – or not sensory-specific – in nature. (In this respect it is similar to the phenomenology distinctive of one's perceptions of approximate number and temporal intervals; Carruthers & Veillet 2017.) There can be a subtle commonality in the way it feels to enjoy a drink when thirsty and the way it feels to enjoy a conversation with a friend; but this is easily dominated by the many and much more vivid sensory differences between the two experiences.

Another reason why it is easy to overlook the phenomenology of valence is that one rarely – if ever – gets to experience the same thing both with and without pleasure for side-by-side comparison. (In contrast, one can compare two tastes one after the other, or two sounds, or two colors literally side-by-side, and so on.) For a conversation that one enjoys and a conversation that one does not will differ in innumerable other respects as well. The closest one can get to a side-by-side comparison is provided by sensory-specific satiety. When one first starts to eat a favorite food it tastes delicious; but as one continues to eat, the pleasure will wane, although many of the sensory properties remain the same. Even here, however, there are sensorially experienced arousal properties that will differ – one's mouth may flood with saliva as one takes one's first bite of a cake, while the same food will cloy in one's mouth as one takes one's last. Moreover, there will be anticipatory positive valence at the outset that is lacking toward the end, and one will experience an urge to eat more at the outset that is no longer there at the end.

The real difficulty for intrinsic-feeling (or "intrinsic-tag") theories of pleasure and displeasure is that it takes only a little reflection to see that they are seriously incomplete. This is because pleasure and displeasure carry information about the current value of the events whose appraisal results in those feelings. Events that are appraised as matching or embodying positive stored values are experienced as pleasant, and those that are appraised as exhibiting negative ones are experienced as unpleasant. Moreover, it is the fact that such feelings or "tags" carry information about current value that explains how their roles in conditioning and evaluative learning have become stabilized, as we have seen. So they qualify as representations of current value – they are *about* the value or disvalue of the events that occasion them. This follows pretty immediately from most if not all informational accounts of intentional content, as we noted in Section 6.1.

6.5 Philosophers on Pleasure (2): Object of Desire

Section 6.4 objected against the intrinsic-feeling theory of pleasure and displeasure endorsed by some philosophers that it is incomplete: it leaves out the fact that these feelings carry information about, and represent, degrees of (adaptive) value and disvalue. In contrast, we saw that some other philosophers have objected against the intrinsic-feeling theory that there is nothing phenomenological in common among all of the varied types of experience that can be described as pleasant or unpleasant. This latter line of thought motivates what is perhaps the dominant view of the nature of pleasure and displeasure among armchair-philosophers, which is that pleasures are simply experiences one wants to have (while wanting them intrinsically, not instrumentally), whereas displeasures are experiences one wants not to have. Those endorsing a desire-theory of pleasure and displeasure include Brandt (1979), Korsgaard (1996), Carruthers (1999), Feldman (2004), Heathwood (2007), and Parfit (2011), among many others.

Desire-theories of pleasure and displeasure face a pair of decisive objections, however. The first is that desires, by their very nature, have distal contents: they are either about the future, or (in the case of wishes and regrets) about the past, or about what might have been. It is quite unclear what it could mean to say that one wants something one is aware of already possessing, or to say that one wants what one is currently experiencing. One can, of course, want to *continue* to possess something, or to keep undergoing an experience. And many pleasures and displeasures are received as input by future-directed appraisal systems and give rise to such states. When one is enjoying the taste of a strawberry, for example, one generally wants it to continue. But pleasure itself is about the value of the currently experienced stimulus. It is present tensed. This is crucial to its role in evaluative learning, as well as to the influence that it has on incentive-salience systems. In effect, desire-theories of pleasure and displeasure fail to keep separate the "liking" system from the "wanting" system, in a way that is inconsistent with the science (Berridge & Kringelbach 2008).

A very similar difficulty infects a more recent class of theories of pleasure and displeasure, which claim that the two valences are really maximally unspecific imperatives, or motor urges (Martínez 2011, 2015; Barlassina & Hayward 2019a, 2019b; Barlassina 2020). According to this set of views, pleasure is an imperative with a content like, *do something to get more of this!*, whereas displeasure has the imperative content, *do something to get less of this!* (Different theories then differ in the proposed referent of "this," making the imperatives either world-directed or experience-directed.) But imperatives, too, are by their nature targeted at distal events. While pleasure often causes future-directed incentive-salience (the pleasant taste makes you want to take another bite), it is distinct from it – and must be, in order for evaluative learning to take place. Evaluative learning requires a comparison between actual (currently experienced, present-tensed) pleasure and the prior tacit expectations of pleasure that constitute the evaluative component of incentive-salience. (Likewise for displeasure.)

The second major objection to desire-theories of pleasure and displeasure is that valence (pleasure and displeasure) is actually itself a component of affective forms of desire. To desire something, as we have seen in

Section 6.2, is to represent that thing with anticipatory pleasure bound into one's representation of it. Likewise, to be averse to something is to represent it with displeasure bound into its representation. Put differently: desire is partly constituted by pleasure; in which case pleasure cannot be constituted by desire. A pleasure is not an experience that one wants; rather, to want an experience is to represent it with anticipatory pleasure. In effect, the desire-theory of pleasure gets the dependence-relations between the two back-to-front.

To reiterate, desires are states that include (besides automatic expressive and/or instrumental motor urges of some sort) a representation of some future action, event, or experience with anticipatory pleasure bound into that representation. (At least, this is true of affective desires, of the kind that can be identified with incentive-salience. The goal-type states described by common sense as desires are different, as we saw in Section 5.1.) Put more simply, desires are states that represent (nonconceptually) their objects as to some degree good. And pleasure itself is a representation of some currently represented action, event, or mental state as being (nonconceptually) good. Likewise, *mutatis mutandis*, for aversions and displeasures.

There are two other accounts of the nature of valence offered by philosophers that may be worth mentioning here. Each is to some degree empirically informed. Schroeder (2004) claims that pleasure represents a net increase in desire-satisfaction relative to one's implicit expectations. This is plainly wrong. First, because it is inward-looking rather than outward-looking. When one enjoys something, it is the event itself that is experienced as pleasant, not the changes taking place in one's own mind. This is better captured by the view being defended here, that pleasure is a nonconceptual representation of value. Second, as we saw earlier, pleasure is actually a component of states of desire. (Recall: to desire something is to have pleasure built into one's representation of that thing.) So desire needs to be explained in terms of pleasure rather than pleasure being explicable in terms of desire, as Schroeder would have it. And then third, Schroeder's account seems more appropriate as a description of the error signal that results from comparing current with anticipated pleasure (issuing in evaluative learning) than as an account of pleasure itself.

Cochrane (2018) presents a very different sort of account. He rightly notes that all affective states produce automatic motor activation. Some of these motor urges are attractant (approach and/or consume) whereas others are avoidant (retreat, avoid contact). Cochrane's claim is then that positive valence is the detection that one's attractant motor plan is succeeding (with the degree of positive valence constituted by the degree of success detected), whereas negative valence is the detection that one's avoidant motor plan is failing. In both cases, the only immediate downstream effect of valence is to increase attention, thereby boosting the motor responses in question. But this view cannot begin to explain the common currency role of valence in decision-making (which must here be characterized in terms of direct competition among motor plans). Nor can it begin to explain the central role that valence plays in evaluative learning and conditioning.

6.6 Philosophers on Desire: Partial Insights

While armchair-philosophers are mostly agreed that desires are attitudes to propositions (mistakenly, as we saw in Section 6.3), there is much less agreement about what that sort of attitude consists in, or what the desiring attitude comprises. Here I will follow the alternatives as laid out by Schroeder (2020). Many of them get at something correct about (some kinds of) desire. But they all also get something wrong, often because they focus on just one form of what common sense counts as a desire (either affective or intention-like) to the exclusion of the other.

Perhaps the most popular account of the attitude of desiring is that it is a disposition toward action (e.g. Anscombe 1957; Smith 1994). To desire that *P* is to be disposed to take actions that one thinks will make it the case that *P*. This fits the kinds of common-sense desire that result from prior decision-making, which are goal-like or intention-like (except that, as we saw in Section 6.3, such desires don't always have propositional contents). It really is true that someone who wants (intends) to cut the grass as soon as lunch is over (having decided to do so) is disposed to take actions that are apt to issue in grass-cutting at the appropriate time.

The disposition-to-act account of desire is false of affective desires, however – that is, states of incentive-salience. Firstly, although affective desires include an automatic motor-urge component, it is one whose action-causing role is independent of belief. And the resulting actions are intentional only in the weak sense of being cortically controlled movements; they aren't intentional in the sense of being chosen or decided upon. (Think of grimacing when in pain, for example, or withdrawing one's hand from something disgusting.) Then second, the evaluative component of states of incentive-salience is comprised of a represented action or outcome with positive valence (i.e. nonconceptual seeming-goodness) attached. This isn't itself a motivational or imperative-like state. Rather, it is a belief-like or perception-like state with correctness-conditions. Its connection with action is indirect, operating only via the influence that it has on decision-making processes.

It is often said by philosophers that desires have a world-to-mind direction of fit (Searle 1983). That is to say, they are apt to get the world to fit their contents. (As opposed to beliefs, whose contents are apt to fit the world and have a mind-to-world direction of fit.) This is true of the goals and intentions that common sense often treats as desires. And it is true of the automatic motor urges that are components of affective desires (states of incentive-salience). But it is false of the components of affective desires that figure directly in decision-making processes. These (like beliefs and perceptual states) have mind-to-world direction of fit. They represent an action or outcome – correctly or incorrectly – as (nonconceptually) good. If this conflicts with philosophers' intuitions, so be it. As I have argued here, and at some length elsewhere, it is what the science warrants (Carruthers 2024).[7]

Other philosophers have theorized that the attitude of desiring can be defined as a disposition to produce pleasure. To desire something is to be disposed to take pleasure in the achievement (or apparent achievement) of that thing (Vadas 1984; Schueler 1995). This is true of goal-type desires (intentions). When one achieves a goal, one is generally pleased to have done so. But this isn't constitutive of what it is to have a goal. Rather, to have a goal is to be disposed to bring about the goal event, and pleasure is produced by an interaction between the satisfied goal-state and the affective system. On the other hand, pleasure *is* partly constitutive of states of incentive-salience. For these embed distally directed pleasure attached to a representation of the desired event. But pleasure doesn't constitute the *attitude* of affective desiring, which is (setting aside the motor-urge component) more perception-like or judgment-like. Rather, pleasure is the vehicle through which the nonconceptual goodness of the desired event is represented, as we saw in Section 6.1.

Some philosophers have argued, in contrast, that to desire something is to perceive it as good (Stampe 1987; Oddie 2005). This is close to being partly correct of the affective form of desire (incentive-salience), except that

[7] Some philosophers think that specific sorts of conceptual judgment of goodness (i.e. judgments of moral goodness or obligation) can be directly motivating (McDowell 1978; Scanlon 1998). In some such cases, however, what is at stake is not really a belief-like judgment, but rather an expression of a prior intention-like *commitment*. One has committed oneself to doing what is right, and the current action is seen as an implementation of that intention. Actual beliefs about goodness, in contrast, can produce motivation, but only via their effects on affective states. They can do so via a sort of top-down generalized placebo effect on affective experience and value. See Section 7.4 for discussion.

it is expressed in terms of conceptual goodness, whereas incentive-salience embeds distally directed pleasure, which represents goodness nonconceptually in an analog-magnitude format. It also misses out the motor-urge component of incentive-salience altogether. Moreover, it is not true at all of goal-like forms of common-sense desires, of course, which generally don't contain any kind of representation of value – albeit having been formed initially via processes involving evaluative appraisal.

Likewise Scanlon (1998), when characterizing what he calls the "directed attention" kind of desire, correctly characterizes one component of affective forms of desire. For incentive-salient actions or events are apt to attract one's attention, as well as to prompt thoughts about them. That is to say: their objects have become salient (more noticeable, more attention-grabbing). But this is by no means a full theory of even incentive-salience, of course. It misses out both the motor-urge component and the representation of the desired event as nonconceptually good (although this may be what Scanlon means by the object of desire being "presented in a favorable light").

One might think that somehow combining together these partially correct theories would be a more promising approach. And indeed, functionalist theories of desire have proposed that desires can be defined in terms of all of our common-sense beliefs about desires and their roles (Lewis 1970, 1972). A desire is whatever occupies the desire-like role. But of course this will only tell us about the folk-psychological notion of desire, not what desires themselves really are. And indeed, since the folk notion actually encompasses states of very different kinds (as we saw in Section 5.1), this is plainly not the way to go. A suitably scientifically informed descendant of this approach is another matter. Instead of asking for the necessary and sufficient conditions for a state to qualify as a desire (as traditional philosophers are apt to do), we should simply describe the various component states and processes, their contents, and their causal roles. That is what I have attempted to do in this chapter.

There are a pair of scientifically informed theories of desire proposed by philosophers that remain to be discussed. One is teleological in nature (Millikan 1984; Papineau 1987), the other is proposed by Schroeder (2004, 2006). We will consider them briefly in turn.

The teleological theory suggests that desires are states of the mind/brain whose proper (biological) function is to produce actions that will bring about the state of affairs that is the content of the desire. This account is correct of goal-like desires. It really is the biological function of intentions (whether active or stored in prospective memory) to motivate actions that one thinks will bring about the intended situation. It is also the teleological function of the instrumental motor urges produced by affective appraisals to bring about or avoid the appraised event (depending on whether the appraisal is positive or negative).

The teleological theory is false, however, of the affective, value-laden, component of incentive-salience. The biological function of attaching anticipatory pleasure to representations of future events, thereby representing those events as nonconceptually good, is to help organisms make adaptive decisions overall. It makes it possible for decision-making to utilize a common currency of valence to compute (along with estimates of likelihood) the expected value of the various things the organism might do in the circumstances, selecting the option with the greatest expected value. Any impact on action is indirect, via an intervening decision-making process.

The teleological theory might be better seen as an account of the stored values, appraisal against which issues in occurrent (active) desires. For it really is the biological function of primary rewards and punishments to increase the likelihood that the organism will pursue adaptive outcomes of various sorts (bodily thermostasis, ingestion of glucose, avoidance of toxins). And likewise, secondary rewards and punishments have what Millikan (1984) calls "derived proper functions," acquired through generally adaptive evaluative learning mechanisms on the basis of generally adaptive primary rewards and punishments.

Schroeder (2004, 2006), although relying on some of the same neuroscientific findings as I do in this book, offers a very different account – although again it is only an account of affective forms of desire, and again while ignoring the automatic motor-activation component of such desires. Schroeder identifies the desire for some thing or event with the organism's use of representations of the current existence of that thing or event to drive reward-based learning. But this is quite wrong on its face. Notice, first, that Schroeder seems here to be characterizing occurrent or active desires, not desire in the sense of a stored inactive state. But if so, the account is obviously mistaken. When one is actively desiring something (is finding it incentive-salient), in advance of getting it there is no reward-based learning taking place. It is only at the consummatory stage, when one acquires the desired thing or event and finds it rewarding (pleasant) that evaluative learning occurs. So if affective desiring is equated with incentive-salience ("wanting") as the science suggests, then Schroeder's account has missed the mark.

But perhaps Schroeder should be read as offering an account of standing or dispositional desires instead, equating them with the stored values appraisal against which issues in incentive-salience. For it is true that these stored values (or differing subsets of them) are used, twice over, to drive evaluative learning. They are used when appraising some distal object or event, issuing in incentive-salience; and then at the consummatory stage they are used again to appraise the actual current value of the thing or event. It is the difference between the two representations that then drives evaluative learning, ramping up or down the value one attaches to that thing by some increment. This would make sense, and is correct as far as it goes. But it leaves Schroeder (2004) with nothing actually said about occurrent desires (incentive-salience itself).

When Schroeder talks about reward-based learning he mostly has in mind instrumental learning, or learning of the actions and action-sequences that issue in reward – not evaluative learning and re-learning of the value of the consummatory-events themselves. But in instrumental learning there may be no need for comparisons between the expected and actual reward-outcomes of the preceding actions. Although this is what traditional "temporal difference" models of instrumental learning assume (Sutton & Barton 1998), more recent modeling and data suggest that such learning occurs via a retrospective search of memory whenever a rewarding event takes place (Jeong et al. 2022), as we noted in Section 4.4. Nevertheless, Schroeder can still say that the standing desire for something is the stored value that is apt to issue in a rewarding event that in turn drives instrumental learning when it occurs.

Schroeder (2004) is quite clear that he is after the essence of desire. That is, he is seeking the core property that can explain all of the other features of desire as causal consequences. His proposal is that reward-based learning is this core property, which in turn depends on the stored values that constitute some events as rewards (when experienced) and others as punishments. But it is quite *un*clear whether it is appropriate to search for essences in cognitive science. Rather, our goal should be to characterize and understand the component processes and networks. In particular, to understand how desire works, we need a theory that encompasses active desire too. Yet Schroeder seemingly offers no account of currently active affective desires.

We saw in Section 6.3 that philosophers have generally gone wrong by taking the way in which we talk about desires on its face, and concluding that (all) desires are propositional attitudes. And we have now seen in the present section that philosophers have at best given partially correct characterizations of some aspects of the attitude(s) of desire, often because they fail to distinguish clearly between affective desires and intention-like ones. (Recall that my own view is that goals and intentions are not properly described as desires at all, however, since they are quite different in nature from paradigmatic affective desires.) Some philosophical theories of the attitude of desiring are correct, or partially correct, of one of these forms of common-sense desire but not of the other.

6.7 Conclusion

Pleasure is a nonconceptual, analog-magnitude representation of (adaptive) value, and displeasure is an analog-magnitude representation of (adaptive) disvalue (inclusive unfitness). Affective forms of desire embed pleasure within one of their three main components (alongside automatic motor activation and arousal). Desires are representations of some future event or outcome in which pleasure is embedded, thereby representing that future event or outcome as (nonconceptually) good. Likewise, *mutatis mutandis*, for displeasures. Decision-making processes then combine these representations of value together with implicit likelihood representations to compute the expected values of the various options open to the agent, as we saw in Sections 5.3 and 5.4.

All existing philosophical accounts of pleasure and desire get something about one or other of these states importantly wrong (although many also contain partial insights, as we saw in Section 6.6). Pleasure is neither a mere "hedonic gloss" on experiences, nor is it just a wanted experience. And desire is not a propositional attitude, nor does it motivate actions directly (except automatically, through its direct motor-activation component). On the contrary, the components of affective forms of desire that figure directly in decision-making have a mind-to-world direction of fit, being comprised of a nonconceptual representation of the goodness of some future event or outcome.

CHAPTER 7

Belief, Judgment, and Knowledge

This chapter argues that beliefs are real, and that they admit of two main kinds: episodic and semantic forms of memory. It also discusses the states often described as beliefs that result from one making up one's mind (forming a judgment), but many of which are actually commitments (a type of intention). The chapter then examines the idea that moral judgments can be directly motivating, as well as a claim that has become popular among armchair-philosophers, that knowledge is a basic kind of intrinsically factive mental state.

7.1 Beliefs Are Real and Structured

BELIEF is a central philosophical concept, integral to both the philosophy of mind and the theory of knowledge.[1] One major fault-line in philosophical debates about the nature of belief contrasts realism with dispositionalism. According to the former view, beliefs are real, internal, structured states, that cause other such states and behavior in interaction with one's desires and other beliefs (Fodor 1981, 1990; Dretske 1988; Burge 2010; Mandelbaum 2016). According to the latter account, beliefs just *are* dispositions to think, feel, and act in ways that are stereotypical of the belief in question (Ryle 1949; Audi 1994; Baker 1995; Schwitzgebel 2002, 2013).[2]

[1] The term is, however, somewhat less common in ordinary speech, where people tend to use "think" instead of "believe," and are apt to restrict "belief" to religious contexts, as in "What are your beliefs?" (Heiphetz et al. 2021). Our interest here, however, is in the state picked out by the concept, not in the terms used.

[2] Another, related, contrast is between realism and instrumentalism, discussed briefly in Section 1.3. According to the latter, for someone to believe that P simply consists in the fact that our best explanation of the person's overall behavior involves attribution of that belief (Dennett 1987). This view suffers from similar problems of order-of-explanation to those faced by dispositionalism, as we will see. The best explanatory package includes the belief that P *because* the person *does* believe that P, not vice versa.

For example, consider Mary's belief that there is beer in the fridge. According to dispositionalism, her having that belief just *is* for her to have a distinctive syndrome of behavioral, affective, and cognitive dispositions. She is disposed to approach the fridge if she wants a beer, and will assert that there is beer in the fridge if asked; she will be disposed to experience surprise if she opens the fridge to find an absence of beer; and in the same circumstances (depending on her other beliefs) she might be disposed to infer that her partner has consumed it all. A realist about belief will allow that Mary has all these dispositions, but will insist that she has them *because* she has a representation of there being beer in the fridge stored and accessible in memory (either semantic or episodic – see Section 7.2). The belief in question *explains* the dispositions, rather than being constituted by them.

Even considered as a debate about the commitments of common-sense psychology, it seems that realism has the upper hand. For notice that dispositionalism, in effect, assimilates beliefs to character traits like irascibility or generosity, which really are dispositions to think, feel, and behave in certain ways. Explaining someone's behavior by appealing to a trait ("He snapped at you because he is an irascible person") is merely explanation by subsumption under a generalization. The explanation says, in effect, that the reaction was of the sort one might have expected, because that is the way in which the agent *generally* responds. Explanation by appeal to belief, in contrast, seems to be much meatier. Such explanations seem, in fact, to cite a token cause of the explanandum. To say that Mary acted as she did because she wanted a beer and believed that there was some in the fridge is to cite a specific cause of her behavior (her belief), not just to say that she behaved in the way that a thirsty beer-in-the-fridge-believer normally would. And likewise, her surprise when she finds no beer there is *caused* by her prior belief interacting with the sight of an empty fridge, rather than just being what one might expect of a beer-believer in the circumstances. Or so I think common sense assumes.

Whatever might be true of folk-psychology, however, almost all work in cognitive science assumes a realist perspective, consistent with the representational theory of mind. On this view, Mary acts as she does because of an active representational state that locates beer in the fridge, interacting with a representation of immediately future beer-drinking as good and attractive. In fact, cognitive science is generally committed to the existence of structured contentful representations that figure in cognitive processes of various sorts, as we noted in Section 1.5. (Whether or not cognitive science vindicates the existence of a single unitary attitude of believing is another matter, however, to which we will return shortly.)

It should be said, however, that some cognitive scientists also use the language of "belief" when describing information that is encoded implicitly in the processing-rules of some cognitive systems. This is especially true of those infancy researchers who attempt to characterize the "core knowledge" that infants possess about other agents and the world around them (Spelke & Kinzler 2007). Thus infants might be said to *believe* that seeing leads to knowing, that objects continue to exist when occluded, that objects cannot move from one place to another without traversing through the intervening space, and so on (Spelke 2022). But there need be no commitment to the claim that infants access a structured representation with the content, *seeing leads to knowing*, or anything like that. Rather, infants are apt to infer directly from the fact that someone sees something that they thereafter know it.

This is quite different from dispositionalism about belief in general, however. For the *products* of core-knowledge systems are generally thought to be explicitly represented. When an infant sees someone looking into a box, for example, the resulting belief that the person knows what is in the box is generally thought to be explicitly represented, even though the processing-rule that generates it is not. In what follows, our focus will be on explicit (but not necessarily conscious) forms of belief – that is to say, on beliefs that are encoded in the form of some sort of symbolic structure (whether sentence-like or map-like).

Although disagreeing about what beliefs are, philosophers are mostly united in thinking that a belief is an attitude, of some sort, to a proposition (such as *that there is beer in the fridge*). And it is certainly true that we generally describe people's beliefs by using propositional that-clauses. It is quite another matter to claim that there is anything in the mind of the subject that maps onto, or is isomorphic with, the proposition ascribed, however. Dispositionalists about belief will deny it, of course (as may instrumentalists). But so will some realists, although for a different reason (Camp 2007, 2018; Rescorla 2009; Carruthers 2015). The latter group argues that many beliefs, in humans as well as other animals, employ map-like representations rather than propositionally structured (sentence-like) ones. Indeed, Mary's belief that there is beer in the fridge might be of this sort, with a representation of beer located in a map-like representation of the contents of her kitchen.

Even honey bees can be said to have beliefs, on some versions of this view, since they have allocentric map-like representations of the space around the hive (coded in terms of solar-compass directions and distances measured by time-of-travel), with landmarks and substances of interest (pollen, nectar, water) located on the map (Menzel et al. 2005; Carruthers 2009; Avarguès-Weber 2012, 2014; Cheeseman et al. 2014).

Less controversially, episodic memories are beliefs that generally have mixed conceptual and nonconceptual components. Such memories might be described and expressed using propositional constructions, but these are often inadequate to capture the real contents of the memory in question. For example, someone might say, "I remember that Mary was sitting opposite me at Thanksgiving dinner." But the real content of the memory is a perception-like perspectival representation of the sight of Mary sitting on the other side of a table with many other features of both her and the surroundings (both sensory and conceptual) also represented.[3]

The contents of episodic memory largely mirror the contents of perception, in fact, which generally comprise a number of object-files into which both conceptual and nonconceptual (analog-magnitude) representations are bound, in various proportions (Carruthers 2015; Quilty-Dunn 2020). At one extreme, when a human infant or an animal lacking the concepts RED, ROUND, and TOMATO, sees a tomato rolling along a surface, the content of the perception can be purely nonconceptual, and might be represented thus: THAT: *SPECIFIC REDS, SPECIFIC ROUNDISH SHAPE, ROLLING AWAY* (using italics here to represent analog-magnitude representations). And then an episodic memory of the event will likewise be wholly nonconceptual. But the same situation viewed by a human adult (and likely some animals too), will have a content carried by a representation somewhat like: THAT: RED, *SPECIFIC REDS*, ROUND, *SPECIFIC ROUNDISH SHAPE*, TOMATO, ROLLING, *ROLLING AWAY*. Here the object-file binds in both conceptual and nonconceptual representations.

It is quite misleading, then, for philosophers to claim that beliefs *are* propositional attitudes. Some are; many are not (but are rather map-like in nature); and many (like episodic memories) have mixed propositional and nonconceptual contents. In fact the propositional-attitude construction is merely something forced on us by our attempts to describe beliefs in natural language.

[3] While episodic memories normally represent the event in question from a first-person perspective, sometimes they adopt a third-personal observer perspective instead. So while all episodic memories are perspectival in content, not all are first-personal.

7.2 Belief: Semantic and Episodic

The distinction between episodic and semantic memory is now familiar to most people, and it corresponds quite closely to the distinction ordinary people draw between *remembering* and *knowing* (Umanath & Coane 2020). In the first instance, the distinction is between types of belief *content*, as we will see. But our question is whether they comprise distinct (real) *kinds* of mental state. I will argue that they do, whether or not the overarching concept BELIEF also succeeds in picking out a real kind. Compare jade. As is now well known, the rocks we call "jade" come it two quite distinct geochemical forms: jadeite and nephrite. Each of these is a natural geological kind. Jade itself, in contrast, is merely a pragmatic kind – both forms can be carved into semi-transparent green artifacts. The term "jade" does *not* pick out a real kind of thing in the world. It is possible that the same is true of the ordinary concept BELIEF. But an alternative view is that episodic and semantic memory stand to one another as do wolves and lions – distinct kinds that nevertheless belong to the same overarching natural kind (beliefs and mammals respectively). I won't attempt to adjudicate this question here.[4]

Episodic memories are event-representations that encode contextual details of the time and place of the event, and in which the event is always both singular and perspectivally represented. In fact, episodic memories are very similar in content to perceptions of events, except with fewer fine-grained details represented and with a representation of approximate past temporal location added.[5]

In contrast, semantic memory is best defined negatively, by the absence of specific perspectivally represented details of the time and place when the memory was formed. Some such memories are purely conceptual, as in one's semantic knowledge that Paris is the capital of France. Others are

[4] I actually suspect that there is not enough in common between episodic and semantic memories to constitute them as a single kind. Both function to carry information forward in time, of course. But so, too, do forms of memory that are almost certainly different in kind, such as implicit memory, core knowledge, procedural memory, and prospective memory.

[5] Tulving (1983) famously claims that episodic memories are also "autonoetic" (self-aware) in character, involving a representation of *oneself* as *experiencing* an event in the past. These facts are implicit in the perspectival and sensory-rich contents distinctive of episodic memory, of course. Whether or not explicit representations of them get formed remains optional, however – some episodic memories have autonoetic content, many don't. Self-referential, meta-representational, content is likely to get added (if at all) when episodic memories are enriched through interaction with one's own mentalizing system. There is no reason to think that the episodic memory system itself is inherently meta-representational or autonoetic (Pan 2022). What may well be true, however, is that people routinely *report* episodic memories in first-person experiential terms ("I remember seeing . . .") as a sort of self-certification of reliability, especially when the facts are in dispute (Mahr & Csibra 2018).

partly nonconceptual, as in one's knowledge of what penguins look like and cows sound like, or in one's knowledge of the layout of a neighborhood. And some are script-like in nature, as in one's expectations for what normally happens when one eats at a restaurant, or when one attends a child's birthday party. All memories are initially formed from specific episodes of seeing, hearing, reading, or being told things, of course. And it seems that many are initially episodic in nature. But then some semantic memories result from the loss of initial contextual detail from an episodic memory, whereas others are formed by overlaying or abstracting across many such memories (e.g. of restaurant meals; Renoult et al. 2019) – processes that Aronowitz (2023) calls "semanticization."

One strand of evidence for the distinctness (or at least partial distinctness) of the episodic and semantic memory systems is the phenomenon of childhood amnesia. Infants and young children – up to the age of around three – are incapable of forming episodic memories that persist for any significant length of time. But these are ages at which children are learning skills and acquiring information (forming semantic memories) at an extraordinarily fast rate. Childhood amnesia is thought to reflect the early reorganization of the hippocampus through neurogenesis (Donato et al. 2021), thus demonstrating that the hippocampus is necessary for the retention of information long-term in the episodic memory system but not the semantic memory one.

Early neuropsychological investigations of people who had suffered brain damage suggested that the two varieties of memory are pretty sharply distinct and doubly dissociable, too – meaning that either one could be lost or damaged while the other remained fully intact (Tulving 1972). Later investigations critiqued that extreme view, however (Squire & Zola 1998). An emerging consensus now suggests the existence of two partially distinct but heavily overlapping systems. Episodic memory depends critically on the hippocampus and nearby regions of the medial temporal lobes (on the inside surfaces of the temporal cortices surrounding the hippocampus), which serve to bind together the various cortically represented components of an experience into a unified event-representation. When these regions are damaged, not only are people unable to form new episodic memories, but access to previously existing episodic information is also lost. (Some forms of autobiographical memory can be retained, however, but lacking in the contextual and sensory details characteristic of episodic remembering.) The impact of hippocampal damage on semantic memory is more complex. While existing semantic knowledge is retained, people are unable to acquire *new* semantic information. It seems that belief acquisition of both types is dependent initially on the hippocampus, whereas an intact hippocampus is only required for retrieval of episodic information (Moscovitch et al. 2016; Renoult et al. 2019).

Semantic memories, while being formed through consolidation into the cortex of initially episodic hippocampus-dependent information, are thought to exist as highly distributed structures that link together representations across large regions of temporal and parietal cortices in content-specific networks (Huth et al. 2016). But these representations are nevertheless organized in accordance with a "hub-and-spoke" model, with a set of amodal (non-sensory) representations in the anterior (frontal) temporal lobes serving as the hub (Lambon Ralph 2017; Renoult et al. 2019). These amodal representations interact with the hippocampus at the learning stage to link together conceptual, sensory, and multisensory information about the kinds and individuals in question, distributed over other regions of temporal and parietal cortices. Thereafter an abstract concept like DOG will link together knowledge of what dogs look like, and their varieties; knowledge of what they sound like (again, with variety); knowledge of how they characteristically move; the ways in which they play; that they are mammals, and much more. Likewise, the concept MARY will link together a range of information about her – where she lives, what she likes, what she looks like, and so on.

When these semantic hubs become progressively damaged bilaterally, as happens in semantic dementia, semantic information is increasingly lost, while leaving episodic memories partially intact. The sparing of episodic memory is only partial, however, because event memories generally comprise not only nonconceptual (sensory) but also conceptual and amodal information. Moreover, it seems to be the conceptual components that often provide the framework for active searches of episodic memory. ("What did I do in France last summer?") As a result, spontaneously evoked (sensory-cued) episodic memory can be relatively preserved in semantic dementia, while such people are deficient at answering conceptually framed questions about past events in their lives.

The hub-and-spoke model coheres nicely with evidence that semantic information about kinds is stored in generic form by default (Leslie et al. 2011; Leslie & Gelman 2012; Gelman et al. 2016). Generics are unqualified statements about a kind, such as "Birds fly" (not all do, of course) or "Mosquitoes bite" (in fact, only females do). When people are given qualified, quantified information about a novel kind ("Some zorks live in trees") they tend to recall it in generic form ("Zorks live in trees"). In addition, people are more likely to assent to a generic like "Birds fly" under speeded conditions or under conditions of cognitive load. Indeed, stereotypes about social groups are generics, too ("Women are gentle," "Asians are good at math," and so on), and are apt to get used inductively in cognition as if they were universally quantified, giving rise to stereotypical expectations about novel members of the group (Leslie 2017). All this makes sense if a semantic kind-concept is an amodal header for a file of distributed information linked to the representation in question. So the header for BIRD will link to FLIES; and recalling that not all birds fly will require one to separately activate the file for PENGUIN or OSTRICH.[6]

Both semantic and episodic memory were traditionally described as declarative, or explicit, in nature, contrasting with the sorts of unconscious statistical information stored within the visual and core-knowledge systems, say, as well as with procedural knowledge and skills. (The latter were discussed in Section 2.4.) Both kinds of memory were once thought to involve consciousness, which was said to underlie one's capacity to express (or "declare") them in speech. But this is now known to be mistaken. Even subliminally presented words will activate their semantic meanings and bias subsequent judgments and processing (Kouider & Dehaene 2009). And conscious episodic recollection is now thought to result from a two-stage process. At the first stage a cue of some sort activates (unconsciously) an episodic memory, which then competes for relevance and attentional resources via the activity of the ventral-attentional or salience networks (Corbetta et al. 2008; Menon & Uddin 2010). If it successfully attracts attention, then it enters working memory and becomes conscious; if it fails to attract attention, it remains unconscious while having other sorts of cognitive effects (Sheldon & Moscovitch 2010; Moscovitch et al. 2016).

In the same way that wolves and lions constitute distinct kinds of animal while nevertheless sharing many properties (since both are predatory mammals), so I suggest that although episodic and semantic memories share a common etiology and involve overlapping brain networks, they are otherwise different enough to qualify as two distinct *kinds* of belief.[7]

[6] What about explicitly quantified beliefs, such as the belief that all people are mortal, or the belief that 80 percent of primary school teachers are women? It seems to me likely – although I won't make anything of it here – that such beliefs incorporate stored linguistic representations of one sort or another, which give them their precision.

[7] Note that the existence of non-believed episodic memories (Otgaar et al. 2014) doesn't really count against their status as beliefs. Some of these are cases where people will disavow remembering while still retaining the corresponding autobiographical belief. An example might be a childhood apparent-memory that one subsequently discovers actually derives from having viewed a video taken by one's parents. Others are cases where people have come to believe, on other grounds, that their apparent-memory is false. The latter kinds of case are similar in structure to unwanted desires. Just as one can

(Recall, though, that I am leaving to one side the question whether *belief* itself is a natural kind, in the way that *mammal* is.) They differ in content (either having or lacking detailed contextual and perspectival information). They differ in neural realization, with episodic memories comprising distributed conceptual and nonconceptual representations held together by sparsely coded spatiotemporal anchoring in the hippocampus, whereas semantic memories comprise a distributed set of representations held together by amodal file-headers in the anterior temporal lobes. Moreover, each form of memory can be lost or damaged while leaving the other largely intact. To the extent that either common sense or philosophers treat *belief* as a single unitary kind, then, they are in error. On the contrary, what we call "beliefs" comprise at least two distinct kinds of mental state.

7.3 What Is Memory For?

The account of memory outlined in Section 7.2 – as involving two partially distinct but overlapping systems involved in the storage and retrieval of episodic and semantic information – is widely accepted among both memory scientists and scientifically oriented philosophers. There has been much more debate about the nature of episodic memory itself, however, and its relationship to imagination. Some in the field claim that each is a manifestation of a single underlying system for constructive episodic simulation, whether of the past, the future, or of counterfactual situations (Addis et al. 2007; Schachter 2012; Addis 2020), a position that has been endorsed by a number of philosophers (de Brigard 2014; Michaelian 2016). This view will be evaluated here.

It has been known for decades that the episodic memory system is at least partly constructive in nature. New (never-experienced) details can be added to any given memory, either at the initial encoding stage or later upon retrieval (Schachter 2001). Indeed, every time a memory is accessed it is apt to become further inferentially elaborated, with the added details thereafter consolidated within it. (This is why it can be so problematic to conduct multiple interviews with a child suspected of having been abused; for the result can be the creation of false memories; Bruck & Ceci 1999.) For instance, people who watch a short video of a car accident are more likely to recall (falsely) seeing broken glass on the ground if asked, "What

have a second-order desire that one not have a given first-order desire, so one can have a second-order belief that a first-order episodic memory is false or confabulated.

happened when the cars *crashed into* each other?" versus, "What happened when the cars *hit* each other?" (Loftus & Hoffman 1989).

More recently has come the discovery that the episodic memory system overlaps heavily with the cortical networks implicated in prospection of the future (Addis et al. 2007; Buckner et al. 2008; Spreng et al. 2009). And it has also been found that people suffering from amnesia, who have damage to the episodic memory system, are equally deficient at envisaging the future (Hassabis et al. 2007; de Brigard 2014). These findings, combined with the constructive nature of memory, are what have led to the proposal that there is just a single system for episodic simulation (or "mental time-travel"), which enables us to flexibly simulate the past when remembering, or to simulate the future when imagining, as well as to simulate counter-factual situations (de Brigard 2014; Michaelian 2016; Addis 2020). The function of the entire episodic-simulation system is forward-looking, concerned with learning for the future and taking adaptive decisions for the future. One advantage of these suggestions is that they are thought to explain *why* episodic memory should be constructive and flexible, rather than just faithfully recording past events. This is to enable flexible construction of future events.

There is a trivial sense in which memory is for the future, of course. Indeed, there is a good sense in which all cognition is for the future. Thus, when one retraces one's steps in episodic memory from the time one re-entered the house in order to recall where one placed one's car keys, this is in the service of future action: driving the car to get groceries. And when one is about to enter a meeting with an irascible and cantankerous colleague, and calls to mind remembered details of one's most recent interaction, this is in the service of knowing how best to approach one's colleague in the upcoming exchange.

Nor, it seems, does the constructive, inferential, nature of episodic memory require any special explanation. For memory makes reuse of the resources of perceptual systems, which are well known to be constructive and inferential in nature. Whenever one observes a moving object, for example, the visual system is continually anticipating its future trajectory (Hecht & Bertamini 2000; Fink et al. 2009). And these predicted futures, because already represented within the visual system, are apt to get stored in memory. Hence the phenomenon called "representational momentum": one will misremember objects as being displaced further along their trajectories than one actually observed (Freyd & Finke 1984; Hubbard 2015). Indeed, it seems that the same phenomenon occurs with all observed changes of physical state, such as an ice-cube melting or a cigarette burning down (Hafri et al. 2022). Such anticipations of the future are reliable enough to be adaptive, it seems, and are built into the design of perceptual and associative-learning systems. The inferential character of memory encoding and retrieval may merely piggy-back on that.

Moreover, as Robins (2022) points out, although memory and imagination may operate on the same body of stored information and employ overlapping brain networks, it is quite doubtful whether the processes involved are the same. Episodic memories, once evoked, are apt to emerge in consciousness "fully formed," or at least spontaneously. Although the underlying processes may include an element of construction, this is not something that remembering agents are aware of. And even in cases where one actively probes memory, any answering content seems to one to emerge automatically in response to the probe. Matters are quite otherwise when one engages in future prospection. Here one is aware of constructing the desired scenario piecemeal, or of mentally rehearsing various potential future actions. It seems that episodic remembering is only tacitly constructive (given the predictive / inferential nature of the systems involved), whereas future simulation is explicitly so (as is counterfactual simulation).

The situation is actually a bit more complex than this suggests, however. For future simulation, too, can also occur spontaneously, as often happens when mind-wandering. One can be attempting to focus on a mundane task when one suddenly finds oneself imagining a stroll along a tropical beach, skimming stones across the glassy sea, for example. The content in question could equally be a memory or a future simulation (although one generally knows which it is), and each can appear equally spontaneous and unintended.

The underlying processes in such cases are quite similar, too. As we saw in Section 4.5, in both cases associatively activated concepts, images, or motor plans are evaluated within the ventral attentional network for relevance to current or recently active goals, as well as to standing values, competing for attentional resources to enter working memory and become conscious. But even here, I suggest, there is a fundamental difference. When a currently unconscious episodic memory is appraised as relevant enough, all it takes for it to become conscious is a redirection of attention. No further decision-making or constructive processes are required. When what is activated unconsciously is a partial future simulation, in contrast, decisions need to be taken to run the simulation and construct and insert the necessary components, redirecting attention to the results.

In short, I suggest that processes of future and counterfactual simulation constitutively involve choice and decision-making (albeit unconscious), in addition to a decision to engage attention, whereas episodic memory only involves the latter. So I agree with Robins (2022) that although future simulation and episodic memory share mechanisms and resources, the processes involved are nevertheless distinct.

7.4 The Motivational Role of Evaluative Belief

There have been extensive debates among philosophers about whether evaluative beliefs and judgments (especially moral beliefs) can be directly motivating. Some have claimed that they are, arguing that moral beliefs can issue in decisions and actions in the absence of any desire to do the moral thing (Nagel 1970; McDowell 1978; Dancy 1993; Scanlon 1998; Shafer-Landau 2003) – a view known as "moral internalism." Others have defended the Humean view that all motivation requires the presence of an affective state of desire, claiming that one is only motivated to act morally if one desires to do so, or wants not to act wrongly (Foot 1972; Williams 1981; Brink 1989; Smith 1994). The science suggests that there is something importantly right (and wrong) in both sets of views.

Recall from Section 3.1 that there are top-down effects of expectations (beliefs) on affective valuation. Numerous studies have shown that expecting something to be pleasurable (as indicated by its label or its price, for example) actually makes it more so – measured not just via verbal report but also from increased activity in known pleasure regions in the brain (Plassmann et al. 2008; Fernqvist & Ekelund 2014; Schmidt et al. 2017). And likewise, there are well-established placebo and nocebo effects on negative affective experiences, such as pain, depression, and anxiety (Ashar et al. 2017; Petrie & Rief 2019). Indeed, such effects can be remarkably strong. For example, a meta-analysis by Khan et al. (2012) found that both drug treatments and psychotherapy are only moderately more effective than placebo pills in treating depression, at least when the clinicians rating the outcomes are blind to the condition. There was a 46 percent improvement from drugs, as opposed to 38 percent from placebo pills. And note that since placebo effects are incorporated within any drug effects, this means that the drugs themselves are responsible for only around one sixth of the improvement in symptoms.

Moreover, expectations don't just have ephemeral effects on affective experience; they can give rise to long-term evaluative change (in one set of studies even being discernible three years later; Sharot et al. 2009, 2012).

For example, affective evaluations of a (fictional) group of people induced by reading a single narrative is able to survive many rounds of associative counter-conditioning (Gregg et al. 2006). Indeed, we have long known from the animal extinction literature that values, once learned, are quite hard to get rid of. An animal that has learned to respond with fear to a light that predicts an electric shock, for example, will gradually cease to do so when shocks are no longer administered, and its negative valuation of the light is said to be "extinguished." But the animal will respond with fear to the light as soon as a shock is administered again. It doesn't need to re-learn the negative value of the light. It seems that extinction is really a form of contextual learning. The animal has learned that the light is not bad *for now*, or in the current context, rather than unlearning its negative value altogether (Quirk & Mueller 2008).

Why are these top-down effects of belief on value so powerful, in humans especially? (There is little evidence of expectation-induced effects among other animals.) It is likely an adaptation for cultural learning (Carruthers 2024). Humans are, and always have been, deeply cultural creatures (Henrich 2016; Boyd 2018). Almost everything that a human infant needs to learn concerns its local culture – the local language, the local ecology, the local practices and customs, and so on. And much of this learning concerns cultural values. To be an accepted and successful member of one's community (especially in small-scale and hunter-gatherer groups) one needs to share the community's values and mores – what is good to eat, what to fear, how to dress, how one should behave, what behaviors are forbidden, and so on. There would have been powerful selective pressures to learn and internalize the local cultural practices and norms (producing intrinsic motivation to comply with them), resulting in what some have called a human "norm psychology" (Sripada & Stich 2006; Chudek & Henrich 2011).

As a result, merely coming to believe that something is bad to do (or is forbidden) or bad not to do (or is required) is likely to be sufficient to produce some degree of matching affective evaluation. I know of no empirical work showing just how strong such effects can be. But extrapolating from the strength of placebo and nocebo effects on affective valuation generally, one would expect them to be quite powerful. In which case, moral and other forms of evaluative judgment can motivate in the absence of any pre-existing desire to perform or refrain from the actions in question – albeit indirectly, via the *creation* of such a desire.

I conclude that while Humeans are correct to claim that all motivation (for so-called "intentional" actions) depends on an affective state of some sort (as we saw in Chapter 5), moral internalists, too, are correct in claiming that moral beliefs can themselves give rise to intrinsic moral motivations (desires) where none had previously existed.

7.5 Judgments and Commitments

Episodic and semantic memories are, for the most part, formed automatically. One observes some salient and/or emotionally significant event and is thereafter capable of bringing to mind important details, experientially represented from the perspective of the original observation. Or one explores a novel environment and gradually builds a mental map of what is located where in that environment, but without being able to recall specific episodes from one's exploration.

There are, of course, things that one can do to enhance memory-formation, but these influences are mostly indirect. Thus one might pay careful attention to an ongoing event with the hope of recalling it later; and one can intentionally revisit one's memory frequently thereafter to help consolidate it (albeit adding extraneous details in the process, as we saw in Section 7.3). And when trying to build a mental map of a new town one might spatially reimagine the relationships among some key landmarks one has visited, and when walking a novel route one might turn around frequently to encode the reverse perspective for purposes of later recognition.[8]

So episodic and semantic memories are not, in general, brought into existence by any sort of judgment-like process. When such memories are thereafter activated by internal or external cues, in contrast, the result is a judgment or judgment-like event. To recall seeing Mary at Thanksgiving dinner is to judge and be disposed to accept the correctness of the mixed-format representation of the event that comes to mind. And to call up one's location on one's mental map of a town, on which the grocery store one wants to visit is located two blocks beyond the church one now recognizes to be in front of one, is to judge (in effect) that the store is two blocks in that direction.

While many beliefs aren't caused by judgments, the reverse is also true. A great many judgments, although they guide decision-making and action in the immediate short-term, fail to express any pre-existing belief, and

[8] It turns out that honey bees, too, do this when leaving a newly discovered pollen or nectar source (Lehrer 1993). On setting out to return to the hive they stop and turn to face the source, hovering from side to side, presumably encoding the appearance of the final stages of the route they will need to follow to return to the source, thereby making their return journey more reliable.

many fail to issue in any new episodic or semantic memories, either. Consider someone participating in a perceptual-judgment experiment in the lab, judging on each trial whether the dominant motion in a random-dot stereogram is to the left or the right. Although a judgment guides their behavior in each instance (given the background goal of complying with the experimenter's instructions), none of those judgments will express a pre-existing belief, and few if any of them will issue in a long-term memory of any sort, either. And in naturalistic environments, of course, we make innumerable such judgments every day – whether the oncoming pedestrian is heading to one's right or one's left on the sidewalk, whether the water-jug one wants to lift is full or empty (and likely to be heavy or light in consequence), and so on.

As we saw in Section 5.6, judgments of this online sort are probably realized in competitive neural accumulators representing each of the options (e.g. *left* or *right*). These populations of neurons build in activity in response to a stimulus or the need for a prediction (e.g. to determine one's grip-strength when lifting the water-jug), doing so in mutually inhibitory fashion until one of them reaches a fixed criterion-level. That event then constitutes a judgment with the relevant content (e.g. *motion to the left*), thereby initiating the relevant response given one's background goals (such as saying "left"). In simple cases like this it seems unlikely that the judgment needs to give rise to any subsequent process of decision-making. Rather, one has a pair of standing intentions – "say 'left' if the motion is to the left; say 'right' if the motion is to the right" – for which the perceptual judgment provides the triggering cue. In other cases (such as walking down a crowded street), multiple concurrent judgments might need to be integrated and evaluated to issue in a separate decision (e.g. "step to one side and allow that frail person to pass").

Although many beliefs aren't caused by judgments, the very paradigm of long-term belief-formation for most philosophers involves a judgment or judgment-like event. One first weighs the evidence, considering the reasons that count in favor of, and against, the truth of some proposition, eventually *making up one's mind*. It is said that one thereby comes to believe that proposition (or one believes it to be false). Jurors in a criminal trial, for example, consider the evidence of the defendant's guilt or innocence before making up their minds. Although the law only requires a simple binary verdict (guilty versus not proven), common sense suggests that there are three psychological states a juror might end up in: belief in guilt, belief in innocence, or undecided. (When one is undecided, of course, then one has *not* made up one's mind about the facts, though one might have made up one's mind that the case is not proven.)

How does this work? The best-known account we have is due to Frankish (2004), building on the work of Cohen (1989) and others. What happens following one's consideration of the evidence is that one *accepts* the defendant's guilt (say), thereby committing oneself to think, reason, and act in the future on that assumption. But one doesn't make this commitment in the same sort of limited way that a defense lawyer might commit herself to her client's innocence. For this latter commitment is for professional purposes only. When the lawyer goes home, she might well confess to her partner that she thinks he is guilty. What Frankish has in mind is rather a sort of unrestricted commitment. When jurors commit themselves to the truth of the proposition, *the defendant is guilty*, their commitment is to treat that proposition as true for all normal practical and theoretical purposes.

Notice that although, on this account, making up one's mind about something is an active process, that doesn't entail the much-maligned claim that one can form new beliefs at will, for purely practical purposes (Williams 1970; O'Shaughnessy 1980; Pettit 1993). Rather, on Frankish's view, in order for a making-up-of-mind to issue in genuine belief, it has to be evidence-based. Just as one cannot genuinely promise something if one believes it to be impossible, so he thinks one can't flat-out commit oneself to a truth without thinking that the evidence warrants one in doing so (Frankish 2007). Just as belief in the possibility of an action is a background enabling condition for a sincere promise to perform it, so a positive evaluation of the evidence supporting a proposition is a background enabling condition for the sort of commitment to truth that is said to constitute believing it.[9]

But how does commitment to truth work? How does committing to the truth of *P* issue in thought and action of the sorts one might expect of someone who believes that *P*? If we think of commitment to truth on the model of promising (or a commitment to act), then it seems it might give rise to an *intention* – in this case the intention to think and act in the future on the assumption that *P* is true. If this is right, then commitment to truth is not really a kind of belief at all (unless intentions are actually beliefs; see

[9] Why? Perhaps because only making up one's mind after considering the evidence will lead one to *believe* that one has come to believe it. Otherwise one likely remains aware that one's making-up-of-mind is merely strategic and limited in scope, like that of the defense lawyer. It may be that committing to truth only issues in (what common sense regards as) a kind of belief when giving rise to a higher-order judgment that one is forming a belief.

Section 5.2). It is a mental state of another kind entirely, but with a content that mimics the effects of belief (thinking and acting as if *P* were true).

Another possibility is that committing oneself to the truth of *P* gives rise to an episodic memory of that very act or event. Then when situations arise in the future to which *P* is relevant, one recalls what one did. Remembering that one had made up one's mind that *P*, one believes that one believes that *P*. Although this is a belief, it is a belief with a different content: one remembers having come to believe the truth of *P*, which is not a belief that *P* per se. (It is higher-order – a belief about a belief – not a first-order belief that *P*.) This can then motivate one to think and reason on the assumption that *P*, given that one values self-consistency. What results from an all-out commitment to truth, then, is generally either an intention to think and act on the assumption that *P*, or it is a motivation to think and act consistently with what one takes oneself to have come to believe, or both. Neither is actually a belief that *P*.

It seems likely that both routes are sometimes operative, either singly or together. For the act of making a commitment, of any sort, generally issues in an intention to do what one has committed oneself to; and one will generally at the same time form an episodic memory of the act of making up one's mind. Thereafter it may be a matter of happenstance whether one's intention becomes activated, or rather one's episodic memory, or both. Notice that the same two routes can be operative in promise-keeping, too. For promise-making will generally issue in an intention to do what one has promised, as well as an episodic memory of one's act of promising. The former (when active and unopposed) will give rise to the promised action directly; the latter will do so in conjunction with an unopposed desire to keep one's promises. I am aware of no attempts to sort out the relative frequency of the two routes empirically.

How else might making up one's mind that *P* work, so as to issue in belief-like thought and behavior? Why not by causing the creation of a new semantic memory with the content *P*? This isn't really an option for Frankish (2004), because for him the first-level mind (System 1, contrasting with the second-level – System 2 – mind that he thinks is comprised of commitments) is associationist in character. (Indeed, Frankish, following Dennett, is an instrumentalist about first-order belief. There is nothing more to being a System 1 *P*-believer than thinking and acting in a way that is best explained by one being described as such.) And it is hard to see how a single act of making up one's mind could give rise to a robust new set of associations.

As soon as we shift to a representational-realist perspective, however, the picture changes. It may be that an act of making up one's mind sometimes issues in a verbal performance, for example, an assertion of "*P*" in outer or inner speech. And that might then give rise to a new semantic memory that *P* in a way that closely resembles the formation of a new belief when someone else tells one that *P*. Hearing oneself as asserting that *P* may sometimes directly cause a new semantic memory with the content, *P*. Indeed, some have gone so far as to claim that whenever one *entertains* a proposition *P* (even if one overtly rejects it), that gives rise to at least some weak degree of belief that *P* (Mandelbaum 2014).

The correct account, here, is almost certainly a pluralist one. There seems little doubt that there is such a thing as an all-out (generalized) commitment to think and act on the assumption that a given proposition is true. And it seems likely that this is what gets created, on some occasions at least, when one makes up one's mind that *P*. There is also little doubt that from a common-sense perspective, to make up one's mind that *P* is to come to believe that *P*. But this is (at least sometimes, if not always) an error. The intention that can result from a commitment to truth is not a belief, and lacks the fine-grained causal profile of a belief that *P* (while mimicking some its effects). And believing that one believes something is not the same as first-order believing it, either – although it, too, can mimic many of the normal effects of a first-order belief.

While Section 7.2 discovered that there are more kinds of belief than common sense may allow (since semantic and episodic memories are distinct kinds of belief-state), here we have found that there are *fewer* types of belief than common sense seems to countenance. For in many cases where one describes oneself or another as believing that *P* one is mistaken. The person in question is really in a state of a different sort (an intention) or with a different content (a belief about their belief) that mimics the normal functional effects of a belief that *P*.[10]

7.6 Knowledge Is Not a Mental State

The traditional view in philosophy is that knowledge is a kind of belief (justified true belief, perhaps, or reliably formed true belief). More recently, Williamson (2000) and others have claimed that knowledge is

[10] Some have argued that religious beliefs constitute another yet category of attitude that common sense treats as a kind of belief, but really is not. Van Leeuwen (2014) suggests, in particular, that religious beliefs are closer to pretense in nature than they are to regular beliefs.

a primitive kind of mental state (as are seeing and remembering) – it is basic, primitive, and not composed out of other properties. It is a state that is intrinsically factive, in the sense that it is partly constituted by the truth of its content.

Much of the defense of this newer view has proceeded as philosophical discussion generally does – considering hypothetical examples and testing proposed analyses in the service of arguing that our *concept* of knowledge is basic and primitive. But some of the arguments for the view have been empirical (although still targeted at the concept, rather than at knowledge itself). It has been claimed that competence with the concept KNOW emerges earlier in development than the concept BELIEF, for example, and is thus the more basic of the two (Nagel 2013; Phillips et al. 2021).

I don't myself find the case for thinking that our concept of knowledge is basic and primitive at all convincing. While Williamson may be right that the concept KNOW is unanalyzable, and is in that sense conceptually primitive, the same is likely to be true of most of our concepts, as Fodor (1998) famously argues. It doesn't follow that the concept isn't learned on the basis of others. Moreover, the data on supposedly early acquisition of competence with the concept KNOW derives from three-year-old and four-year-old children, using verbal tests. In contrast, we now have dozens of studies conducted with infants as young as six months using indirect measures showing that competence in reasoning about belief and false belief is achieved a great deal earlier (Southgate & Vernetti 2014; Baillargeon et al. 2016; Scott & Baillargeon 2017; Hyde et al. 2018). Moreover, despite the so-called "replication crisis," new studies employing even more stringent methods continue to find the same thing (Király et al. 2018, 2023; Buttelmann & Kovács 2019; Forgács et al. 2019, 2020; Kampis & Kovács 2021; Kovács et al. 2021; Ting et al. 2021; Woo & Spelke 2022, 2023). Furthermore, the tasks that have been employed with children and (especially) other primates that are said to show competence in understanding the difference between knowledge and ignorance can just as well be said to show understanding of the difference between true-belief and no-belief – in hardly any of them is any attempt made to test for the distinctive properties of knowledge.[11]

[11] There are a few experiments with children and apes that do test for knowledge-understanding against otherwise equivalent Gettier cases where knowledge is said to be lacking (Kaminski et al. 2008; Oktay-Gür & Rakoczy 2017; Horschler et al. 2019). But these admit of alternative explanations in terms of disrupted attention. And in any case, hardly anyone other than philosophers thinks that knowledge is really absent in these cases (Starmans & Friedman 2020).

For our purposes, however, all this is by-the-by. Even if our concept of knowledge were basic and simple, and even if our common-sense psychology were to treat it as such, this would fail to address the real – metaphysical – nature of the state. To discover the structure and state-types that the mind contains we should look to cognitive science, not common sense. And it is no defense for Williamson to point out, as he does (Williamson 2020), that all science has to be grounded in common sense (e.g. about the general reliability of perception). For the point is that one shouldn't rely on common sense when there is well-established science on the very same topic (the mind and its contents), as there is here. To make claims about the structure and contents of the mind on the basis of common-sense theorizing might once have been justifiable but is, now, intellectually indefensible.

So what does the science tell us? It is true that cognitive scientists are interested in explaining cognitive success. The core problem in vision science, for example, is to explain how the brain extracts, in real time and in a generally reliable manner, a three-dimensional representation of the world on the basis of patterns of two-dimensional stimulation of the retina. But it is quite another matter to claim that the central target of explanation here is knowledgeable seeing, with *sight* treated as a primitive and factive psychological state. Indeed, vision scientists themselves are generally quite happy to use the word "see" as encompassing all conscious outputs of visual processing, whether illusory or not. Something similar is true of the cognitive scientists who study memory, as the literature on false memory attests (Brainerd & Rayna 2002; Loftus 2005).

In both cases (vision science and memory science) the goal is to understand the processes that give rise to visual and mnemonic phenomena. It may be a background constraint on theorizing that the processes in question are generally reliable ones, tending to issue in correct visual representations and true memories. But capturing and explaining patterns of error is equally important to the enterprise. The goal is to understand how these systems actually work, not just to explain the subset of outputs that qualify as forms of knowledge. Hence cognitive science doesn't treat memory as a factive state, but rather uses the term "memory" as a label for the results of a more-or-less reliable process of encoding, storage, and retrieval. Whatever gets stored and consolidated is a memory, while often including properties added through inference at the time of encoding, or added when the memory is accessed, which can be false of the actual event remembered (Schacter et al. 1998). Nevertheless, these are regarded as parts of the memory, and of what one remembers. In science as opposed to philosophy, then, memory is not a factive mental state. The subset of states that constitute (factive) seeing, (factive) memory, and (factive) knowledge don't in any sense provide a privileged target of explanation.

What of the concept of a memory *trace*, however (Robins 2023)? To the extent that memory science vindicates the existence of such traces, doesn't this introduce an intrinsically factive state into the ontology of the science? In fact it does not. For a memory trace is a record of a previous *experience*; but the memory itself represents the event that the experience was an experience *of* – which may or may not have been veridical. Illusory experiences and hallucinatory experiences may leave memory traces just as do any other experiences. When those traces are reactivated, one may be left with a false memory of an event that never took place.

In response to these points, it might be suggested that although factive mental states aren't *targets* of explanation in cognitive science, they might nevertheless serve as primitive *explainers*. But this is not the case, either. What is true is that externally individuated forms of *content* play a role in scientific explanation. Cognitive science explanations often need to appeal to the content of the states cited in the explanations. Some forms of content result from map-like correspondences between cognitive representations and the domain represented; others can perhaps best be characterized as the subset of information carried by a state that explains how the role of states of that sort have become stabilized, as we saw in Section 6.1 (Shea 2018). The former presupposes that the correspondence in question is at least partially correct. And the latter presupposes that, on the occasions that did the stabilizing, the representations in question *were* correct. But it is a far cry from this to claiming that cognitive science explanations make appeal to primitive factive states like *know*. Indeed, the idea seems inconsistent with the core commitment of almost all cognitive science, which is to the reality of the representational mind.

All talk of representations, their correctness-conditions, and the processes that compute over those representations presupposes that cognitive states are comprised of a pair of distinct components: a representation or structured symbol of some sort, and the content / correctness-conditions of that representation. There is no place here for a type of mental state that already has correctness somehow built into it (as – allegedly – does knowledge). The actual correctness of a representation (as well as its production via a generally reliable process, and together with any other signature properties of knowledge), are extraneous, relational, properties of the representation (the belief, percept, or memory), not intrinsic to it.

It might be objected that the representational theory operates at a lower level of explanation, and is about the way mental states are realized in the brain rather than the mental states themselves. In that case knowledge could be a unitary and basic kind of state, but realized at lower levels of organization by representations and their relations. In fact, however, the representational theory of mind maintains that mental states *are* representations with correctness-conditions. This is not a lower (e.g. physical) level of explanation, but a reductive proposal about the nature of the mental itself. Admittedly, the computations that are postulated to take place over these representations occur at a lower level of explanation. But these are intended to explain transitions among mental states, not the natures of those states themselves.

Mental states are also individuated by their functional properties, of course. Roughly, beliefs guide planning and action-selection, while desires make the desired options seem good and choice-worthy, and intentions initiate and guide online acting. (See Chapters 5 and 6.) There are no differences between true beliefs and false beliefs in terms of functional role, however: both are apt to influence planning and action-selection in exactly the same manner. It is true that actions undertaken on the basis of false information are less likely to succeed, but this is a distal probabilistic effect rather than a difference in role. The same is true of knowledge: states of knowing will influence decision-making in exactly the same ways that both true beliefs and false beliefs do, but the actions undertaken on the basis of the former will be somewhat less vulnerable to failure.

One final consideration: it is widely agreed that the notion of causation is at least closely tied to the idea of manipulability (Woodward 2003). If A is a cause of B, then manipulating A should have an influence on B. But by this measure, knowledge is not a cause of behavior. For one can manipulate knowledge by manipulating the circumstances without impacting belief, and so without any subsequent effects on behavior. Consider, for instance, situations that are said to destroy knowledge without changing belief: someone first observes a ball being placed in a box, and then in their absence the ball is removed from the box before being placed back into it again. This is said (by philosophers) to destroy the person's state of knowledge, but it leaves belief intact.[12] (Indeed, it leaves intact justified true belief, as well as subsequent successful retrieval of the ball.) Plainly there can be no impact on the person's behavior, here, unless we choose to disclose what happened.

[12] On this point philosophers are extreme outliers relative to both other academics (in the humanities as well as the sciences) and laypeople (Starmans & Friedman 2020). Hardly any non-philosophers share the intuition that knowledge is destroyed in so-called "authentic-evidence" Gettier cases of the sort used in the example here.

This seems like sufficient reason to claim that only representations and their contents are causes of behavior (at the non-algorithmic / intentional level of explanation). Substituting one representation for another, even while holding their correctness-conditions constant, will be apt to alter behavior, even if only subtly. (Consider the pairs, "evening star" / "morning star"; "Jocasta" / "mother"; and "Clark Kent" / "Superman.") And of course substituting a belief with one content for a belief with another will generally do likewise. But substituting mere belief in place of knowledge (or vice versa) generally won't.

I conclude that, whatever might be true of the concept KNOW, knowledge itself (the putative mental state, not the concept) is not itself a real aspect or component of the mind. While beliefs of at least two kinds (semantic and episodic) are real, knowledge itself is not (except insofar as it is a kind – albeit perhaps an unspecifiable or indefinable kind – of belief).

It remains true, of course, that knowledge might be a pragmatic kind of some sort, rather like the property of being a weed or being a bush. And of course there are truths involving the concept KNOW, just as there are truths involving the concepts WEED and BUSH – as in, "He knows where the car keys are," "The neighbors' yard is overrun with weeds," and "The drought has killed the bush I planted last spring." But no one thinks that the concepts WEED or BUSH pick out real – natural – kinds in the world. Nor should anyone think that about KNOWS, I have argued.

7.7 Conclusion

This chapter has argued that beliefs are real, and that they admit of two kinds: semantic and episodic. It has also argued for the distinctness of imagination from episodic memory, and has argued that the states that result from making up one's mind are sometimes not beliefs at all, but rather intentions to think and reason as if one had such a belief, or are sometimes beliefs with a different content (second-order beliefs). The chapter has shown how evaluative judgments can motivate in the absence of any pre-existing desire, but only by giving rise to a new desire. Finally, the chapter has argued that the recent trend among philosophers to treat knowledge as a metaphysically basic component of the mind is mistaken.

CHAPTER 8

Do Attitudes Come in Degrees?

This chapter takes up an idea that is arguably a central component of common-sense thinking, as well as one that is widely accepted among philosophers. This is that all kinds of attitude – desires, beliefs, and goals / intentions – come in degrees. They can admit of differing strengths or causal efficacy. Although rarely fully articulated, some versions of the view go along with a distinctive picture of the nature of decision-making (called here "the push-push theory"). As we will see, there is an element of truth in some of these claims, but also much that is mistaken.

8.1 Intrinsic versus Extrinsic Degrees

We first need to delineate our target, separating it from some nearby ideas. Our question is whether attitudes like belief differ in strength intrinsically rather than extrinsically or relationally. The ordinary claim that one can believe (or desire) something more or less strongly is ambiguous between these two sorts of view. It might mean, for example, that a belief can be more or less deeply embedded in one's web of beliefs (Quine & Ullian 1970), in such a way that giving up on that belief would occasion a great many changes in one's other beliefs. Put differently, a strongly held belief can be one that supports and is supported by a great many others. As a result, it would require much more evidence to overturn it or to get one to give up that belief than would be required for others that are less deeply embedded.

In contrast, one version of the view that beliefs can vary in strength intrinsically might derive from the commonly accepted idea that beliefs are dispositions to act when combined with a desire. (Another version is provided by the philosophical theory of *credences,* which are an alleged kind of belief that admit of degrees. See Section 8.5.) It might be said that one can be more or less strongly disposed to act on a given belief. That is, one belief might be more likely to issue in action when combined with a desire of a given strength than another, even though the contents of the two beliefs are identical, and even though those beliefs are equally deeply embedded.

A similar distinction can be drawn for desires. One affective state of desire might be stronger than another in the sense that it manifests appraisals against many more of one's stored values. Compare wanting a slice of chocolate cake (manifesting just a single appraisal of taste) with longing to purchase the property that is one's dream home. The latter feeling might manifest a great many values – for elegance, for neighborhood, for accessibility, for long-term financial security, and more. Here one would have to give up much more of what one values if the desire had to be set aside than one would give up by opting not to have the cake.

In contrast, compare the ordinary desire for cake with one's desire for a drink of water when one returns from a desert hike and is thoroughly dehydrated (having run out of water, perhaps). Although the two desires each manifest just a single dimension of value (for a specific taste versus slaking one's thirst), intuitively it seems that one desire is much stronger than the other, and would easily dominate the latter in any head-to-head competition. ("What would you prefer: a slice of chocolate cake or a glass of water?")

Essentially the same distinction can be drawn for goals and intentions. A given intention (like the intention to place a bid on that dream home) can be embedded in a much deeper network of values and other already existing intentions than another (such as the intention to ask for a slice of cake when the waiter passes by). As a result, it would take much more to make one reconsider one's intention in the one case than the other. This, too, is a relational (and uncontroversial) sort of strength of intention.

In contrast, consider the ordinary idea of strength-of-will, or willpower. On this view, a given goal or intention can be held more or less firmly, not because of the way in which it is embedded in a network of values and other intentions, but simply because one is strong-willed (or strong-willed in this instance). In psychology, this idea has manifested in the theory that willpower can become depleted: after exerting self-control in one task (holding firm to one's intention to complete that task) it is said to be harder to exert control in a follow-up task (Masicampo & Baumeister 2008). The only difference between the intentions in the two cases seems to be the strength with which the intention is held. One intends less strongly when willpower is depleted than when it is not.

The *contents* of one's attitudes can differ by degrees, too, of course. For example, an episodic memory of an event can be more or less rich and detailed. But the one is not more of a memory than the other (whatever that might mean). Likewise, an intention can be highly specific and detailed in content (comprising a detailed plan of some sort) or it can remain abstract and unspecific. ("I'll vacation somewhere in the Caribbean this year.") Although such differences are intrinsic to the attitudes in question, they are differences in content, not differences in the strength of the attitude one takes to those contents.

Finally, it is worth mentioning that stored (or "standing-state") attitudes can be more or less *accessible*. Some memories are easy to recall, some take hard work and systematic probing. Likewise, a prospective memory (a stored intention) can be more or less easily evoked into activity, depending on the number of triggering cues it contains and the time that has elapsed since it was formed. But again, these are not differences in the attitudes themselves. They are, rather, relational differences not unlike the depth-of-embedding variations discussed earlier.

Our focus in this chapter will be on the idea that attitudes can differ in strength intrinsically – not because of the way they are embedded among other attitudes, and not because of differences in their contents or their accessibility, but simply in the strength or degree of efficacy of the attitude one takes to those contents.

8.2 The Push-Push Theory of Decision-Making

How would differing attitude strengths figure in decision-making? One natural way to develop the idea is in terms of imperative-like causal "oomph." A strong desire pushes harder for its own satisfaction when in competition with others. And a strong belief pushes harder for any goal that it can facilitate. These degrees of strength then combine together to issue in a decision to pursue the desire that has the greatest *overall* strength – the strongest push wins. The contents of the various states determine which desires fit together with which beliefs to issue in a represented way of securing the object of desire. But (on this view) it is the combined strengths of the component attitudes that determine choice.

This sort of account is at least suggested by theories of desire as dispositions to bring about the desired state of affairs (Anscombe 1957; Smith 1994) – interpreted here as a theory of affective forms of desire rather than as a theory of the goal-states (intentions) that are often described as desires. The idea would be that a desire pushes for its own satisfaction (with greater or lesser causal efficacy in competition with others), initiating a search for beliefs that would enable pursuit of the object of desire. While it is less intuitive to think of beliefs having any sort of imperative role, the suggestion could be that their strength consists in their power to modulate the strength of any desire with which they are paired. So a medium-strength desire combined with a strong belief will come out overall stronger than a competing medium-strength desire combined with a weak belief. When combined together, then, both beliefs and desires make an independent contribution to the overall push toward action that might satisfy the desire – hence the name, the "push-push" theory of decision-making.

A view of this sort is also suggested by imperative theories of valence and desire. If a desire is a representation of an event or outcome with some degree of positive valence attached, and positive valence has imperative content of the sort, *do something to get that!*, then the upshot is an imperative theory of desire. On some versions of the account, the "that" in "get that!" refers to the worldly event or outcome; on other versions it refers to the *experience* of that event or outcome. (Martínez 2011 tentatively suggests a version of the first view; Barlassina & Hayward 2019a, 2019b suggest the latter.) Either way, a desire is a kind of high-level, unspecific, urge toward action. And it is then hard to see how imperatives of this sort could fit together with the strengths of the various implementation-beliefs to determine choice unless strength-of-belief served to modulate the strength of the imperative urges.

Although such views are coherent, and successfully flesh out the common-sense idea that both beliefs and desires come in varying strengths, they play no role in cognitive science. On the contrary, as we saw in Chapter 5, the science has converged on a view of decision-making as resulting from computations of expected value. Desires assign some degree of value to their objects, and beliefs embed representations of likelihood, enabling an overall expected value for each alternative to be computed. Here the degrees are all in the contents of the attitudes in question (represented value and represented likelihood), not in the attitudes themselves.[1]

Chapter 6 has already outlined the account of desire that is best supported by the science. Section 8.3 will briefly revisit that account to bring out what is right, and what is wrong, about the idea that desires are imperative-like, with their varying strengths being a matter of how strongly they push for implementation. Section 8.4 will discuss the role of degrees of arousal, especially within strong emotions. Section 8.5 will then discuss the

[1] See also Carruthers (2024) for an extended cognitive-science-based critique of imperative theories of pleasure and desire.

philosophical theory of credences. These are held to be a distinct category of graded belief-like attitudes that (on some views) exist alongside our more familiar categorical belief-states. And then finally, Section 8.6 will consider strength of will, or willpower.

8.3 Strength of Desire

Talk about the strength of one's desires is ubiquitous in common-sense psychology. One can be said to somewhat want to do something, to want to do it very much, or to have an overwhelmingly strong desire to do it. And as we will see in Section 8.5, one reason for taking degrees of belief seriously and accepting the reality of credences as a type of attitude is that, given that desires vary in strength, one should expect beliefs to vary in strength too. For those strengths would need to be compared and traded off against one another somehow when one engages in practical reasoning and decision-making.

As we saw in Section 6.2, however, desires actually comprise two distinct graded components (in addition to degrees of arousal and de-arousal, which can be set aside for the moment, to be returned to in Section 8.4). One is the degree of value represented by the valence component of the desire, which makes the object of desire seem better or worse, more or less attractive and choice-worthy. But the sort of "strength" here is indicative rather than imperative and belongs to the content of the desire. It is an analog-magnitude representation of the value attaching to the object of desire. It is these representations that play the main role in decision-making, interacting with estimates of likelihood and the costs or disvalue of acting to issue in decisions.

But alongside valence, desires also comprise an automatically produced motoric component, and these do vary in imperative-like strength. The appraisals of value that issue in affective states of desire and emotion automatically activate motor urges of various sorts (of greater or lesser strength), either innate or acquired through previous instrumental conditioning. Desiring the last piece of chocolate cake, one has an urge to reach out and take it. The motoric component of desire will issue in action unless inhibited. As a result, as we saw in Chapter 3, in many cases the actions that desires and emotions motivate don't result from decision-making processes at all. Rather, they are direct products of the appraisals that issue in the affective state in question. (Sometimes, as we noted, one might take a decision not to inhibit the motoric urge, and then the subsequent action is an indirect product of decision-making.)

The automatic motor-urge components of desire and emotion do enter into decision-making, however, but indirectly. For it takes executive effort to suppress them. When one has a desire with a strong motor-urge component, one's decision will depend not just on the positive valence attaching to the object of desire, the likelihood of achieving it, and the costs of acting, but also on the costs of *not* acting – that is, on how difficult or unpleasant it would be to suppress the urge to act. For as is well known, exerting executive control is experienced as effortful (negatively valenced) by default. Indeed, there is now a well-established literature on decision-making that includes estimates of the costs of cognitive control (Kurzban et al. 2013; Shenhav et al. 2014, 2017; Inzlicht et al. 2018).

The account outlined here both supports and is supported by recent models of addiction that emphasize impaired and inconsistent control as opposed to irresistibly strong motor urges (Holton & Berridge 2013; Pickard 2022). Indeed, as Sripada (2022) reviews, self-reports offered by people struggling with addiction only rarely mention the presence of especially strong behavioral urges. And in fact all forms of addiction are responsive to incentives, with addicts being well-capable of avoiding drug use when negative consequences are clearly and saliently present ("the policeman at the elbow"). Sripada emphasizes, instead, the way in which addiction influences and distorts the patterns of one's automatic thoughts, leading to illusion-like mis-evaluations of the costs and benefits of drug use, eventually culminating in a decision to use the drug again.

Decision-making itself, then, involves indicative representations only (albeit ones that admit of degrees). One weighs the estimated outcome value (some degree of positive or negative valence) against the estimated physical effort involved in acting (represented by the magnitude of negative valence that attaches to acting), while also weighing the estimated cognitive effort (if any) involved in *not* acting (the estimated negative valence involved in repressing or inhibiting the urge to act); combining these together with an estimate of the likelihood of achieving the outcome if one does act.[2] So the main components of desire do admit of degrees; but the graded components of desire that figure in decision-making are properties of the contents of desire, not of the attitude of desiring. (Similar points hold for emotions, of course, and for affective states generally.)

[2] Notice that this implies that all beliefs (or all beliefs that can figure in practical decision-making, at any rate) must already have representations of likelihood built into their content, whether numerically (as in 0.75 PROBABLE), or conceptual (as in LIKELY), or analog-magnitude in nature. Jackson's (2022) argument against the reduction of credence to belief goes awry by overlooking this possibility.

8.4 Degrees of Arousal

For the most part in this book we have been able to treat desires and emotions alongside one another, since they share a common structure of appraisal, automatic motor output, arousal, and valence attaching either to the represented object of appraisal or to the anticipated action (or both). But the arousal component of affective states can vary much more dramatically in emotions (especially emotions like anger and fear), issuing in an especially salient dimension of strength-of-attitude in such cases. This will be discussed here.

While all affective states have some impact on the autonomic nervous system (albeit often fairly minor), emotions (especially strongly felt emotions) can issue in a suite of dramatic bodily changes. These include increases in heart rate and respiration rate, pupil dilation, increased sweating, redirection of blood flow from the periphery to the core organs, and release of chemicals like adrenaline and cortisol into the bloodstream. All of these changes can happen by degrees, from relatively minor in connection with mere annoyance or anxiety to a full-blown "fight or flight" response in cases of fury or terror.

Large increases in arousal can be thought of as degrees of preparation for urgent action and possible injury. But they also have general effects on cognition, such as automatically enhancing memory for subsequent events (Kensinger & Corkin 2004), in addition to emotion-specific ones. (Anger increases confidence and enhances risk-taking, fear reduces confidence and inhibits risk-taking; Lerner & Keltner 2000.) Especially relevant for our purposes, however, increases in arousal (both large and small) give rise to a domain-general "urgency" signal that enhances rates of neural gain in both decision-making and motor-control networks (Murphy et al. 2016; Thura & Cisek 2016; Hanks & Summerfield 2017; Carland et al. 2019). That is, decision-related evidence in sensory and cognitive systems builds up faster than it otherwise would, and decision-making at all levels happens quicker. With a domain-general injection of additional neural activity added to the noisy competitive accumulators that underlie judgment and decision-making, they are quicker to reach their fixed criterion-level, issuing in swifter decisions and swifter actions.

Not only do affective states vary in the degrees of valence directed at their objects, then, and in their degrees of associated motor activation, but they also come with degrees of physiological arousal. The latter is especially salient and impactful in connection with high-arousal emotions like anger and fear. And as we have just seen, degrees of arousal can have direct impacts on decision-making processes. Specifically, higher arousal makes decision-making take place faster, at all levels, including the sensorimotor decisions that make any resulting actions take place quicker. So there is a real sense in which high arousal creates an extra "push" within desires and emotions, but it is a push for *faster* decision-making and quicker responding, rather than a push for one decision over another. Put differently, high arousal has no influence on *what* one decides to do, just on how quickly one decides to do it. It doesn't strengthen one desire or emotion in relation to others.

These findings present little or no challenge to common sense, I think. For it is familiar to most of us that states of high emotion tend to cause heightened alertness and a sense of urgency. But such findings can nevertheless help explain why the automatic motor outputs produced by strong emotions are more likely to evade executive suppression, as when in a state of extreme anger one says things one knows (after even a moment's reflection) one shouldn't, or when one (stupidly) turns to run from an aggressive black bear in the forest. This is because the arousal component of any strong emotion will push the neural accumulators involved in sensorimotor systems to reach criterion even quicker than normal. So the automatic motor-network activity produced by the emotion will sometimes initiate action before executive decision-making processes have a chance to engage.

8.5 Strength of Belief: Credences

Notice that all three of the main (putative) varieties of belief discussed in Chapter 7 are categorical in nature. One either possesses them or one does not. They don't come in degrees. Information about individuals, places, and kinds of thing is either stored in semantic memory or it is not. Although that information can be more or less accessible, or more or less easily recalled and used, it is either known or it is not. Likewise, while episodic memories can be more or less rich in content, more or less accurate, and more or less easily evoked, their existence as memories doesn't admit of degrees, either. And philosophers who have maintained that the (putative) sorts of belief that result from a making-up-of-mind, and are constituted by commitments to think and reason on the assumption that a proposition is true, have been explicit that these are categorical states (Frankish 2004). One has either made a commitment to truth or one has not.[3]

[3] As we saw in Section 7.5, however, many of these states are really either intentions or beliefs about beliefs, not beliefs in their own right, although they mimic some of the behavioral effects of first-order belief.

On the face of it, common sense seems to imply that beliefs can come in degrees, however. One can say, "He believes it very strongly," for example. But as we noted in Section 8.2, there are various things that this might mean without one needing to be committed to a distinct type of graded belief. It could mean that it would take a lot of evidence or persuasion for the person to change their belief, for instance, since it is deeply embedded in and supported by a wide range of other beliefs (Harman 1986). But this doesn't make the attitude of believing into one that admits of degrees. And intentions and commitments, too, can be more or less firmly embedded in one's value systems, as we saw. It can require a larger change in circumstances – events that were not envisaged when the intention was formed, for example – to make one give up on some intentions rather than others.

Alternatively, a strongly held belief can be one that someone is very confident of, where confidence is a separate metacognitive attitude taken toward the belief. One can believe of one's belief that it is strongly supported by the evidence, or is almost certainly true, for example. But that doesn't turn it into a graded kind of belief, either. Put differently, both of the possibilities mentioned so far are extrinsic and relational, depending on a given belief's relationships with others, not intrinsic properties of the attitude of believing considered in isolation from others.

Given that common sense also seems to assume that desires can come in different strengths (as we saw in Section 8.3), one might be attracted to a picture of practical decision-making as involving competition among beliefs and desires of various strengths. And indeed, it is common to see philosophers claiming that people will act on their strongest desire all else being equal, for example, or saying that whether someone acts on a given desire depends partly on the strength of their supporting beliefs. But as we saw in Chapter 6 (and briefly again in Section 8.3), it is a mistake to think that the attitude of desiring admits of variations in strength, or that desires come in degrees, at least in respect of those aspects of desire that figure directly in decision-making. So we don't *need* to think of beliefs as coming in degrees, either, in order to make sense of practical reasoning and decision-making. Indeed, I will suggest the opposite.

It is common for philosophers to claim, however, that alongside our categorical beliefs there is an important class of graded beliefs, or levels-of-confidence attitudes, that they call "credences." These are generally represented on a scale of real numbers between zero and one, where credence-0 in *P* is complete certainty of the falsehood of *P* and credence-1 in *P* is certainty that *P* is true. There are varying views, however, about the relationship between credences and categorical beliefs (Jackson 2020). Some think that credences are basic, and that beliefs are either just credences of 1, or credences above some threshold between 0.5 and 1 (Jeffrey 1970; Levi 1991; Foley 1993; Bouvens & Hawthorne 1999). Others maintain that beliefs and credences are both equally basic (Pollock 1983; Sosa 2011; Friedman 2013b; Staffel 2017; Jackson 2019, 2022), at least in the sense that neither can be reduced to the other.[4] And yet other philosophers claim that it is beliefs that are basic, where the fine-grained numerical features of credences can be built into the contents of (some) beliefs (Harman 1986; Schiffer 2003; Holton 2008; Moon 2017). On this latter view, then, rather than having a 0.75 degree of belief in *P* (a credence of 0.75 in *P*), one can believe (flat-out) that *P is 0.75 probable or likely*.

What reason is there to prefer either of the first two options over the third? Given that one can get all of the explanatory benefits of numerical measurement by supposing that the degrees in question are embedded in the content of the beliefs, what reason is there for insisting that there is, in addition, a special kind of fine-grained belief-like attitude (credence) instead or as well? One set of arguments has concerned the notion of probability that would be embedded in the contents of one's beliefs (Christensen 2004; Staffel 2013). For objective chances (such as the likelihood of throwing three "heads" in a row using a fair coin) and frequencies (like the proportion of people who have cheated on an exam in the past) can't do the work, it is said; and yet subjective probabilities seem to beg the question (or to reduce to credences).

As Moon and Jackson (2020) show, however, epistemic probabilities broadly construed (encompassing concepts like MIGHT, as well as POSSIBLE, PROBABLE, and LIKELY) can do all of the work required; where the epistemic probability of something happening is a function of the extent to which it is predicted by one's total (or total accessible) evidence. Thus one can believe, of each claim in one's carefully researched book considered individually, that it is highly likely to be true, while also believing – without contradiction – that it is highly likely that one has

[4] Frankish (2009) thinks that credences are more basic in a different sense. He thinks they are a more *primitive* ("System 1") type of state, shared with animals, whereas beliefs are commitments, belonging to System 2, which is likely to be human-specific.

made a mistake somewhere, and that one of those claims is false. One doesn't need to appeal to credences to capture such facts. Admittedly, one might also simply think, of each claim in the book, that it is true (without qualification) while also believing that one has surely made some mistakes. But this, too, can be explained without appealing to credences, as we will see in due course.

It is true that ordinary discourse about beliefs is shot-through with certainty talk. People say that they are certain, fairly certain, mildly certain, or uncertain that *P*, suggesting that what is in question might be a graded attitude of some sort toward *P*. Talk of degrees of confidence is equally ubiquitous. One is said to be fully confident, fairly confident, mildly confident, or not at all confident that *P*. In short, our talk about belief and belief-like attitudes seems to support the existence of graded confidence-levels in the truth or falsity of a proposition, mapping smoothly onto the credences postulated by philosophers. But these forms of discourse at best reflect the assumptions of our folk-psychology, of course, which – as we have seen throughout this book – we should distrust. So what does the science say?

The vast majority of psychological investigations of certainty and uncertainty in humans have concerned explicit (verbal or scalar) metacognitive judgments (Dunlosky & Metcalfe 2009; Fleming & Daw 2017; Fleming 2021). Typically, participants might be asked to make a first-order judgment or discrimination of some sort (such as indicating which is the longest of a set of lines on a screen), and are then asked how certain they are of the correctness of the judgment just made, or they might be asked to place a bet on its correctness. (Typical findings are that confidence is only moderately correlated with accuracy.) Here a judgment of uncertainty seems to be, not a graded attitude toward a proposition (e.g. 0.6: *that the top line is longest*), but rather a judgment about a previous judgment: that it is or is not likely to be correct. It expresses a likelihood-belief about a belief, not a graded first-order belief.

It might be said, however, that the basis on which one makes a judgment of certainty or uncertainty is by introspecting and expressing a first-order graded attitude. But in fact people have to rely, at least in part, on indirect cues when reporting their own degrees of certainty. These include their own reaction times (expressing more certainty about first-order judgments that are made swiftly; Kiani et al. 2014) as well as affective feelings of fluency or disfluency (expressing more certainty about judgments that less effortful to arrive at; Rhodes & Castel 2009; Kornell et al. 2011). Moreover,

Nicholson et al. (2019, 2021) provide direct experimental evidence that there are no resources shared between the first-order judgments involved and people's subsequent judgments of degrees of certainty. So there is nothing here to suggest that the underlying attitudes are themselves graded ones.

Indeed, theoretical models built to explain data from human first-order judgment tasks that simultaneously measure levels of certainty suggest, not the existence of graded belief-like attitudes, but rather judgments that embed within their contents analog-magnitude (nonconceptual) representations of likelihood (Pouget et al. 2016). For example, van den Berg et al. (2016a) asked participants to judge the direction of motion of a random-dot stimulus on each trial, indicating whether the dominant motion was leftwards or rightwards. Participants made their choice by moving a cursor to one of four positions on the screen using a joystick beneath the table. The two left-most positions indicated leftward motion, and the two right-most positions indicated rightward motion. But the upper and lower positions on each side came with different payoffs in terms of points won or lost. The upper positions were high-risk, giving a 2-point gain for a correct choice but a 3-point loss for an incorrect one; the lower positions were low-risk, with a 1-point gain or a 1-point loss. (Participants saw a running tally of their point scores throughout.) In effect, then, the upper positions expressed high confidence, but were not described to participants in these terms, and no explicit judgments of confidence needed to be made.

This setup enabled van den Berg et al. (2016a) to collect data on accuracy, reaction times, confidence, and also changes of mind about the correct choice and/or about confidence made while moving the joystick, which they then set out to model and explain. Like many others in cognitive science, they assume that decisions are grounded in accumulating neural activity (which can be thought of as accumulating *evidence*, or as a strengthening representation of direction of motion following the onset of the stimulus). Accumulating activity in each of two competing neural populations (representing leftward motion and rightward motion respectively) takes a fluctuating "walk" toward a criterion.[5]

It is assumed that evidence begins to accumulate in noisy fashion from a few milliseconds following stimulus onset until the decision-criterion is

[5] Traditionally the decision-criterion was thought to be set by the participants themselves in light of a speed / accuracy trade-off. But as we noted in Section 8.4, many now think that the criterion-level for a decision is fixed, and what varies is the speed of neural gain in the competing accumulators, modulated by a generalized urgency-signal that reflects one's degree of arousal.

reached, with confidence-levels being fixed by the extent of the difference between the two sets of signals (leftward versus rightward). And although participants are required to make binary choices (left versus right as well high-risk versus low-risk) what underlies these choices are analog-magnitude representations of extent. Van den Berg and colleagues interpret the confidence-signal, in particular, as representing the likelihood that the overall motion is in one particular direction rather than the other, and Carruthers & Williams (2022) draw on Shea's (2018) semantic framework to show that they are correct.

Recall from Section 6.1 that the content of a representation is best understood as the subset of information carried by that representation that explains how the representation's role has become stabilized, either by evolution or by learning. The difference between the rates of accumulating activity in the two neural accumulators representing leftward motion and rightward motion carries information about the comparative strength of the evidence for *left* versus *right*. And it is this information about epistemic likelihood that explains and makes sense of the signal's role in determining one's high-risk or low-risk choices. For it is adaptive to take a high-risk decision when epistemic likelihood is high and to take a low-risk decision when it is low.[6]

What is emerging is a strong case for denying the existence of credences as attitudes. Rather, estimates of likelihood are built into the contents of at least many ordinary beliefs and judgments. One of the main objections to such a view, however, has been that it implausibly over-intellectualizes what is involved in judgment-under-uncertainty. For it seems to require that nonhuman animals possess concepts like PROBABLE, LIKELY, UNLIKELY, CERTAIN, and so on (Frankish 2009). But all that it actually requires is that animals possess analog-magnitude representations of degrees of likelihood, of the sort involved in the experiment by van den Berg et al. (2016a) just discussed. And in fact we know that animals are extremely adept at tracking the changing likelihoods of reward, and adapting their behavior accordingly. Thus Balci et al. (2009) and Kheifets and Gallistel (2012) show that mice approximate to ideal Bayesian reasoners in probabilistic-reward experiments where the likelihoods of reward from the two options change frequently. Moreover, we

[6] Indeed, van den Berg et al. (2016b) go on to show how people make adaptive use of the epistemic-likelihood signal in tasks where success depends on a sequence of correct decisions. People are faster to make a judgment about the second of the two discriminations when they estimate that the likelihood of being correct on the first is low, taking more time when it is high. (The strategy here is: "don't waste time if you are unlikely to succeed.")

know that humans routinely make use of perception-like representations of probability in addition to conceptual ones (Balci et al. 2009; Gallistel et al. 2014). This option might have been overlooked by philosophers because they falsely assume that beliefs have exclusively propositional / purely conceptual contents.

In fact, virtually all living creatures need to draw on their past experience to estimate the likelihoods of things and events in their environment. They build up implicit statistical knowledge over time of the distributions of the things and events in their world, and use that information when deciding what to do. But they don't need the concept LIKELY to do this. Rather, their background knowledge serves to deliver an analog-magnitude representation of likelihood that gets built into their representation of potential future events. This enables foraging animals to make near-optimal decisions about when to switch from one foraging patch to another, for example, or how much time to spend foraging versus information-seeking (Pyke et al. 1977; Stephens & Krebs 1986; Vasconcelos et al. 2015).

Note that optimal foraging requires animals to estimate the likelihood that there is another foraging patch nearby, while also estimating its likely returns (its likely value), enabling them to compute the expected value of the two options (stay or go). Just as analog-magnitude representations of approximate number ("numerosity") are widespread across the animal kingdom and are even present in newborn infants (Gallistel et al. 2001; Jordan et al. 2008; Izard et al. 2009; Gennari et al. 2023), so too, it seems, are analog-magnitude representations of approximate likelihood (Lebreton et al. 2015).

How might a believer in credences respond to these (and many similar) findings? It might be said that although animals and humans compute likelihoods and the changing rates of likelihood, the upshot of those computations gets built into the resulting attitude itself (its credence or strength) rather than into its content. But this is mysterious. Why should representational change lead to a change in attitude strength? Given that analog-magnitude likelihood is already represented, why should those representations not be embedded into the content of the resulting belief? If we already knew, of course, that desires admit of degrees of strength, and that decision-making takes some sort of push-push format, then the proposal might make sense. But we have already seen that the best accounts of desire and decision-making involve integrating representations of value with beliefs. And the best account of human and animal decision-making involves computations of expected value which then determine choice.

Note, too, that the formalisms employed by decision-theorists and Bayesian epistemologists are actually neutral on the question of credences, although they are generally interpreted by philosophers in those terms. Thus for example, "*p*(H/E)" (the probability of a hypothesis given the evidence) can either be interpreted as a graded belief in the hypothesis given the evidence (a credence), or it can be seen as the *content* of a categorical belief, a belief that has some degree of likelihood embedded in its content. Likewise the formalisms used by decision-theorists for computing expected utilities can either be read in terms of graded beliefs and desires, or in terms of beliefs and desires with graded contents. And the latter is the standard interpretation employed in the cognitive-science literature in the field of "neuroeconomics," it should be said (Huys et al. 2011; Orsini et al. 2015; O'Doherty et al. 2017) – and for good reason. For one of the core commitments of cognitive science is to seek causal explanations of cognitive processes in terms of computations over content-bearing representations, as we noted in Section 1.5.

It might be helpful at this point to revisit the paradox of the preface. The content of each individual belief one expresses in one's book can embed an analog-magnitude representation of very high likelihood, just as does the content of one's acknowledgment in the preface that one will have made some mistakes. There is no contradiction between these contents, of course. But when those contents are expressed directly in speech (whether outer or inner), if the likelihoods are high enough one might speak categorically. Hence one might say, without qualification, of each individual content that it is true while also saying (again without qualification) that at least one of them is false. One can explain away the apparent contradiction here by pointing out that one almost certainly lacks introspective access to small differences in degrees of likelihood, leading one to express high-likelihood beliefs categorically.

Before concluding this section it is worth considering a recent scientifically informed philosophical theory of subjective probability. This is Icard's (2016) *propensity sampling* account. The idea is that one judges the likelihood of some situation or event by sampling from one's internal model of similar situations or events. If the first few samples contain the event then one estimates high likelihood, otherwise not. There is no doubt that people frequently use this heuristic. Asked to judge how likely it is that new couples will split up during their first year together one swiftly calls to mind instances of this happening and estimates likelihood on the basis of how easily accessible such memories are, for example (Tversky & Kahneman 1973, 1974; MacLeod & Campbell 1992). Notice that the target of explanation here is explicit judgments of likelihood, however, where the degree of likelihood is built into the content of the judgment. So the account provides no support for the existence of credences, where gradations would need to be built into the attitude itself rather than its content. Moreover, it is hard to see how to apply the account to the sorts of online estimates of likelihood that underlie much human and animal behavior of the sort discussed earlier.

A closely related idea is more promising, however. This is that the relative *accessibility* of information stored in memory may influence how quickly the neural realizers of that information reach criterion when activated, thereby issuing in a stronger likelihood-signal. In effect, recency (among other factors that influence accessibility) may function as a proxy for likelihood. Similarly, information that is more deeply embedded in a web of related beliefs will be apt to reach criterion more swiftly and reliably, issuing in a higher approximate likelihood-representation. This is because stored information, when initially accessed, will associatively activate related beliefs, receiving reciprocal activation in turn. Hence higher likelihood estimates for deeply embedded beliefs will be generated "on the fly" whenever those stored beliefs become activated into a judgment. Plausibly, it is in just such ways that analog-magnitude representations of likelihood can get built into the contents of judgments that are activated from episodic or semantic memories, which may not themselves embed stored likelihood-representations.

The upshot of this section, then, is that this is yet another case where armchair-philosophers have made claims about the kinds of mental state that the mind contains while paying scant attention to the science. Rather than containing graded attitudes of believing (credences), the mind contains beliefs with graded contents (analog-magnitude representations of approximate likelihood). And if folk-psychology is committed to graded strengths of belief then it, too, is in error.

8.6 Strength of Will

Common sense assumes that there is such a thing as strength of will, or strength of intention – although whether this is really a commitment to variations in the intrinsic strengths of the attitude of intending, rather than differing depths of embedding, is perhaps moot. What seems clear, however, is that the common-sense commitment to some *people* being more strong-willed than others presupposes some version of the degrees-of-intending view. For a strong-willed person is someone who is more disposed than others to stick with the goals and intentions they have decided upon. And it is hard to see how one person's intentions *in general* or *as a whole* could be more deeply embedded in their own values and other intentions than another person's. In any case, a graded-attitude view will be evaluated here.

There is a well-known theory in scientific psychology that, if true, would vindicate the idea of strength of intention. This is the theory of "ego-depletion" (Baumeister & Vohs 2007; Masicampo & Baumeister 2008) – so-named, presumably, because the ego or self is identified with the goals one adopts after reflection involving one's beliefs and desires. The scientific finding on which it is based is that when people perform a series of cognitively effortful / attentionally demanding tasks, they tend to perform worse in the follow-up tasks. Since one can presume that participants retain an intention to do well in each of the tasks, it is said that weakening performance reflects a weakening will, which can be analogized to a tiring prefrontal "brain-muscle." More mechanistically, it has been argued that ego-depletion is caused by reductions in the glucose necessary to fuel optimal functioning of the prefrontal cortex, which houses the executive systems of the mind.

The ego-depletion theory is now thought to be highly problematic, however, for a variety of reasons. One is that there have been difficulties in replicating the original data (Hagger et al. 2014). Another is that the evidence supporting the depleted-glucose explanation is both theoretically ill-motivated and empirically weak (Kurzban 2010; Vadillo et al. 2016). And a third is that the effect itself (insofar as it exists) appears to depend on participants' folk-beliefs that willpower gets depleted by cognitive effort, and such beliefs turn out to be culture-relative rather than universal (Savani & Job 2017). It is people who *believe* that willpower is a depleting resource – rather than nonlimited – who tend to perform worse in a series of attentionally demanding tasks; and interventions to induce nonlimited beliefs can improve performance quite significantly (Job et al. 2010, 2013, 2015; Duckworth et al. 2019).

Nevertheless, rats as well as humans find executively demanding tasks to be aversive by default (Winstanley & Floresco 2016; Inzlicht et al. 2018). In the case of the rats, this can be tested by giving the animals a choice between two different tasks to secure a reward. If they choose one option then they have to pay careful attention, selecting a location indicated by a briefly flashed light, say; the other option allows them to identify the target location easily. The finding is that it requires significantly higher rewards to induce the rats to select the former task. But rats, like humans, can nevertheless learn to evaluate demanding tasks positively, issuing in a kind of learned industriousness (Eisenberger 1992; Hosking et al. 2016). Hence humans can come to enjoy chess, or crossword puzzles, or even reading philosophy. Recent models of decision-making among tasks suggest, in fact, that in addition to computing outcome values, likelihoods, and physical effort, many creatures also integrate into their decisions the estimated costs (or value) of the *mental* effort involved (Kurzban et al. 2013; Kurzban 2016; Shenhav et al. 2017; Inzlicht et al. 2018).

Why is it that attentionally demanding tasks are experienced as aversive by default? The answer is probably that attention is a limited but valuable resource. When an animal is focused on any one task it has less attentional resources available to monitor its surroundings, potentially making it vulnerable to attack or predation. The same would have been true of humans in ancestral conditions. But even today, attention focused on one task withdraws attention from others, such as reviewing the past or planning for the future. In fact, Kurzban (2016) suggests that the default aversiveness of cognitive effort implicitly encodes an estimated opportunity-cost – one *could* be using one's executive resources for other, potentially more valuable, activities.

The literature reviewed so far, then, provides no support for the idea that intentions and goals come in various strengths that can become weakened with exercise. Rather, the longer one focuses on completing any given goal (or whenever one sort of cognitively demanding goal-pursuit is followed by another), then the stronger the anticipated aversiveness-signal attached to the thought of continuing will become, designed to motivate one to switch one's attention elsewhere. Or at least, this will be so in cases where the activities involved have not come to be intrinsically rewarding and/or where one fails to appraise continued performance as a challenge rather than a burden.

There is a separate literature that might seem to support the idea of gradable willpower, or goal strength, however, at least as a stable trait of individual people. This dates back to the now-famous marshmallow test (Mischel et al. 1972). Young children were offered a choice: to have one marshmallow now or at any point during the wait, or to get two marshmallows when the experimenter returned. (In each case the child's favorite treat was employed, rather than a marshmallow in every instance.) The finding was that children displayed a lot of variation in their waiting-times. Longitudinal follow-up studies then suggested that childhood self-control is a significant predictor of a great many adolescent and adult outcomes, from school grades to the likelihood of drug abuse (Mischel et al. 1988;

Shoda et al. 1990; Ayduk et al. 2000). In addition, a longitudinal study of a cohort of all children born in a single year in Dunedin, New Zealand, found essentially the same thing using a different set of composite measures of childhood self-control (Moffit et al. 2011). Even when controlling for IQ and socioeconomic status, childhood self-control was a significant predictor of many adult outcomes between the ages of 26 and 32, including degrees of health, wealth, numbers of criminal convictions, and more.

From the outset, however, what the data really suggested was not a trait-like strength of willpower, but rather (at most) a kind of trait-like metacognitive intelligence (Mischel et al. 1972, 2011). The children who waited longest employed smart attentional strategies of various sorts to help them resist the immediate temptation to eat the marshmallow – they turned their backs, played with a toy, or otherwise distracted themselves. Moreover, later findings suggest that development of the trait in question might be an adaptive response to the character of the children's home environments (Watts et al. 2018). And when children are tested by an experimenter who first displays evidence of her trustworthiness, almost all of the children succeed in waiting for the full amount of time, whereas when tested by an experimenter who shows evidence of untrustworthiness, hardly any of them do (Kidd et al. 2013). It seems that the stability or predictability of the home environment might be what sets people's default expectations and decision-making strategies.

More-convincing evidence of something genuinely resembling trait willpower is provided by studies showing how maturation of the prefrontal cortex predicts capacities for self-control (Chambers et al. 2003; Vijayakumar et al. 2014; Caballero et al. 2016), as well as from studies of how delays in the maturation of these networks are responsible for the symptoms of ADHD (Sripada et al. 2014). As is well known, children (especially toddlers) have limited capacities for self-control, with those capacities gradually increasing into young adulthood. There are especially dramatic changes during and after adolescence, when the prefrontal cortex is still maturing along with the strength of its connectivity to subcortical systems involved in emotion and motivation. It seems that the overall balance between goals and intentions, on the one hand, and currently felt desires and emotions, on the other, shifts dramatically during this period. As teenagers mature, it becomes easier for them to stick with their long-term goals and to resist short-term temptations and risky behavior.

If what changes with the development of the prefrontal cortex is that previously formed goals and intentions are more likely to win any given competition with a current desire or emotion, then that suggests, either that those intentions increase in average strength during this time, or that desires somehow become less compelling, or both. One of the maturational changes during this period is cortical thinning of the prefrontal cortex as a result of extensive neural pruning of synapses, however (Caballero et al. 2016). Since such pruning is experience-dependent, it might be suggested that what happens is that adolescents gradually acquire more effective metacognitive strategies for managing their own emotions. And that would suggest that the increases in self-control result from the increasing use of intelligent strategies to "weaken" the influence of one's affective states when they conflict with existing intentions, rather than intrinsic changes in the strength of the latter.

This may well be part of the story. But it cannot easily explain the role played by increases in the myelination of the long-distance pathways between the prefrontal cortex and subcortical affective networks. (Neural myelination makes transmission of information between neurons faster and more efficient.) Nor can it account for the effects of increasing functional connectivity between the two regions (Chambers et al. 2003; Caballero et al. 2016). I think, in consequence, that at least part of the explanation for developmental increases in willpower during this time can rightfully be interpreted as a strengthening of the causal efficacy of goals and intentions, which in turn suggests a graded-attitude view of the latter.

Consider what happens when the goal of studying for a test comes into conflict with an affective desire to play a favorite video game. There is a neural population in the prefrontal cortex that becomes activated from prospective memory ("study for the test"). As we saw in Section 5.6, this goal will then direct attention to study-relevant stimuli and study-relevant memories ("where did I leave the textbook?"), and will activate related motor plans. In so doing, however, competing stimuli, memories, and motor activity will be correspondingly suppressed. A reasonable hypothesis is that age-dependent prefrontal-network maturation increases the strength and efficacy of these suppressive signals, thereby making goal-pursuit in the face of temptation more effective.

This account is admittedly speculative. But it fits quite well with everything we know about the implementation of decision-making in the brain. Does it imply any change in the *attitude* of intending with development, however? The *content* of the goal of studying in a 12-year-old and in a 20-year-old presumably remains the same. What has changed is the strength and efficacy of the prefrontal goal-dependent signals that serve to suppress competing motivations (Sripada 2020). Given that the attitude of intending is constituted by its overall functional role (i.e. not only its role in guiding attention, memory search, and action-selection, but at the same time suppressing competing stimuli, memories, and motor plans), it appears to follow that it is the attitude itself that has been strengthened. In which case willpower does genuinely admit of degrees, and does so intrinsically, not just through depth of relational embedding.

8.7 Conclusion

This chapter has discussed and evaluated the common-sense idea that some or all of the main kinds of attitude (desires, emotions, beliefs, and intentions) admit of degrees, or variations in their attitude strength. We have focused, in particular, on the claim that such variations are intrinsic rather than extrinsic or relational.

There is an element of truth in the claim that desires and emotions come in a variety of strengths, since their automatically induced motoric-urge components do. But the degrees of desire that figure in decision-making are all of them degrees in the *contents* of desire, rather than in the attitude. These are the degrees of value attaching to the object of desire and the degrees of disvalue attaching to the physical and mental effort required to obtain it. There is also some truth in the idea that emotions come in various strengths, both because they share the structure of desires, and because the arousal component of affective states can vary dramatically in cases of strong emotion, with a variety of downstream effects on cognition and decision-making (speeding up the latter, in particular). And as we have just seen, goals and intentions can admit of differing intrinsic strengths (willpower), especially as a function of developmental brain maturation. There is, however, no element of truth in the claim that there are graded beliefs (credences). Rather, what are graded are the analog-magnitude signals of likelihood that are built into the content of some or all beliefs.

CHAPTER 9

Summary and Conclusions

This concluding chapter briefly summarizes the main findings from previous ones, noting what is right and what is wrong about the standard model of action and action-explanation. It then draws out some methodological morals for the way in which the philosophy of mind should properly be conducted.

9.1 Summary of Findings

The standard belief-desire model gets a few things right, but multiple things wrong. One thing it gets wrong is its ill-motivated exclusive focus on so-called "intentional" actions: actions that are caused by interactions among one's beliefs and desires. This ignores habitual actions that are cued directly by features of the context. It ignores speeded and skilled actions that depend on decision-like processes within sensorimotor systems. And it ignores actions that are direct products of affective appraisals. Taken together, these amount to a very significant proportion of one's everyday behavior. And many of these actions are just as distinctively human and just as expressive of one's self as are many intentional actions.

Expanding the range of actions to include those that are habitual, skilled, or directly affect-caused comes with a payoff, as we saw in Chapter 4. For we can then chart how some mental actions are more similar to some of these kinds than others; and many of the resulting kinds of mental action fail to conform to the standard model. Moreover, proper understanding of the processes that issue in some of these (putative) mental actions leads to conclusions that conflict with claims often made by philosophers. Specifically, both mind-wandering and creative insight turn out to be active in nature, whereas most judgments and decisions are not.

While the standard model is right about the real existence of the explaining attitudes to which it appeals (beliefs, desires, and intentions), and is right that these play a causal role in the production of at least some actions ("intentional actions"), it is wrong about the nature of those attitudes. To begin, it is wrong in thinking that all are *propositional* attitudes. On the contrary, all desires, as well as some beliefs and some intentions, have contents that are at least partly nonconceptual / analog-magnitude in nature (and some have contents that are entirely nonconceptual). Moreover, only intentions, of these three types, have a world-to-mind direction of fit. In contrast with most philosophers' views, not only do all beliefs have correctness-conditions rather than satisfaction-conditions but so do all desires. For all desires represent their objects as to some degree nonconceptually good.

The standard model is also mistaken in thinking that the attitudes of believing and desiring admit of degrees. They do not. It is their contents that do, embedding analog-magnitude representations of likelihood and value, respectively. The standard model is correct, however, to the extent that it claims that goals and intentions admit of trait-like degrees of efficacy, varying across individuals and across development.

Although not strictly part of the standard model itself, philosophers who endorse it are also mistaken about the nature of pleasure and its relationship to desire. Pleasure is neither a motivating mere intrinsic feeling, nor is it an experience or sensation that is desired. Rather, pleasure is an analog-magnitude representation of the current value one attaches to something, and desires are representations of distal states of affairs with anticipatory pleasure built into their contents.

Philosophers who endorse the standard model are also apt to under-count and/or over-count the number of types of belief that there are. Some treat belief as a unitary kind of state, whereas in fact episodic and semantic memories constitute distinct kinds. And some of the states that philosophers are apt to characterize as beliefs aren't really, but are rather intention-like commitments to think and reason as if their contents were true.

In conclusion, and as I remarked prospectively near the outset in Section 1.2, the philosophy of action needs a complete make-over. It gets more things wrong than right.

9.2 Methodological Morals

Philosophers typically address metaphysical (and other) questions by eliciting, systematizing, and arguing from intuitive judgments (including the deliverances of introspection).[1] The same is true of much of the work underlying the standard model of action and action-explanation. Indeed, the same is true of most work in the philosophy of mind generally. So one can be asked to imagine someone who has had color-inverting lenses inserted into his eyes without his knowledge who is then transported to a world in which the actual colors of things are the inverse of those on Earth (Block 1990). Or one might be asked to imagine a creature who is a physical, functional, and intentional duplicate of oneself, but for whom everything is "dark on the inside," completely lacking in phenomenal experience (Chalmers 1996). Such examples are used to elicit judgments that then get theorized and argued from to show something about the mind itself – in this case, about the nature of consciousness.

Where do intuitive judgments themselves come from? What is their source? Hardly anyone now thinks that they derive from direct unmediated insight into the nature of reality (Williamson 2007), and many now allow, too, that introspection is at least partly theory-dependent (Carruthers 2011; Cassam 2014). Rather, they have a multiplicity of more-mundane sources. They might sometimes reflect implicit statistical knowledge acquired through previous learning. Or they might be products of background theories, such as our common-sense psychology (either explicit or implicit). Or they might reflect something about the structure and interconnectedness of the concepts in question. What standard philosophical methods do, therefore, is enable us to draw out the implications of things that on some level we already believe. And then in the absence of evidence to the contrary, it may be rational to accept the resulting claims. If you have nothing else to go on, then it is reasonable to rely on common-sense theories, beliefs, and concepts when forming general beliefs about questions of metaphysics.

When it comes to questions about the structure and contents of the mind, however, there already exists a vast body of scientific knowledge on the topic. Philosophical theorizing should surely take its start from that. At the very least, philosophical claims about the mind need to be tested for *consistency* with scientific findings, and arguably they are best arrived at

[1] It might appear that the relatively recent movement of experimental philosophy is an exception. But in fact its practitioners are quite clear that they are attempting to characterize folk concepts and folk theories, rather than the actual metaphysical structure of the world or mind (Knobe et al. 2012; Sytsma & Buckwalter 2016). As such, I have no principled objections – except that the studies in question are often poorly controlled, and that direct questioning is generally not a reliable way to elicit the nature of implicit theories. This is because a great many factors can influence what people will say in answer to a question in addition to the cognitive structures that are the target of inquiry (Schwarz 1999).

though linking, systematizing, and explaining those findings. For if we are interested in knowing what the mind is really like, then what could be the point of considering what our folk-theories and implicit beliefs tell us, or what they imply? For example, what could be the interest of showing that intentions can be conceptually reduced to combinations of beliefs and desires (Sinhababu 2013), if the result conflicts with the science of prospective memory and action-initiation, as we saw in Section 5.2?

Plainly, folk theories can be false, and often are. (Consider the histories of common-sense physics and folk biology.) And this can be the case even if those theories work fine for everyday and practical purposes. Likewise, human conceptual structures (even if innate and universal) can fail to map onto the real kinds of thing that there are – in the cases that concern us, the real kinds of mental state and process that comprise the human mind. If folk theories were all we had to go on, then it would make sense to employ standard philosophical methods, constructing examples, counterexamples, and counterfactual scenarios to elicit our intuitions, which could then serve as a basis for further theorizing. But such methods are no longer appropriate in domains where there already exists a substantial body of scientific knowledge.

Similar points hold in relation to philosophical methods that rely on syntactic and semantic analysis of natural language, examining and theorizing about how we talk about the mind as evidence of the latter's structure. As we saw in Section 2.7, some have argued on these sorts of grounds that know-how and skills are really forms of propositional knowledge, or knowledge *that* (Stanley & Williamson 2001, 2017; Stanley 2011a). There would be reason to be skeptical of this sort of argument even if there weren't a substantial body of scientific knowledge on the topic pointing in other directions. For at least folk theories that function successfully in everyday life are likely to be approximately true, since their success may best be explained by at least approximate or partial truth. But there are many other pressures besides truth-tracking on the development of natural languages, having to do with ease of learnability, ease of sentence-construction, ease of comprehension, and ease of expression (Gibson et al. 2019). So if folk theories are an unreliable source of knowledge about the nature of the mind, syntactic and/or semantic analysis is doubly so.

Even if traditional philosophers retreat from making claims about the actual nature of the mind and its states, and claim instead to be characterizing what might be called the "manifest image" of the mind, or the way in which our minds *appear* to us, a similar point holds. For there is now a great deal of well-established scientific work on the nature and development of human mentalizing or "theory of mind" abilities, too – albeit with some remaining scientific controversies. This is a field to which philosophers have made useful contributions since near the outset, in fact (Gordon 1986; Goldman 1989; Davies 1994; Carruthers & Smith 1996). But it is not one in which philosophers can now hope to make any real progress alone, using traditional methods independently of the science.[2]

If the message is that we should follow the science, however, then what role is there left for philosophy to play? One answer is that philosophers are free to range broadly across all fields of cognitive science, bringing related findings to bear on one another, and constructing theories that can integrate them successfully – an approach that some describe as "synthetic philosophy" (Schliesser 2019). Most cognitive scientists, in contrast, are focused somewhat more narrowly, constrained by their expertise with particular experimental methods and empirical research programs. They can also fail to draw relevant distinctions (something philosophers are generally pretty good at). Moreover, scientists are sometimes too quick to adopt a particular interpretation of their findings, and can fail to consider alternative explanations. Thus many comparative psychologists have in my view been too quick to endorse metacognitive explanations of their "uncertainty monitoring" paradigms conducted with monkeys. I have argued, in contrast, that the data are better explained in terms of first-order likelihood estimation (Carruthers 2014, 2017; Carruthers & Williams 2019, 2022).

Most philosophical work on the metaphysics of mind actually proceeds as follows. One first immerses oneself in what other philosophers have said about a topic, considering their theories, arguments, and counter-arguments. One then proposes a new thesis, building on what others have done, or one puts forward a new counter-example to an existing thesis and drives the argument home, or one attempts to reconcile or find middle ground between a pair of existing theories, and so on. If some of the extant literature incorporates or otherwise makes use of scientific findings, then one might acquaint oneself with those out of professional duty. And one might also go looking for specific findings to refute or support some philosophical claim one is interested in. But one doesn't immerse oneself in the scientific literature, either on the topic in question or in general.

[2] And in any case, if philosophers were to take this route then they would have to give up on making unqualified metaphysical claims about the states and processes that make up the human mind. They could only make claims about how people are apt to *think about* the metaphysics of the mind.

The approach taken in this book, in contrast (and the approach that I think philosophers of mind *should* adopt, and that increasingly many *are* now using) is almost the exact inverse of this. To begin work on a particular topic, one should first immerse oneself in what appear to be the relevant scientific findings in psychology and cognitive neuroscience, learning of key results, major theories, open questions, and points of agreement and disagreement. At the same time, one should read widely (albeit, of necessity, shallowly) across both nearby and more distant areas of cognitive science. This is to help constrain later theory choice, since one good-making feature of a theory is that it should cohere well with other well-grounded theories and existing discoveries. Then one can think about what the science shows, how it should best be interpreted, and what the upshot is for questions of philosophical interest, reasoning by inference to the best explanation of the scientific facts and theories. Having done all that, one can then have a look around to see if other philosophers have engaged with the same or similar regions of the science, taking account of or disputing what they say as necessary.

The contrast drawn here is one that admits of degrees, of course. And my impression is that the field as a whole has become increasingly scientifically informed and engaged in recent decades. (One possible exception is the field of consciousness-studies, which remains the "wild West" of ungrounded claims and rampant philosophical speculation.) My hope is that this book may help to nudge things along even further in that direction.

References

Addis, D. (2020). Mental time travel? A neurocognitive model of event simulation. *Review of Philosophy and Psychology*, 11, 233–259.

Addis, D., Wong, A., & Schacter, D. (2007). Remembering the past and imagining the future: Common and distinct neural substrates during event construction and elaboration. *Neuropsychologia*, 45, 1363–1377.

Adolphs, R. & Anderson, D.J. (2018). *The Neuroscience of Emotion*. Princeton University Press.

Ahrens, A., Singer, B., Fitzpatrick, C., Morrow, J., & Robinson, T. (2016). Rats that sign-track are resistant to Pavlovian but not instrumental extinction. *Behavioral Brain Research*, 296, 418–430.

Allen, G., Barnard, H., McColl, R., Hester, A., Fields, J., Weiner, M., Ringe, W., Lipton, A., Brooker, M., McDonald, E., Rubin, C., & Cullum, C.M. (2007). Reduced hippocampal functional connectivity in Alzheimer's disease. *Archives of Neurology*, 64, 1482–1487.

Anderson, B.A. (2016). The attention habit: How reward learning shapes attentional selection. *Annals of the New York Academy of Sciences*, 1369, 24–39.

Anscombe, G.E. (1957). *Intention*. Blackwell.

Aristei, S., Milinger, A., & Rahman, R. (2011). Electrophysiological chronometry of semantic context effects in language production. *Journal of Cognitive Neuroscience*, 23, 1567–1586.

Aronowitz, S. (2023). Semanticization challenges the episodic-semantic distinction. *British Journal for the Philosophy of Science*. Online first.

Ashar, Y., Chang, L.J., & Wager, T. (2017). Brain mechanisms of the placebo effect: An affective appraisal account. *Annual Review of Clinical Psychology*, 13, 73–98.

Audi, R. (1973). Intending. *Journal of Philosophy*, 70, 387–403.

Audi, R. (1994). Dispositional beliefs and dispositions to believe. *Noûs*, 28, 419–434.

Avarguès-Weber, A., d'Amaro, D., Metzler, M., & Dyer, A. (2014). Conceptualization of relative size in honeybees. *Frontiers in Behavioral Neuroscience*, 8, #80.

Avarguès-Weber, A., Dyer, A., Combe, M., & Giurfa, M. (2012). Simultaneous mastering of two abstract concepts by the miniature brain of bees. *Proceedings of the National Academy of Sciences*, 109, 7481–7486.

Averbeck, B., Latham, P., & Pouget, A. (2006). Neural correlations, population coding and computation. *Nature Reviews Neuroscience*, 7, 358–366.

Ayduk, O., Mendoza-Denton, R., Mischel, W., Downey, G., Peake, P., & Rodriguez, M. (2000). Regulating the interpersonal self: Strategic self-regulation for coping with rejection sensitivity. *Journal of Personality and Social Psychology*, 79, 776–792.

Baillargeon, R., Scott, R., & Bian, L. (2016). Psychological reasoning in infancy. *Annual Review of Psychology*, 67, 110–118.

Baird, B., Smallwood, J., Mrazek, M., Kam, J., Franklin, M., & Schooler, J. (2012). Inspired by distraction: Mind wandering facilitates creative incubation. *Psychological Science*, 23, 1117–1122.

Baker, L. (1995). *Explaining Attitudes*. Cambridge University Press.

Balci, F., Freestone, D., & Gallistel, C.R. (2009). Risk assessment in man and mouse. *Proceedings of the National Academy of Sciences*, 106, 2459–2463.

Balleine, B. & O'Doherty, J. (2010). Human and rodent homologies in action control: Corticostriatal determinants of goal-directed and habitual action. *Neuropsychopharmacology*, 35, 48–69.

Barbey, A., Koenigs, M., & Grafman, J. (2013). Dorsolateral prefrontal contributions to human working memory. *Cortex*, 49, 1195–1205.

Barch, D., Shirtcliff, E., Elsayed, N., Whalen, D., Gilbert, K., Vogel, A., Tillman, R., & Luby, J. (2020). Testosterone and hippocampal trajectories mediate the relationship of poverty to emotion dysregulation and depression. *Proceedings of the National Academy of Sciences*, 117, 22015–22023.

Barlassina, L. & Hayward, M. (2019a). Loopy regulations: The motivational profile of affective phenomenology. *Philosophical Topics*, 47, 233–261.

Barlassina, L. & Hayward, M. (2019b). More of me! Less of me!: Reflexive imperativism about affective phenomenal character. *Mind*, 128, 1013–1044.

Barlassina, L. (2020). Beyond good and bad: Reflexive imperativism, not evaluativism, explains valence. *Thought*, 9, 274–284.

Barrett, L.F. (2017). *How Emotions Are Made*. Mariner Books.

Barsalou, L. (1999). Perceptual symbol systems. *Behavioral and Brain Sciences*, 22, 577–660.

Barsalou, L. (2009). Simulation, situated conceptualization, and prediction. *Philosophical Transactions of the Royal Society B*, 364, 1281–1289.

Bateson, M., Desire, S., Gartside, S., & Wright, G. (2011). Agitated honeybees exhibit pessimistic cognitive biases. *Current Biology*, 21, 1070–1073.

Baumeister, R. & Vohs, K. (2007). Self-regulation, ego depletion, and motivation. *Psychology Compass*, 1, 115–128.

Bedny, M. & Caramazza, A. (2011). Perception, action, and word meanings in the human brain: The case from action verbs. *Annals of the New York Academy of Sciences*, 1224, 81–95.

Benoit, R. & Schacter, D. (2015). Specifying the core network supporting episodic simulation and episodic memory by activation likelihood estimation. *Neuropsychologia*, 75, 450–457.

Benoit, R., Szpunar, K., & Schacter, D. (2014). Ventromedial prefrontal cortex supports affective future simulation by integrating distributed knowledge. *Proceedings of the National Academy of Sciences*, 111, 16550–16555.

Berridge, K. & Kringelbach, M. (2008). Affective neuroscience of pleasure: Reward in humans and animals. *Psychopharmacology*, 199, 457–480.

Bird, C. & Emery, N. (2009). Rooks use stones to raise the water level to reach a floating worm. *Current Biology*, 19, 1410–1414.

Bisley, J. (2011). The neural basis of visual attention. *Journal of Physiology*, 589, 49–57.

Block, N. (1990). Inverted Earth. *Philosophical Perspectives*, 4, 53–79.

Block, N. (2007). Consciousness, accessibility, and the mesh between psychology and neuroscience. *Behavioral and Brain Sciences*, 30, 481–499.

Block, N. (2011). Perceptual consciousness overflows cognitive access. *Trends in Cognitive Sciences*, 12, 567–575.

Bourget, D. & Chalmers, D. (2023). Philosophers on philosophy: The 2020 PhilPapers Survey. *Philosophers' Imprint*, 23, 11.

Bouvens, L. & Hawthorne, J. (1999). The preface, the lottery, and the logic of belief. *Mind*, 108, 241–264.

Boyd, R. (2018). *A Different Kind of Animal: How culture transformed our species.* Princeton University Press.

Boyd, R., Richerson, P., & Henrich, J. (2011). The cultural niche: Why social learning is essential for human adaptation. *Proceedings of the National Academy of Sciences*, 108, 10918–10925.

Boyer, P. (2001). *Religion Explained: The evolutionary origins of religious thought.* Basic Books.

Brainerd, C. & Rayna, V. (2002). Fuzzy-trace theory and false memory. *Current Directions in Psychological Science*, 11, 164–169.

Brandt, R. (1979). *A Theory of the Good and the Right.* Oxford University Press.

Bratman, M. (1987). *Intentions, Plans, and Practical Reason.* Harvard University Press.

Bratman, M. (1999). *Faces of Intention.* Cambridge University Press.

Bridges, A., MaBouDi, H., Procenko, O., Lockwood, C., Mohammed, Y., Kowalewska, A., Romero González, J., Woodgate, J., & Chittka, L. (2023). Bumblebees acquire alternative puzzle-box solutions via social learning. *PLoS Biology*, 21, e300219.

Brink, D. (1989). *Moral Realism and the Foundations of Ethics.* Cambridge University Press.

Briscoe, R. & Schwenkler, J. (2015). Conscious vision in action. *Cognitive Science*, 39, 1435–1467.

Bromberg-Martin, E. & Hikosaka, O. (2009). Midbrain dopamine neurons signal preference for advance information about upcoming rewards. *Neuron*, 63, 119–126.

Brooks, R. (1991). Intelligence without representation. *Artificial Intelligence*, 47, 139–159.

Brown, D. (2001). *Human Universals.* McGraw-Hill.

Bruck, M. & Ceci, S. (1999). The suggestibility of children's memory. *Annual Review of Psychology*, 50, 419–439.

Buckner, R. (2010). The role of the hippocampus in prediction and imagination. *Annual Review of Psychology*, 61, 27–48.

Buckner, R., Andrews-Hanna, J., & Schacter, D. (2008). The brain's default network: Anatomy, function, and relevance to disease. *Annals of the New York Academy of Sciences*, 1124, 1–38.

Burge, T. (2010). *Origins of Objectivity*. Oxford University Press.

Burke, K., Franz, T., Miller, D., & Schoenbaum, G. (2008). The role of the orbitofrontal cortex in the pursuit of happiness and more specific rewards. *Nature*, 454, 340–345.

Burton, A., Nakamura, K., & Roesch, M. (2015). From ventral-medial to dorsal-lateral striatum: Neural correlates of reward-guided decision-making. *Neurobiology of Learning and Memory*, 117, 51–59.

Buttelmann, F. & Kovács, A. (2019). 14-month-olds anticipate others' actions based on their belief about an object's identity. *Infancy*, 24, 738–751.

Caballero, A., Granberg, R., & Tseng, K. (2016). Mechanisms contributing to prefrontal cortex maturation during adolescence. *Neuroscience and Biobehavioral Reviews*, 70, 4–12.

Cammaerts, M. (2004). Operant conditioning in the ant *Myrmica sabuleti*. *Behavioral Processes*, 67, 417–425.

Camp, E. (2007). Thinking with maps. *Philosophical Perspectives*, 21, 145–182.

Camp, E. (2018). Why maps are not propositional. In A. Grzankowski & M. Montague (eds.), *Non-Propositional Intentionality*. Oxford University Press.

Carland, M., Thura, D., & Cisek, P. (2019). The urge to decide and act: Implications for brain function and dysfunction. *The Neuroscientist*, 25, 491–511.

Carrasco, M. & McElree, B. (2001). Covert attention accelerates the rate of visual information processing. *Proceedings of the National Academy of Sciences*, 98, 5363–5367.

Carruthers, P. (1999). Sympathy and subjectivity. *Australasian Journal of Philosophy*, 77, 465–482.

Carruthers, P. (2000). *Phenomenal Consciousness*. Cambridge University Press.

Carruthers, P. (2006). *The Architecture of the Mind*. Oxford University Press.

Carruthers, P. (2009). Invertebrate concepts confront the Generality Constraint (and win). In R. Lurz (ed.), *The Philosophy of Animal Minds*. Cambridge University Press.

Carruthers, P. (2011). *The Opacity of Mind*. Oxford University Press.

Carruthers, P. (2014). Two concepts of metacognition. *Journal of Comparative Psychology*, 128, 138–139.

Carruthers, P. (2015). *The Centered Mind*. Oxford University Press.

Carruthers, P. (2017). Are epistemic emotions metacognitive? *Philosophical Psychology*, 30, 58–78.

Carruthers, P. (2018). Basic questions. *Mind & Language*, 22, 130–147.

Carruthers, P. (2019). *Human and Animal Minds: The consciousness questions laid to rest*. Oxford University Press.

Carruthers, P. (2021). The contents and causes of curiosity. *British Journal for the Philosophy of Science*. Online first.

Carruthers, P. (2024). *Human Motives: Hedonism, altruism, and the science of affect.* Oxford University Press.

Carruthers, P. & Smith, P.K. (eds.) (1996). *Theories of Theories of Mind.* Cambridge University Press.

Carruthers, P. & Veillet, B. (2017). Consciousness operationalized, a debate realigned. *Consciousness and Cognition*, 55, 79–90.

Carruthers, P. & Williams, D. (2019). Comparative metacognition. *Animal Behavior and Cognition*, 6, 278–288.

Carruthers, P. & Williams, D. (2022). Model-free metacognition. *Cognition*, 225, e105117.

Cassam, Q. (2014). *Self-Knowledge for Humans.* Oxford University Press.

Cesana-Arlotti, N., Kovács, Á., & Téglás, E. (2020). Infants recruit logic to learn about the social world. *Nature Communications*, 11, 5999.

Cesana-Arlotti, N., Martín, A., Téglás, E., Vorobyova, L., Cetnarski, R., & Bonatti, L. (2018). Precursors of logical reasoning in preverbal infants. *Science*, 359, 1263–1266.

Chalmers, D. (1996). *The Conscious Mind.* Oxford University Press.

Chambers, R.A., Taylor, J., & Potenza, M. (2003). Developmental neurocircuitry of motivation in adolescence: A critical period of addiction vulnerability. *American Journal of Psychiatry*, 160, 1041–1052.

Cheeseman, J., Millar, C., Greggers, U., Lehmann, K., Pawley, M., Gallistel, C., Warman, G., & Menzel, R. (2014). Way-finding in displaced clock-shifted bees proves bees use a cognitive map. *Proceedings of the National Academy of Sciences*, 111, 8949–8954.

Chemero, A. (2009). *Radical Embodied Cognitive Science.* MIT Press.

Cheney, P., Fetz, E., & Sawyer Palmer, S. (1985). Patterns of facilitation and suppression of antagonist forelimb muscles from motor cortex sites in the awake monkey. *Journal of Neurophysiology*, 53, 805–820.

Chikazoe, J., Lee, D., Kriegeskorte, N., & Anderson, A. (2014). Population coding of affect across stimuli, modalities and individuals. *Nature Neuroscience*, 17, 1114–1122.

Christensen, D. (2004). *Putting Logic in Its Place.* Oxford University Press.

Chudek, M. & Henrich, J. (2011). Culture-gene coevolution, norm-psychology and the emergence of human prosociality. *Trends in Cognitive Sciences*, 15, 218–226.

Chudek, M., McNamara, R., Birch, S., Bloom, P., & Henrich, J. (2018). Do minds switch bodies? Dualist interpretations across ages and societies. *Religion, Brain & Behavior*, 8, 354–368.

Chukoskie, L., Snider, J., Mozer, M., Krauzlis, R., & Sejnowski, T. (2013). Learning where to look for a hidden target. *Proceedings of the National Academy of Sciences*, 110, 10438–10445.

Chun, M., Golomb, J., & Turk-Browne, N. (2011). A taxonomy of external and internal attention. *Annual Review of Psychology*, 62, 73–101.

Cisek, P. (2007). Cortical mechanisms of action selection: The affordance competition hypothesis. *Philosophical Transactions of the Royal Society B*, 362, 1585–1599.

Cisek, P. & Kalaska, J. (2010). Neural mechanisms for interacting with a world full of action choices. *Annual Review of Neuroscience*, 33, 269–298.

Clark, A. (2001). Visual experience and motor action: Are the bonds too tight? *Philosophical Review*, 110, 495–519.

Clark, A. (2008). *Supersizing the Mind*. Oxford University Press.

Clark, A. & Chalmers, D. (1998). The extended mind. *Analysis*, 58, 7–19.

Cochrane, T. (2018). *The Emotional Mind*. Cambridge University Press.

Cohen, E., Burdett, E., Knight, N., & Barrett, J. (2011). Cross-cultural similarities and differences in person-body reasoning: Experimental evidence from the United Kingdom and Brazilian Amazon. *Cognitive Science*, 35, 1282–1304.

Cohen, L.J. (1989). Belief and acceptance. *Mind*, 98, 367–389.

Corbetta, M., Patel, G., & Shulman, G. (2008). The reorienting system in the human brain: From environment to theory of mind. *Neuron*, 58, 306–324.

Corley, M., Brocklehurst, P., & Moat, H. (2011). Error biases in inner and overt speech: Evidence from tongue twisters. *Journal of Experimental Psychology: Learning, Memory, and Cognition*, 37, 162–175.

Cos, I., Duque, J., & Cisek, P. (2014). Rapid prediction of biomechanical costs during action decisions. *Journal of Neurophysiology*, 112, 1256–1266.

Cowan, N. (2001). The magical number 4 in short-term memory: A reconsideration of mental storage capacity. *Behavioral and Brain Sciences*, 24, 87–185.

Cummins, R. (1996). *Representations, Targets, and Attitudes*. MIT Press.

Damasio, A. (1994). *Descartes' Error*. Putnam Press.

Dancy, J. (1993). *Moral Reasons*. Blackwell.

Darwin, C. (1872). *The Expression of Emotion in Man and Animals*. John Murray.

Davidson, D. (1963). Actions, reasons, and causes. *Journal of Philosophy*, 60, 685–699.

Davies, M. (1994). The mental simulation debate. *Proceedings of the British Academy*, 83, 99–127.

De Brigard, F. (2014). Is memory for remembering? Recollection as a form of episodic hypothetical thinking. *Synthese*, 191, 155–185.

De Brigard, F. (2019). Know-how, intellectualism, and memory systems. *Philosophical Psychology*, 32, 720–759.

de Gelder, B., Tamietto, M., van Boxtel, G., Goebel, R., Sahraie, A., van den Stock, J., Stienen, B., Weiskrantz, L., & Pegna, A. (2008). Intact navigation skills after bilateral loss of striate cortex. *Current Biology*, 18 (24), R1128–R1129.

de Leon, M., Golomb, J., George, A., Convit, A., Tarshish, C., McRae, T., De Santi, S., Smith, G., Ferris, S., Noz, M., & Rusinek, H. (1993). The radiologic prediction of Alzheimer disease: The atrophic hippocampal formation. *American Journal of Neuroradiology*, 14, 987–906.

De Petrillo, F. & Rosati, A. (2021). Variation in primate decision-making under uncertainty and the roots of human economic behavior. *Philosophical Transactions of the Royal Society B*, 376, 20190671.

Dehaene, S. (2014). *Consciousness and the Brain*. Viking Press.

Deneve, S., Latham, P., & Pouget, A. (1999). Reading population codes: A neural implementation of ideal observers. *Nature Neuroscience*, 2, 740–745.

Dennett, D. (1971). Intentional systems. *Journal of Philosophy*, 68, 87–106.

Dennett, D. (1987). *The Intentional Stance*. MIT Press.

Dennett, D. (1991a). *Consciousness Explained*. Penguin Press.

Dennett, D. (1991b). Real patterns. *The Journal of Philosophy*, 88, 27–51.

Dennett, D. & Kinsbourne, M. (1992). Time and the observer: The where and when of consciousness in the brain. *Behavioral and Brain Sciences*, 15, 183–201.

Di Nucci, E. (2013). *Mindlessness*. Cambridge Scholars Publishing.

Diedrichsen, J. & Kornysheva, K. (2015). Motor skill learning between selection and execution. *Trends in Cognitive Sciences*, 19, 227–233.

Diekelmann, S., Wilhelm, I., & Born, J. (2009). The whats and whens of sleep-dependent memory consolidation. *Sleep Medicine Reviews*, 13, 309–321.

DiFeliceantonio, A. & Berridge, K. (2016). Dorsolateral neostriatum contribution to incentive salience: Opioid or dopamine stimulation makes one reward cue more motivationally attractive than another. *European Journal of Neuroscience*, 43, 1203–1218.

Doll, B., Simon, D., & Daw, N. (2012). The ubiquity of model-based reinforcement learning. *Current Opinion in Neurobiology*, 22, 1075–1081.

Donald, M. (2005). Imitation and mimesis. In S. Hurley & N. Chater (eds.), *Perspectives on Imitation*. MIT Press.

Donato, F., Alberini, C., Amso, D., Dragoi, G., Dranovsky, A., & Newcombe, N. (2021). The ontogeny of hippocampus-dependent memories. *Journal of Neuroscience*, 41, 920–926.

Dorsch, F. (2009). Judging and the scope of mental agency. In L. O'Brien & M. Soteriou (eds.), *Mental Actions*. Oxford University Press.

Doyon, J., Bellec, P., Amsel, R., Penhune, V., Monchi, O., Carrier, J., Lehéricy, S., & Benali, H. (2009). Contributions of the basal ganglia and functionally related brain structures in motor learning. *Behavioral Brain Research*, 199, 61–75.

Dretske, F. (1988). *Explaining Behavior*. MIT Press.

Dretske, F. (1995). *Naturalizing the Mind*. MIT Press.

Dreyfus, H. (2002). Intelligence without representation: Merleau Ponty's critique of representation. *Phenomenology and the Cognitive Sciences*, 1, 367–383.

Driskell, J., Copper, C., & Moran, A. (1994). Does mental practice enhance performance? *Journal of Applied Psychology*, 79, 481–492.

Duckworth, A., Taxer, J., Eskreis-Winkler, L., Galla, B., & Gross, J. (2019). Self-control and academic achievement. *Annual Review of Psychology*, 70, 373–299.

Dunlosky, J. & Metcalfe, J. (2009). *Metacognition*. Sage Publications.

Duque, J. & Ivry, R. (2009). Role of corticospinal suppression during motor preparation. *Cerebral Cortex*, 19, 2013–2024.

Edwards, M., Goodhew, S., & Badcock, D. (2021). Using perceptual tasks to selectively measure magnocellular and parvocellular performance: Rationale and user's guide. *Psychonomic Bulletin & Review*, 28, 1029–1050.

Eichenbaum, H. (2017). Time (and space) in the hippocampus. *Current Opinion in Behavioral Sciences*, 17, 65–70.

Eisenberger, R. (1992). Learned industriousness. *Psychological Review*, 99, 248–267.

Ekman, P. (1980). *The Face of Man: Universal expressions of emotion in a New Guinea Village*. Garland Press.

Ekman, P. (2007). The micro-expression training tool, version 2 (METT2). Available at: www.mettonline.com.

Ekman, P., Sorenson, E., & Friesen, W. (1969). Pan-cultural elements in facial displays of emotion. *Science*, 164, 86–88.

Eldar, E., Pessiglione, M., & van Dillen, L. (2021). Positive affect as a computational mechanism. *Current Opinion in Behavioral Sciences*, 39, 52–57.

Eldar, E., Rutledge, R., Dolan, R., & Niv, Y. (2016). Mood as representation of momentum. *Trends in Cognitive Sciences*, 20, 15–24.

Elfenbein, H. & Ambady, N. (2002). On the universality and cultural specificity of emotion recognition: A meta-analysis. *Psychological Bulletin*, 128, 203–235.

Elman, J., Bates, E., Johnson, M., Karmiloff-Smith, A., Parisi, D., & Plunkett, K. (1999). *Rethinking Innateness: A connectionist perspective on development*. MIT Press.

Emery, N. (2023). *Naturalism Beyond the Limits of Science*. Oxford University Press.

Erdogan, G., Yildirim, I., & Jacobs, R.A. (2015). From sensory signals to modality-independent conceptual representations: A probabilistic language of thought approach. *PLoS Computational Biology*, 11, e1004610.

Farina, N., Young, J., Tabet, N., & Rusted, J. (2013). Prospective memory in Alzheimer-type dementia: Exploring prospective memory performance in an age-stratified sample. *Journal of Clinical and Experimental Neuropsychology*, 35, 983–992.

Favela, L. (2020). Dynamical systems theory in cognitive science and neuroscience. *Philosophy Compass*, 15, e12695.

Feinberg, T., Schindler, R., Gilson Flanagan, N., & Haber, L. (1992). Two alien hand syndromes. *Neurology*, 42(1), e19.

Feldman, F. (1997). Two questions about pleasure. In F. Feldman (ed.), *Utilitarianism, Hedonism, and Desert*. Cambridge University Press.

Feldman, F. (2004). *Pleasure and the Good Life*. Oxford University Press.

Fernández-Abascal, E., Cabello, R., Fernández-Berrocal, P., & Baron-Cohen, S. (2013). Test-retest reliability of the "Reading the Mind in the Eyes" test: A one-year follow-up study. *Molecular Autism*, 4, 33.

Fernqvist, F. & Ekelund, L. (2014). Credence and the effect on consumer liking of food: A review. *Food Quality and Preference*, 32, 340–353.

Ferrer, R., Macley, A., Litvak, P., & Lerner, J. (2017). Revisiting the effects of anger on risk-taking: Empirical and meta-analytic evidence for differences between males and females. *Journal of Behavioral Decision Making*, 30, 516–526.

Ferrigno, S., Huang, Y., & Cantlon, J. (2021). Reasoning through the disjunctive syllogism in monkeys. *Psychological Science*, 32, 292–300.

Fiebelkorn, I. & Kastner, S. (2020). Functional specialization in the attention network. *Annual Review of Psychology*, 71, 221–249.

Fink, P., Foo, P., & Warren, W. (2009). Catching fly balls in virtual reality: A critical test of the outfielder problem. *Journal of Vision*, 9(13), article #14.

Fleming, S.M. (2021). *Know Thyself: The science of self-awareness*. Basic Books.

Fleming, S.M. & Daw, N. (2017). Self-evaluation of decision-making: A general Bayesian framework for metacognitive computation. *Psychological Review*, 124, 91–114.

Fodor, J. (1975). *The Language of Thought*. Harvester.

Fodor, J. (1981). *Representations*. MIT Press.

Fodor, J. (1990). *A Theory of Content*. MIT Press.

Fodor, J. (1998). *Concepts: Where cognitive science went wrong*. Oxford University Press.

Fodor, J. & Pylyshyn, Z. (1988). Connectionism and cognitive architecture: A critical analysis. *Cognition*, 28, 3–71.

Foley, R. (1987). *The Theory of Epistemic Rationality*. Harvard University Press.

Foley, R. (1993). *Working without a Net: A study of egocentric epistemology*. Oxford University Press.

Foley, R.T., Whitwell, R., & Goodale, M. (2015). The two-visual-systems hypothesis and the perspectival features of visual experience. *Consciousness and Cognition*, 35, 225–233.

Foot, P. (1972). Morality as a system of hypothetical imperatives. *The Philosophical Review*, 81, 305–316.

Forgács, B., Gervain, J., Parise, E., Csibra, G., Gergely, G., Baross, J., & Király, I. (2020). Electrophysiological investigation of infants' understanding of understanding. *Developmental Cognitive Neuroscience*, 43, 100783.

Forgács, B., Parise, E., Csibra, G., Gergely, G., Jacquey, L., & Gervain, J. (2019). Fourteen-month-old infants track the language comprehension of communicative partners. *Developmental Science*, 22, e12751.

Forstmann, B.U., Ratcliff, R., & Wagenmakers, E.-J. (2016). Sequential sampling models in cognitive neuroscience: Advantages, applications, and extensions. *Annual Review of Psychology*, 67, 641–666.

Forstmann, M. & Burgmer, P. (2015). Adults are intuitive mind-body dualists. *Journal of Experimental Psychology: General*, 144, 222–235.

Frankfurt, H. (1978). The problem of action. *American Philosophical Quarterly*, 15, 157–162.

Frankish, K. (2004). *Mind and Supermind*. Cambridge University Press.

Frankish, K. (2007). Deciding to believe again. *Mind*, 116, 523–547.

Frankish, K. (2009). Partial belief and flat-out belief. In F. Huber & C. Schmidt-Petri (eds.), *Degrees of Belief*. Springer.

Freyd, J. & Finke, R. (1984). Representational momentum. *Journal of Experimental Psychology: Learning, Memory, and Cognition*, 10, 126–132.

Fridland, E. (2017). Automatically minded. *Synthese*, 194, 4337–4363.

Fridland, E. (2019). Longer, smaller, faster, stronger: On skills and intelligence. *Philosophical Psychology*, 32, 760–784.

Friedman, J. (2013a). Question-directed attitudes. *Philosophical Perspectives*, 27, 145–174.

Friedman, J. (2013b). Rational agnosticism and degrees of belief. In T. Gendler & J. Hawthorne (eds.), *Oxford Studies in Epistemology 4*. Oxford University Press.

Frijda, N. (2010). Impulsive action and motivation. *Biological Psychiatry*, 84, 570–579.

Frith, C., Blakemore, S.-J., & Wolpert, D. (2000). Abnormalities in the awareness and control of action. *Philosophical Transactions of the Royal Society of London B*, 355, 1771–1788.

Galea, J., Vazquez, A., Pasricha, N., Orban de Xivry, J.-J., & Celnik, P. (2011). Dissociating the roles of the cerebellum and motor cortex during adaptive learning: The motor cortex retains what the cerebellum learns. *Cerebral Cortex*, 21, 1761–1770.

Gallistel, C.R. & Gibbon, J. (2001). Time, rate, and conditioning. *Psychological Review*, 108, 289–344.

Gallistel, C.R. & King, A. (2010). *Memory and the Computational Brain*. Blackwell.

Gallistel, C.R., Krishan, M., Liu, Y., Miller, R., & Latham, P. (2014). The perception of probability. *Psychological Review*, 121, 96–123.

Gallistel, C.R., Mark, T.A., King, A.P., & Latham, P.E. (2001). The rat approximates an ideal detector of rates of reward. *Journal of Experimental Psychology: Animal Behavior Processes*, 27, 354–372.

Ganel, T. & Goodale, M. (2019). Still holding after all these years: An action-perception dissociation in patient DF. *Neuropsychologia*, 128, 249–254.

García Carrasco, D. & Aboitiz Cantalapiedra, J. (2016). Effectiveness of motor imagery or mental practice in functional recovery after stroke: A systematic review. *Neurología*, 31, 43–52.

Gazzaley, A., Cooney, J., McEvoy, K., Knight, R., & D'Esposito, M. (2005). Top-down enhancement and suppression of the magnitude and speed of neural activity. *Journal of Cognitive Neuroscience*, 17, 507–517.

Gelman, S., Sánchez Tapia, I., & Leslie, S.-J. (2016). Memory for generic and quantified sentences in Spanish-speaking children and adults. *Journal of Child Language*, 43, 1231–1244.

Gennari, G., Dehaene, S., Valera, C., & Dehaene-Lambertz, G. (2023). Spontaneous supra-modal encoding of number in the infant brain. *Current Biology*, 33, 1906–1915.

Gheysen, F., Van Opstal, F., Roggeman, C., Van Waelvelde, H., & Fias, W. (2010). Hippocampal contribution to the early and late stages of implicit motor sequence learning. *Experimental Brain Research*, 202, 795–807.

Gibbons, M., Versace, E., Crump, A., Baran, B., & Chittka, L. (2022). Motivational trade-offs and modulation of nociception in bumblebees. *Proceedings of the National Academy of Sciences*, 119, e2205821119.

Gibson, E., Futrell, R., Piantadosi, S., Dautriche, I., Mahowald, K., Bergen, L., & Levy, R. P. (2019). How efficiency shapes human language, *Trends in Cognitive Sciences*, 23, 309–407.

Gigerenzer, G. & Gaissmaier, W. (2011). Heuristic decision making. *Annual Review of Psychology*, 62, 451–482.

Gigerenzer, G., Todd, P., & the ABC Research Group (2000). *Simple Heuristics That Make Us Smart*. Oxford University Press.

Gilbert, D. & Wilson, T. (2007). Prospection: Experiencing the future. *Science*, 317, 1351–1354.

Gilbert, D. & Wilson, T. (2009). Why the brain talks to itself: Sources of error in emotional prediction. *Philosophical Transactions of the Royal Society B*, 364, 1335–1341.

Gilby, I. & Wrangham, R. (2007). Risk-prone hunting by chimpanzees increases during periods of high diet quality. *Behavioral Ecology and Sociobiology*, 61, 1771–1779.

Gläscher, J., Daw, N., Dayan, P., & O'Doherty, J. (2010). Prediction error signals underlying model-based and model-free reinforcement learning. *Neuron*, 66, 585–595.

Gneezy, A., Gneezy, U., & Lauga, D. (2014). A reference-dependent model of the price-quality heuristic. *Journal of Marketing Research*, 51, 153–164.

Goldman, A. (1989). Interpretation psychologized. *Mind & Language*, 4, 161–185.

Goldman, A. (1999). *Knowledge in a Social World*. Oxford University Press.

Goodale, M. & Milner, D. (2018). Two visual pathways: Where have they taken us and where will they lead in future? *Cortex*, 98, 283–292.

Goodfellow, I., Shlens, J., & Szegedy, C. (2015). Explaining and harnessing adversarial examples. arXiv:1412.6572.

Goodman, N., Tenenbaum, J., Feldman, J., & Griffiths, T. (2008). A rational analysis of rule-based concept learning. *Cognitive Science*, 32, 108–154.

Gordon, R. (1986). Folk psychology as simulation. *Mind & Language*, 1, 158–171.

Gordon, R. (1987). *The Structure of Emotions*. Cambridge University Press.

Gould, J. & Gould, C. (1994). *The Animal Mind*. Scientific American Library.

Grabenhorst, F. & Rolls, E. (2011). Value, pleasure and choice in the ventral prefrontal cortex. *Trends in Cognitive Sciences*, 15, 56–67.

Greenspan, P. (1988). *Emotions and Reasons*. Routledge.

Gregg, A., Seibt, B., & Banaji, M. (2006). Easier done than undone: Asymmetry in the malleability of implicit preferences. *Journal of Personality and Social Psychology*, 90, 1–20.

Grieves, R. & Jeffery, K. (2017). The representation of space in the brain. *Behavioral Processes*, 135, 113–131.

Griffin, D. & Strick, P. (2020). The motor cortex uses active suppression to sculpt movement. *Science Advances*, eabb8395.

Gruber, M., Gelman, B., and Ranganath, C. (2014). States of curiosity modulate hippocampus-dependent learning via the dopaminergic circuit. *Neuron*, 84, 486–496.

Gruber, R., Schiestl, M., Boeckle, M., Frohnwieser, A., Miller, R., Gray, R., Clayton, N. & Taylor, A.H. (2019). New Caledonian crows use mental representations to solve metatool problems. *Current Biology*, 29, 686–692.

Hafri, A., Boger, T., & Firestone, C. (2022). Melting ice with your mind: Representational momentum for physical states. *Psychological Science*, 33, 725–735.

Hagger, M., Chatzisarantis, N., Alberts, H., Anggono, C., Batailer, C., Birt, A., Brand, R., Brandt, M., Brewer, G., Bruyneel, S., Calvillo, D., Campbell, W., Cannon, P., Carlucci, M., Carruth, N., Cheung, T., Crowell, A., De Ridder, D., Dewitte, S., Elson, M., Evans, J.R., Fay, B., Fennis, B., Finley, A., Francis, Z., Heise, E., Hoemann, H., Inzlicht, M., Koole, S., Koppel, S., Kroese, F., Lange, F., Lau, K., Lynch, B., Martijn, C., Merckelbach, H., Mills, N., Michirev, A., Miyake, A., Mosser, A., Muise, M., Muller, D., Muzi, M., Nalis, D., Nurwanti, R., Otgaar, H., Philipp, M., Primoceri, P., Rentzsh, K., Ringos, L., Schlinkert, C., Schmeichel, B., Schoch, S., Schrama, M., Schütz, A., Stamos, A., Tinghög, G., Ullrich, J., vanDellen, M., Wimbarti, S., Wolff, W., Yusainy, C., Zerhouni, O., & Zwienenberg, M. (2014). A multilab preregistered replication of the ego-depletion effect. *Perspectives on Psychological Science*, 11, 546–573.

Haidt, J. (2001). The emotional dog and its rational tail: A social intuitionist approach to moral judgment. *Psychological Review*, 108, 814–834.

Haidt, J. (2007). The new synthesis in moral psychology. *Science*, 316, 998–1002.

Hanks, T. & Summerfield, C. (2017). Perceptual decision making in rodents, monkeys, and humans. *Neuron*, 93, 15–31.

Hanus, D., Mendes, N., Tennie, C., & Call, J. (2011). Comparing the performances of apes (*Gorilla gorilla, pan troglodytes, Pongo pymaeus*) and human children (*Homo sapiens*) in the floating peanut task. *PLoS One*, 6, e19555.

Hardwick, R., Caspers, S., Eickhoff, S., & Swinnen, S. (2018). Neural correlates of action: Comparing meta-analyses of imagery, observation, and execution. *Neuroscience and Biobehavioral Reviews*, 94, 31–44.

Harman, G. (1986). *Change in View*. MIT Press.

Hassabis, D., Kumaran, D., Vann, S., & Maguire, E. (2007). Patients with hippocampal amnesia cannot imagine new experiences. *Proceedings of the National Academy of Sciences*, 104, 1726–1731.

Havermans, R. & Jansen, A. (2007). Increasing children's liking of vegetables through flavor-flavor learning. *Appetite*, 48, 259–262.

Heathwood, C. (2007). The reduction of sensory pleasure to desire. *Philosophical Studies*, 133, 23–44.

Hecht, H. & Bertamini, M. (2000). Understanding projectile acceleration. *Journal of Experimental Psychology: Human Perception and Performance*, 26, 730–746.

Heiphetz, L., Landers, C., & Van Leeuwen, N. (2021). Does *think* mean the same thing as *believe?* Linguistic insights into religious cognition. *Psychology of Religion and Spirituality*, 13, 287–297.

Hendrycks, D., Zhao, K., Basart, S., Steinhardt, J., & Song, D. (2021). Natural adversarial examples. *Proceedings of the Conference on Computer Vision and Pattern Recognition (CVPR)*, 15262–25271.

Henrich, J. (2016). *The Secret of Our Success*. Princeton University Press.

Henrich, J. & Muthukrishna, M. (2024). What makes us smart? *Topics in Cognitive Science*, 16, 322–342.

Hickey, C. & Peelen, M. (2015). Neural mechanisms of incentive salience in naturalistic human vision. *Neuron*, 85, 512–518.

Hickok, G. & Poeppel, D. (2007). The cortical organization of speech processing. *Nature Reviews Neuroscience*, 8, 393–402.

Holton, R. (2008). Partial belief, partial intention. *Mind*, 117, 27–58.

Holton, R. & Berridge, K. (2013). Addiction between compulsion and choice. In N. Levy (ed.), *Addiction and Self-Control*. Oxford University Press.

Honda, T., Nagao, S., Hashimoto, Y., Ishikawa, K., Yakota, T., Mizusawa, H., & Ito, M. (2018). Tandem internal models execute motor learning in the cerebellum. *Proceedings of the National Academy of Sciences*, 115, 7426–7433.

Horschler, D., Santos, L., & MacLean, E. (2019). Do non-human primates really represent others' ignorance? A test of the awareness relations hypothesis. *Cognition*, 190, 72–80.

Hosking, J., Crocker, P., & Winstanley, C. (2016). Prefrontal cortical inactivations decrease willingness to expend cognitive effort on a rodent cost/benefit decision-making task. *Cerebral Cortex*, 26, 1529–1538.

Hsieh, N.-h. & Andersson, H. (2021). Incommensurable values. In E. Zalta (ed.), *Stanford Encyclopedia of Philosophy*. https://plato.stanford.edu/archives/fall2021/entries/value-incommensurable/.

Hubbard, T. (2015). The varieties of momentum-like experience. *Psychological Bulletin*, 141, 1081–1119.

Hull, C. (2020). Prediction signals in the cerebellum: Beyond supervised motor learning. *eLife*, 9, e54073.

Humphrey, N. (1986). *The Inner Eye*. Faber and Faber.

Hurlburt, R., Heavey, C., & Kelsey, J. (2013). Toward a phenomenology of inner speaking. *Consciousness and Cognition*, 22, 1477–1494.

Hurlburt, R. & Schwitzgebel, E. (2007). *Describing Inner Experience? Proponent meets skeptic*. MIT Press.

Huth, A., de Heer, W., Griffiths, T.L., Theunissen, F., & Gallant, J. (2016). Natural speech reveals the semantic maps that tile human cerebral cortex. *Nature*, 532, 453–458.

Hutto, D. & Myin, E. (2013). *Radical Enactivism: Basic minds without content*. MIT Press.

Huys, Q., Cools, R., Gölzer, M., Friedel, E., Heinz, A., Dolan, R., & Dayan, P. (2011). Disentangling the roles of approach, activation and valence in instrumental and Pavlovian responding. *PLoS Computational Biology*, 7, e1002028.

Hyde, D., Simon, C., Ting, F., & Nokolaeva, J. (2018). Functional organization of the temporal-parietal junction for theory of mind in preverbal infants: A near-infrared spectroscopy study. *Journal of Neuroscience*, 38, 4264–4274.

Icard, T. (2016). Subjective probability as sampling propensity. *Review of Philosophy and Psychology*, 7, 863–903.

Ilyas, A., Santurkar, S., Tsipras, D., Engstrom, L., Tran, B., & Madry, A. (2019). Adversarial examples are not bugs, they are features. *Advances in Neural Information Processing Systems*, 32.

Inzlicht, M., Shenhav, A., & Olivola, C. (2018). The effort paradox: Effort is both costly and valued. *Trends in Cognitive Sciences*, 22, 337–349.

Irving, Z. (2021). Drifting and directed minds: The significance of mind-wandering for mental agency. *The Journal of Philosophy*, 118, 614–644.

Iwasaki, M. & Noguchi, Y. (2016). Hiding true emotions: Micro-expressions in eyes retrospectively concealed by mouth movements. *Nature Scientific Reports*, 6, e22045.

Izard, V., Sann, C., Spelke, E., & Streri, A. (2009). Newborn infants perceive abstract numbers. *Proceedings of the National Academy of Sciences*, 106, 10382–10385.

Jackson, E. (2019). How belief-credence dualism explains away pragmatic encroachment. *Philosophical Quarterly*, 69, 511–533.

Jackson, E. (2020). The relationship between belief and credence. *Philosophy Compass*, 15, e12668.

Jackson, E. (2022). Why credences are not beliefs. *Australasian Journal of Philosophy*, 100, 360–370.

Jacobacci, F., Armony, J., Yeffal, A., Lerner, G., Amaro, E., Jovicich, J., Doyon, J., & Della-Maggiore, V. (2020). Rapid hippocampal plasticity supports motor sequence learning. *Proceedings of the National Academy of Sciences*, 117, 23898–23903.

James, W. (1890). *Principles of Psychology*. Henry Holt.

Jaworska, A. (2007). Caring and internality. *Philosophy and Phenomenological Research*, 74, 529–568.

Jeannerod, M. (2006). *Motor Cognition*. Oxford University Press.

Jeffrey, R. (1970). Dracula meets wolfman: Acceptance vs partial belief. In M. Swain (ed.), *Induction, Acceptance, and Rational Belief*, Reidel.

Jensen, O., Kaiser, J., & Lachaux, J.-P. (2007). Human gamma-frequency oscillations associated with attention and memory. *Trends in Neurosciences*, 30, 317–324.

Jeong, H., Taylor, A., Floeder, J., Lohmann, M., Mihalas, S., Wu, B., Zhou, M., Burke, D., & Namboodri, V. (2022). Mesolimbic dopamine release conveys causal associations. *Science*, 378, eabq6740.

Ji, M. & Wood, W. (2007). Purchase and consumption habits: Not necessarily what you intend. *Journal of Consumer Psychology*, 17, 261–276.

Jiang, Y. (2018). Habitual versus goal-driven attention. *Cortex*, 102, 107–120.

Job, V., Dweck, C., & Walton, G. (2010). Ego depletion: Is it all in your head? Implicit theories about willpower affect self-regulation. *Psychological Science*, 21, 1686–1693.

Job, V., Walton, G., Bernecker, K., & Dweck, C. (2013). Beliefs about willpower determine the impact of glucose on self-control. *Proceedings of the National Academy of Sciences*, 110, 14837–14842.

Job, V., Walton, G., Bernecker, K., & Dweck, C. (2015). Implicit theories about willpower predict self-regulation and grades in everyday life. *Journal of Personality and Social Psychology*, 108, 637–647.

Jones, C.R., Simonoff, E., Baird, G., Pickles, A., Marsden, A., Tregay, J., Happé, F., & Charman, T. (2018). The association between theory of mind, executive function, and the symptoms of autism spectrum disorder. *Autism Research*, 11, 95–109.

Jordan, K., MacLean, E., & Brannon, E. (2008). Monkeys match and tally quantities across senses. *Cognition*, 108, 617–625.

Joyce, J. (1999). *The Foundations of Causal Decision Theory*. Cambridge University Press.

Juechems, K. & Summerfield, C. (2019). Where does value come from? *Trends in Cognitive Sciences*, 23, 836–850.

Kahneman, D. (2011). *Thinking, Fast and Slow*. Farrar, Straus & Giroux.

Kaminski, J., Call, J., & Tomasello, M. (2008). Chimpanzees know what others know, but not what they believe. *Cognition*, 109, 224–234.

Kampis, D. & Kovács, Á. (2021). Seeing the world from others' perspective: 14-month-olds show altercentric modulation effects by others' beliefs. *Open Mind: Discoveries in Cognitive Science*, 5, 189–207.

Kaplan, H., Hill, K., Lancaster, J., & Hurtado, A.M. (2000). A theory of human life history evolution: Diet, intelligence, and longevity. *Evolutionary Anthropology*, 9, 156–185.

Kelemen, D., Rottman, J., & Seston, R. (2013). Professional physical scientists display tenacious teleological tendencies: Purpose-based reasoning as a cognitive default. *Journal of Experimental Psychology: General*, 142, 1074–1083.

Kelso, J. (1995). *Dynamic Patterns: The self-organization of brain and behavior*. MIT Press.

Keltner, D. (1995). Signs of appeasement: Evidence for the distinct displays of embarrassment, amusement, and shame. *Journal of Personality and Social Psychology*, 68, 441–454.

Kensinger, E. & Corkin, S. (2004). Two routes to emotional memory: Distinct neural processes for valence and arousal. *Proceedings of the National Academy of Sciences*, 101, 3310–3315.

Khan, A., Faucett, J., Lichtenberg, P., Kirsch, I., & Brown, W.A. (2012). A systematic review of the comparative efficacy of treatments and controls for depression. *PLoS ONE*, 7, e41778.

Kheifets, A. & Gallistel, C.R. (2012). Mice take calculated risks. *Proceedings of the National Academy of Sciences*, 109, 8776–8779.

Kiani, R., Corthell, L., & Shadlen, M. (2014). Choice certainty is informed by both evidence and decision time. *Neuron*, 84, 1329–1342.

Kidd, C., Palmeri, H., & Aslin, R. (2013). Rational snacking: Young children's decision-making on the marshmallow task is moderated by beliefs about environmental reliability. *Cognition*, 126, 109–114.

Kim, P., Evans, G.W., Angstadt, M., Ho, S.S., Sripada, C., Swain, J., Liberzon, I., & Phan, K.L. (2013). Effects of childhood poverty and chronic stress on emotion regulatory brain function in adulthood. *Proceedings of the National Academy of Sciences*, 110, 18442–18447.

Király, I., Oláh, K., Csibra, G., & Kovács, Á. (2018). Retrospective attribution of false beliefs in 3-year-old children. *Proceedings of the National Academy of Sciences*, 115, 11477–11482.

Király, I., Oláh, K., & Kovács, Á. (2023). Can 18-month-olds revise attributed beliefs? *Open Mind: Discoveries in Cognitive Science*, 7, 435–444.

Knight, R. & Grabowecky, M. (1995). Escape from linear time: Prefrontal cortex and conscious experience. In M. Gazzaniga (ed.), *The Cognitive Neurosciences*. MIT Press.

Knobe, J., Buckwalter, W., Nichols, S., Robbins, P., Sarkissian, H., & Sommers, T. (2012). Experimental philosophy. *Annual Review of Psychology*, 63, 81–99.

Kobayashi, K. & Hsu, M. (2019). Common neural code for reward and information value. *Proceedings of the National Academy of Sciences*, 16, 13061–13066.

Kobayashi, S., Kojima, S., Yamanaka, M., Sadamoto, H., Nakamura, H., Fujito, Y., Kawai, R., Sakakibara, M., & Ito, E. (1998). Operant conditioning and escape behavior in the pond snail, *Lymnaea stagnalis*. *Zoological Science*, 15, 683–690.

Kornell, N., Rhodes, M., Castel, A., & Tauber, S. (2011). The ease-of-processing heuristic and the stability bias: Dissociating memory, memory beliefs, and memory judgments. *Psychological Science*, 22, 787–794.

Korsgaard, C. (1996). *The Sources of Normativity*. Cambridge University Press.

Kosslyn, S., Thompson, W., & Ganis, G. (2006). *The Case for Mental Imagery*. Oxford University Press.

Kouider, S. & Dehaene, S. (2009). Subliminal number priming within and across the visual and auditory modalities. *Experimental Psychology*, 56, 418–433.

Kovács, Á., Téglás, E., & Csibra, G. (2021). Can infants adopt underspecified contents into attributed beliefs? Representational prerequisites of theory of mind. *Cognition*, 213, 104640.

Kravitz, D., Saleem, K., Baker, C., & Mishkin, M. (2011). A new neural framework for visuospatial processing. *Nature Reviews Neuroscience*, 12, 217–230.

Krieglmeyer, R., Deutsch, R., De Houwer, J., & De Raedt, R. (2010). Being moved: Valence activated approach-avoidance behavior independently of evaluation and approach-avoidance intentions. *Psychological Science*, 21, 607–613.

Kurakin, A., Goodfellow, I., & Bengio, S. (2018). Adversarial examples in the physical world. In R. Yampolskiy (ed.), *Artificial Intelligence Safety and Security*. Chapman & Hall.

Kurzban, R. (2010). Does the brain consume additional glucose during self-control tasks? *Evolutionary Psychology*, 8, 244–259.

Kurzban, R. (2016). The sense of effort. *Current Opinion in Psychology*, 7, 67–70.

Kurzban, R., Duckworth, A., Kable, J., & Myers, J. (2013). An opportunity cost model of subjective effort and task performance. *Behavioral and Brain Sciences*, 36, 661–679.

La Corte, V., Ferrieux, S., Abram, M., Bertrand, A., Dubois, B., Teichmann, M., & Piolino, P. (2021). The role of semantic memory in prospective memory and episodic future thinking: New insights from a case of semantic dementia, *Memory*, 29, 943–962.

Labukt, I. (2012). Hedonic tone and the heterogeneity of pleasure. *Utilitas*, 24, 172–199.

Lambon Ralph, M. (2017). Neurocognitive insights on conceptual knowledge and its breakdown. *Philosophical Transactions of the Royal Society B*, 369, 20120392.

Langland-Hassan, P. (2016). Hearing a voice as one's own: Two views of inner-speech self-monitoring deficits in schizophrenia. *Review of Philosophy and Psychology*, 7, 675–699.

LaPointe, L. (2005). *Aphasia and Related Neurogenic Language Disorders*, 3rd edition. Theime Medical Publishers.

Lau, H., Michel, M., LeDoux, J., & Fleming, S.M. (2022). The mnemonic basis of subjective experience. *Nature Reviews Psychology*, 1, 479–488.

Laukka, P. & Elfenbein, H. (2021). Cross-cultural emotion recognition and in-group advantage in vocal expression: A meta-analysis. *Emotion Review*, 13, 3–11.

Lebreton, M., Abitol, R., Daunizeau, J., & Pessiglione, M. (2015). Automatic integration of confidence in the brain valuation signal. *Nature Neuroscience*, 18, 1159–1167.

Lecouvey, G., Morand, A., Gonneaud, J., Piolino, P., Orriols, E., Pélerin, A., Ferreira Da Silva, L., de La Sayette, V., Eustache, F., & Desgranges, B. (2019). An impairment of prospective memory in mild Alzheimer's disease: A ride in a virtual town. *Frontiers in Psychology*, 10, #241.

Ledberg, A., Bressler, S., Ding, M., Coppola, R., & Nakamura, R. (2007). Large-scale visuomotor integration in the cerebral cortex. *Cerebral Cortex*, 17, 44–62.

LeDoux, J. (2012). Rethinking the emotional brain. *Neuron*, 73, 653–676.

Lehrer, M. (1993). Why do bees turn and look back? *Journal of Comparative Physiology A*, 172, 549–563.

Leknes, S., Berna, C., Lee, M., Snyder, G., Biele, G., & Tracey, I. (2013). The importance of context: When relative relief renders pain pleasant. *Pain*, 154, 402–410.

Lerner, J., Gonzalez, R., Small, D., & Fischhoff, B. (2003). Effects of fear and anger on perceived risks of terrorism: A national field experiment. *Psychological Science*, 14, 144–150.

Lerner, J. & Keltner, D. (2000). Beyond valence: Toward a model of emotion-specific influences on judgment and choice. *Cognition and Emotion*, 14, 473–493.

Leslie, S.-J. (2017). The original sin of cognition: Fear, prejudice, and generalization. *The Journal of Philosophy*, 114, 393–421.

Leslie, S.-J. & Gelman, S. (2012). Quantified statements are recalled as generics: Evidence from preschool children and adults. *Cognitive Psychology*, 64, 186–214.

Leslie, S.-J., Khemlani, S., & Glucksberg, S. (2011). All ducks lay eggs: The generic overgeneralization effect. *Journal of Memory and Language*, 65, 887–900.

Levelt, W. (1989). *Speaking*. MIT Press.

Levi, I. (1991). *The Fixation of Belief and its Undoing*. Cambridge University Press.

Levy, D. & Glimcher, P. (2012). The root of all value: A neural common currency for choice. *Current Opinion in Neurobiology*, 22, 1027–1038.

Levy, N. (2014). *Consciousness and Moral Responsibility*. Oxford University Press.

Lewis, D. (1970). How to define theoretical terms. *The Journal of Philosophy*, 67, 427–446.

Lewis, D. (1972). Psychophysical and theoretical identifications. *Australasian Journal of Philosophy*, 50, 249–258.

Lewis, M. (2015). *The Biology of Desire*. Perseus Books.

Lhermitte, F. (1983). "Utilization behavior" and its relation to lesions of the frontal lobe. *Brain*, 106, 237–255.

Lhermitte, F. (1986). Human autonomy and the frontal lobes, II. Patient behavior in complex and social situations: The "environmental dependency syndrome." *Annals of Neurology*, 19, 335–343.

Li, M., Tan, H.-E., Lu, Z., Tsang, K., Chung, A., & Zuker, C. (2022). Gut-brain circuits for fat preference. *Nature*, 610, 722–730.

Lind, A., Hall, L., Breidegard, B., Balkenius, C., & Johansson, P. (2014). Speakers' acceptance of real-time speech exchange indicates that we use auditory feedback to specify the meaning of what we say. *Psychological Science*, 25, 1198–1205.

Litman, J. (2005). Curiosity and the pleasures of learning: Wanting and liking new information, *Cognition and Emotion*, 19, 793–814.

Loftus, E. (2005). Planting misinformation in the human mind: A 30-year investigation of the malleability of memory. *Learning and Memory*, 12, 361–366.

Loftus, E. & Hoffman, H. (1989). Misinformation and memory: The creation of new memories. *Journal of Experimental Psychology: General*, 118, 100–104.

MacLeod, C. (1992). The Stroop task: The "gold standard" of attentional measures. *Journal of Experimental Psychology: General*, 121, 12–14.

MacLeod, C. & Campbell, L. (1992). Memory accessibility and probability judgments: An experimental evaluation of the availability heuristic. *Journal of Personality and Social Psychology*, 63, 890–902.

Mahon, B. & Caramazza, A. (2008). A critical look at the embodied cognition hypothesis and a new proposal for grounding conceptual content. *Journal of Physiology: Paris*, 102, 59–70.

Mahr, J. & Csibra, G. (2018). Why do we remember? The communicative function of episodic memory. *Behavioral and Brain Sciences*, 41, e1.

Mandelbaum, E. (2014). Thinking is believing. *Inquiry*, 57, 55–96.

Mandelbaum, E. (2016). Attitude, inference, association: On the propositional structure of implicit bias. *Noûs*, 50, 629–658.

Manes, F., Sahakian, B., Clark, L., Rogers, R., Antoun, N., Aitken, M., & Robbins, T. (2002). Decision-making processes following damage to the prefrontal cortex. *Brain*, 125, 624–639.

Marks, J. (1982). A theory of emotion. *Philosophical Studies*, 42, 227–242.

Marr, D. (1982). *Vision: A computational investigation into the human representation and processing of visual information*. W.H. Freeman.

Marsh, A. & Ambady, N. (2007). The influence of the fear facial expression on prosocial responding. *Cognition and Emotion*, 21, 225–247.

Martin, T., McDaniel, M., Guynn, M., Houck, J., Woodruff, C., Pearson Bish, J., Moses, S., Kičič, D., & Tesche, C. (2007). Brain regions and their dynamics in prospective memory retrieval: A MEG study. *International Journal of Psychophysiology*, 64, 247–258.

Martínez, M. (2011). Imperative content and the painfulness of pain. *Phenomenology and the Cognitive Sciences*, 10, 67–90.

Martínez, M. (2015). Pains as reasons. *Philosophical Studies*, 172, 2261–2274.

Marušić, B. & Schwenkler, J. (2018). Intending is believing: A defense of strong cognitivism. *Analytic Philosophy*, 59, 309–340.

Masicampo, E. & Baumeister, R. (2008). Toward a physiology of dual-process reasoning and judgment: Lemonade, willpower, and expensive rule-based analysis. *Psychological Science*, 19, 255–260.

Matsumoto, R., Nair, D., LaPresto, E., Jajm, I., Bingaman, W., Shibasaki, H., & Lüders, H. (2004). Functional connectivity in the human language system: A cortico-cortical evoked potential study. *Brain*, 127, 2316–2330.

McCall, S. (1987). Decision. *Canadian Journal of Philosophy*, 17, 261–287.

McDaniel, M., LaMontagne, P., Beck, S., Scullin, M., & Braver, T. (2013). Dissociable neural routes to successful prospective memory. *Psychological Science*, 24, 1791–1800.

McDowell, J. (1978). Are moral requirements hypothetical imperatives? *Proceedings of the Aristotelian Society*, 52, 13–29.

McNamara, J. & Houston, A. (1986). The common currency for behavioral decisions. *The American Naturalist*, 127, 358–378.

McNamee, D. & Wolpert, D. (2019). Internal models in biological control. *Annual Review of Control, Robotics, and Autonomous Systems*, 2, 339–364.

Mele, A. (2000). Deciding to act. *Philosophical Studies*, 100, 81–108.

Mele, A. (2003). *Motivation and Agency*. Oxford University Press.

Mele, A. (2021). Deciding: How special is it? *Philosophical Explorations*, 24, 359–375.

Mendola, J. (2006). Intuitive hedonism. *Philosophical Studies*, 128, 441–477.

Menon, V. & D'Esposito, M. (2022). The role of PFC networks in cognitive control and executive function. *Neuropsychopharmacology*, 47, 90–103.

Menon, V. & Uddin, L. (2010). Saliency, switching, attention and control: A network model of insula function. *Brain Structure and Function*, 214, 655–667.

Menzel, R., Greggers, U., Smith, A., Berger, S., Brandt, R., Brunke, S., Bundrock, G., Hülse, S., Plümpe, T., Schaupp, F., Schüttler, E., Stach, S., Stindt, J., Stollhoff, N., & Watzl, S. (2005). Honey bees navigate according to a map-like spatial memory. *Proceedings of the National Academy of Sciences*, 102, 3040–3045.

Mercier, H. & Sperber, D. (2017). *The Enigma of Reason*. Harvard University Press.

Merel, J., Botvinick, M., & Wayne, G. (2019). Hierarchical motor control in mammals and machines. *Nature Communications*, 10, 5489.

Michaelian, K. (2016). *Mental Time Travel*. MIT Press.

Miller, K., Ludvig, E., Pezzulo, G., & Shenhav, A. (2018). Realigning models of habitual and goal-directed decision-making. In R. Morris, A. Bornstein, & A. Shenhav (eds.), *Goal-Directed Decision Making*. Academic Press.

Miller, K., Shenhav, A., & Ludvig, E. (2019). Habits without values. *Psychological Review*, 126, 292–311.

Millikan, R. (1984). *Language, Thought, and Other Biological Categories*. MIT Press.

Millikan, R. (1989). Biosemantics. *The Journal of Philosophy*, 86, 281–297.

Milner, D. & Goodale, M. (1995). *The Visual Brain in Action*. Oxford University Press.

Miloyan, B. & Suddendorf, T. (2015). Feelings of the future. *Trends in Cognitive Sciences*, 19, 196–200.

Mischel, W., Ayduk, O., Berman, M., Casey, B., Gotlib, I., Jonides, J., Kross, E., Teslovich, T., Wilson, N., Zayas, V., & Shoda, Y. (2011). "Willpower" over the life span: Decomposing self-regulation. *SCAN*, 6, 252–256.

Mischel, W., Ebbesen, E., & Raskoff Zeiss, A. (1972). Cognitive and attentional mechanisms in delay of gratification. *Journal of Personality and Social Psychology*, 21, 204–218.

Mischel, W., Shoda, Y., & Peake, P. (1988). The nature of adolescent competencies predicted by preschool delay of gratification. *Journal of Personality and Social Psychology*, 54, 687–699.

Mischiati, M., Lin, H.-T., Herold, P., Imler, E., Olberg, R., & Leonardo, A. (2014). Internal models direct dragonfly interception steering. *Nature*, 517, 333–338.

Mishra, S. (2014). Decision-making under risk: Integrating perspectives from biology, economics, and psychology. *Personality and Social Psychology Review*, 18, 280–307.

Mobbs, D., Headley, D., Ding, W., & Dayan, P. (2020). Space, time, and fear: Survival computations along defensive circuits. *Trends in Cognitive Sciences*, 24, 228–241.

Moffitt, T., Arseneault, L., Belsky, D., Dickson, N., Hancox, R., Harrington, H., Houts, R., Poulton, B., Ross, S., Sears, M., Thomson, W.M., & Caspi, A.

(2011). A gradient of childhood self-control predicts health, wealth, and public safety. *Proceedings of the National Academy of Sciences*, 108, 2693–2698.

Molnar-Szakacs, I. & Uddin, L. (2022). Anterior insula as a gatekeeper of executive control. *Neuroscience and Biobehavioral Reviews*, 139, 104736.

Momennejad, I. & Haynes, J.-D. (2013). Encoding of prospective tasks in the human prefrontal cortex under varying task loads. *Journal of Neuroscience*, 33, 17342–17349.

Montague, P.R. & Berns, G. (2002). Neural economics and the biological substrates of valuation. *Neuron*, 36, 265–284.

Moon, A. (2017). Beliefs do not come in degrees. *Canadian Journal of Philosophy*, 47, 760–778.

Moon, A. & Jackson, E. (2020). Credence: A belief-first approach. *Canadian Journal of Philosophy*, 50, 652–669.

Moore, G.E. (1903). *Principia Ethica*. Cambridge University Press.

Moors, A., Ellsworth, P., Scherer, K., & Frijda, N. (2013). Appraisal theories of emotion: State of the art and future development. *Emotion Review*, 5, 119–124.

Morillo, C. (1995). *Contingent Creatures*. Rowman & Littlefield.

Morsella, E., Ben-Zeev, A., Lanska, M., & Bargh, J. (2010). The spontaneous thoughts of the night: How future tasks breed intrusive cognitions. *Social Cognition*, 28, 641–650.

Moscovitch, M., Cabeza, R., Winocur, G., & Nadel, L. (2016). Episodic memory and beyond: The hippocampus and neocortex in transformation. *Annual Review of Psychology*, 67, 105–134.

Murakami, M., Vicente, M.I., Costa, G., & Mainen, Z. (2014). Neural antecedents of self-initiated actions in secondary motor cortex. *Nature Neuroscience*, 17, 1574–1582.

Murphy, P., Boonstra, E., & Nieuwenhuis, S. (2016). Global gain modulation generates time-dependent urgency during perceptional choice in humans. *Nature Communications*, 7, 13526.

Mylopoulos, M. & Pacherie, E. (2017). Intentions and motor representations: The interface challenge. *Review of Philosophy and Psychology*, 8, 317–336.

Nagel, J. (2013). Knowledge as a mental state. In T. Gendler & J. Hawthorne (eds.), *Oxford Studies in Epistemology*, volume 4. Oxford University Press.

Nagel, T. (1970). *The Possibility of Altruism*. Oxford University Press.

Nakamura, J. & Csikszentmihalyi, M. (2002). The concept of flow. In C. Snyder & S. Lopez (eds.), *Handbook of Positive Psychology*. Oxford University Press.

Neal, D., Wood, W., Labrecque, J., & Lally, P. (2012). How do habits guide behavior: Perceived and actual triggers of habits in daily life. *Journal of Experimental Social Psychology*, 48, 492–498.

Neal, D., Wood, W., Wu, M., & Kurlander, D. (2011). The pull of the past: When do habits persist despite conflict with motives? *Personality and Social Psychology Bulletin*, 37, 1428–1437.

Neander, K. (2017). *A Mark of the Mental: In defense of informational semantics*. MIT Press.

Negri, G., Rumiati, R., Zadini, A., Ukmar, M., Mahon, B., & Caramazza, A. (2007). What is the role of motor simulation in action and object recognition? Evidence from apraxia. *Cognitive Neuropsychology*, 24, 795–816.

Nguyen, D., Naffziger, E., & Berridge, K. (2021). Positive affect: Nature and brain bases of liking and wanting. *Current Opinion in Behavioral Sciences*, 39, 72–78.

Nicholson, T., Williams, D.M., Grainger, C., Lind, S., & Carruthers, P. (2019). Relationships between implicit and explicit uncertainty monitoring and mind-reading: Evidence from autism spectrum disorder. *Consciousness and Cognition*, 70, 11–24.

Nicholson, T., Williams, D.M., Grainger, C., Lind, S., & Carruthers, P. (2021). Linking metacognition and mindreading: Evidence from autism and dual-task investigations. *Journal of Experimental Psychology: General*, 150, 206–220.

Novick, J., Trueswell, J., & Thompson-Schill, S. (2010). Broca's area and language processing: Evidence for the cognitive control connection. *Language and Linguistics Compass*, 4, 906–924.

Nozari, N., Dell, G., & Schwartz, M. (2011). Is comprehension necessary for error detection? A conflict-based account of monitoring in speech production. *Cognitive Psychology*, 63, 1–33.

Nussbaum, M. (2001). *Upheavals of Thought*. Cambridge University Press.

O'Doherty, J., Cockburn, J., & Pauli, W. (2017). Learning, reward, and decision making. *Annual Review of Psychology*, 68, 73–100.

O'Keefe, J. (1976). Place units in the hippocampus of the freely moving rat. *Experimental Neurology*, 51, 78–109.

O'Shaughnessy, B. (1980). *The Will: A dual aspect theory*. Cambridge University Press.

Oddie, G. (2005). *Value, Reality, and Desire*. Oxford University Press.

Oktay-Gür, N. & Rakoczy, H. (2017). Children's difficulty with true belief tasks: Competence deficit or performance problem? *Cognition*, 166, 28–41.

Olney, J., Warlow, S., Naffzinger, E., & Berridge, K. (2018). Current perspectives on incentive salience and applications to clinical disorders. *Current Opinion in Behavioral Sciences*, 22, 59–69.

Olsson, A., McMahon, K., Papenberg, G., Zaki, J., Bolger, N., & Ochsner, K. (2016). Vicarious fear learning depends on empathic appraisals and trait empathy. *Psychological Science*, 27, 25–33.

Oppenheim, G. & Dell, G. (2008). Inner speech slips exhibit lexical bias, but not the phonemic similarity effect. *Cognition*, 106, 528–537.

Oppenheim, G. & Dell, G. (2010). Motor movement matters: The flexible abstractness of inner speech. *Memory & Cognition*, 38, 1147–1160.

Optician, L. & Pretegiani, E. (2017). What stops a saccade? *Philosophical Transactions of the Royal Society B*, 372, 20160194.

Orsini, C., Moorman, D., Young, J., Setlow, B., & Floresco, S. (2015). Neural mechanisms regulating different forms of risk-related decision-making: Insights from animal models. *Neuroscience and Biobehavioral Reviews*, 58, 147–167.

Otgaar, H., Scoboria, A., & Mazzoni, G. (2014). On the existence and implications of nonbelieved memories. *Current Directions in Psychological Science*, 23, 349–354.

Overlan, M., Jacobs, R., & Piantadosi, S. (2017). Learning abstract visual concepts via probabilistic program induction in a Language of Thought. *Cognition*, 168, 320–334.

Pacherie, E. & Mylopoulos, M. (2021). Beyond automaticity: The psychological complexity of skill. *Topoi*, 40, 649–662.

Pan, S. (2022). What is so special about episodic memory: Lessons from the system-experience distinction. *Synthese*, 200, #5.

Papineau, D. (1987). *Reality and Representation*. Blackwell.

Papineau, D. (2013). In the zone. *Royal Institute of Philosophy Supplement*, 73, 175–196.

Parfit, D. (2011). *On What Matters*. Oxford University Press.

Pavese, C. (2017). Know-how and gradability. *Philosophical Review*, 126, 345–383.

Pavese, C. & Beddor, B. (2023). Skills as knowledge. *Australasian Journal of Philosophy*, 101, 609–624.

Peacocke, A. (2021). Mental action. *Philosophy Compass*, 16, e12741.

Peacocke, C. (2008). *Truly Understood*. Oxford University Press.

Perenin, M. & Vighetto, A. (1988). Optic ataxia: A specific disruption in visuomotor mechanisms. *Brain*, 111, 643–674.

Peters, J. & Büchel, C. (2011). The neural mechanisms of inter-temporal decision-making: Understanding variability. *Trends in Cognitive Sciences*, 15, 227–239.

Petersen, S. & Posner, M. (2012). The attention system of the human brain: 20 years after. *Annual Review of Neuroscience*, 35, 73–89.

Petrie, K. & Rief, W. (2019). Psychobiological mechanisms of placebo and nocebo effects: Pathways to improve treatments and reduce side effects. *Annual Review of Psychology*, 70, 599–625.

Pettit, P. (1993). *The Common Mind*. Oxford University Press.

Pezzulo, G. & Cisek, P. (2016). Navigating the affordance landscape: Feedback control as a process model of behavior and cognition. *Trends in Cognitive Sciences*, 20, 414–424.

Phillips, J., Buckwalter, W., Cushman, F., Friedman, O., Martin, A., Turri, J., Santos, L., & Knobe, J. (2021). Knowledge before belief. *Behavioral and Brain Sciences*, 44, e140.

Piantadosi, S. & Jacobs, R. (2016). Four problems solved by the probabilistic language of thought. *Current Directions in Psychological Science*, 25, 54–59.

Pickard, H. (2022). Is addiction a brain disease? A plea for agnosticism and heterogeneity. *Psychopharmacology*, 239, 993–1007.

Pickering, M. & Garrod, S. (2013). An integrated theory of language production and comprehension. *Behavioral and Brain Sciences*, 36, 329–347.

Piñeros Glasscock, J. & Tenenbaum, S. (2023). Action. In E. Zalta & U. Nodelman (eds.), *The Stanford Encyclopedia of Philosophy*. https://plato.stanford.edu/archives/spr2023/entries/action.

Plassmann, H., O'Doherty, J., Shiv, B., & Rangel, A. (2008). Marketing actions can modulate neural representations of experienced pleasantness. *Proceedings of the National Academy of Sciences*, 105, 1050–1054.

Pleskac, T. & Busemeyer, J. (2010). Two-stage dynamic signal detection: A theory of choice, decision time, and confidence. *Psychological Review*, 117, 864–901.

Pollock, J. (1983). Epistemology and probability. *Synthese*, 55, 231–252.

Poppenk, J., Moscovitch, M., McIntosh, A., Ozcelik, E., & Craik, F. (2010). Encoding the future: Successful processing of intentions engages predictive brain networks. *NeuroImage*, 49, 905–913.

Porter, S., ten Brinke, L., & Wallace, B. (2012). Secrets and lies: Involuntary leakage in deceptive facial expressions as a function of emotional intensity. *Journal of Nonverbal Behavior*, 36, 23–37.

Pouget, A., Dayan, P., & Zemel, R. (2000). Information processing with population codes. *Nature Reviews Neuroscience*, 1, 125–132.

Pouget, A., Drugowitsch, J., & Kepecs, A. (2016). Confidence and certainty: Distinct probabilistic quantities for different goals. *Nature Neuroscience*, 19, 366–374.

Prinz, J. (2004). *Gut Reactions*. Oxford University Press.

Purushothaman, G. & Bradley, D. (2005). Neural population code for fine perceptual decisions in area MT. *Nature Neuroscience*, 8, 99–106.

Pyke, G., Pulliam, H., & Charnov, E. (1977). Optimal foraging: A selective review of theory and tests. *Quarterly Review of Biology*, 52, 137–154.

Qi, S., Hassabis, D., Sun, J., Guo, F., Daw, N., & Mobbs, D. (2018). How cognitive and reactive fear circuits optimize escape decisions in humans. *Proceedings of the National Academy of Sciences*, 115, 3186–3191.

Quilty-Dunn, J. (2020). Perceptual pluralism. *Noûs*, 54, 807–838.

Quilty-Dunn, J., Porot, N., & Mandelbaum, E. (2023). The best game in town: The re-emergence of the language of thought hypothesis across the cognitive sciences. *Behavioral and Brain Sciences*, 46, e261.

Quine, W.V. & Ullian, J. (1970). *The Web of Belief*. Random House.

Quirk, G. & Mueller, D. (2008). Neural mechanisms of extinction learning and retrieval. *Neuropsychopharmacology*, 33, 56–72.

Raz, J. (1986). *The Morality of Freedom*. Oxford University Press.

Renoult, L., Irish, M., Moscovitch, M., & Rugg, M. (2019). From knowing to remembering: The semantic-episodic distinction. *Trends in Cognitive Sciences*, 23, 1041–1057.

Rescorla, M. (2009). Cognitive maps and the language of thought. *British Journal for the Philosophy of Science*, 60, 377–407.

Rhodes, M. & Castel, A. (2009). Metacognitive illusions for auditory information: Effects on monitoring and control. *Psychonomic Bulletin & Review*, 16, 550–554.

Ritchie, J.B. (2019). The content of Marr's information-processing framework. *Philosophical Psychology*, 32, 1079–1099.

Ritchie, J.B., Montesinos, S., & Carter, M. (2024). What is a visual stream? *Journal of Cognitive Neuroscience*, 36, 2627–2638.

Roazzi, M., Nyhof, M., & Johnson, C. (2013). Mind, soul and spirit: Conceptions of immaterial identity in different cultures. *International Journal for the Psychology of Religion*, 23, 75–86.

Robins, S. (2022). Episodic memory is not for the future. In A. Sant'Anna, C. McCarroll, & K. Michaelian (eds.), *Current Controversies in the Philosophy of Memory*. Routledge.

Robins, S. (2023). The 21st century engram. *WIREs Cognitive Science*, 14, e1653.

Rolls, E. (1999). *The Brain and Emotion*. Oxford University Press.

Rosenthal, D. (2010). How to think about mental qualities. *Philosophical Issues*, 20, 368–393.

Ruff, C. & Fehr, E. (2014). The neurobiology of rewards and values in social decision-making. *Nature Reviews Neuroscience*, 15, 549–562.

Rupert, R. (2018). Representation and mental representation. *Philosophical Explorations*, 21, 204–225.

Russell, J.A. (1994). Is there universal recognition of emotion from facial expression? A review of the cross-cultural studies. *Psychological Bulletin*, 115, 102–141.

Ryle, G. (1949). *The Concept of Mind*. Barnes and Noble.

Sauter, D., Eisner, F., Ekman, P., & Scott, S.K. (2010). Cross-cultural recognition of basic emotions through nonverbal emotional vocalizations. *Proceedings of the National Academy of Sciences*, 107, 2408–2412.

Sauter, D., LeGuen, O., & Haun, D. (2011). Categorical perception of emotional facial expressions does not require lexical categories. *Emotion*, 11, 1479–1483.

Savani, K. & Job, V. (2017). Reverse ego-depletion: Acts of self-control can improve subsequent performance in Indian cultural contexts. *Journal of Personality and Social Psychology*, 112, 589–607.

Scanlon, T. (1998). *What We Owe to Each Other*. Harvard University Press.

Schacter, D. (2001). *The Seven Sins of Memory*. Houghton Mifflin.

Schacter, D. (2012). Adaptive constructive processes and the future of memory. *American Psychologist*, 67, 603–613.

Schacter, D. (2019). Implicit memory, constructive memory, and imagining the future: A career perspective. *Perspectives on Psychological Science*, 14, 256–272.

Schacter, D. & Addis, D. (2007). The cognitive neuroscience of constructive memory: Remembering the past and imagining the future. *Philosophical Transactions of the Royal Society B*, 362, 773–786.

Schacter, D., Norman, K., & Koutstaal., W. (1998). The cognitive neuroscience of constructive memory. *Annual Review of Psychology*, 49, 289–318.

Schiffer, S. (2003). *The Things We Mean*. Oxford University Press.

Schliesser, E. (2019). Synthetic philosophy. *Biology & Philosophy*, 34, 1–9.

Schmidt, L., Skvortsova, V., Kullen, C., Weber, B., & Plassmann, H. (2017). How context alters value: The brain's valuation and affective regulation system link price cues to experienced taste pleasantness. *Nature Scientific Reports*, 7, 8098.

Schmidtmann, G., Logan, A., Carbon, C.-C., Loong, J., & Gold, I. (2020). In the blink of an eye: Reading mental states from briefly presented eye regions. *i-Perception*, 11, 1–17.

Schrittwieser, J., Antonoglou, I., Hubert, T., Simonyan, K., Sifre, L., Schmitt, S., Guez, A., Lockhart, E., Hassabis, D., Graepel, T., Lillicrap, T., & Silver, D. (2020). Mastering Atari, Go, chess and shogi by planning with a learned model. *Nature*, 588, 604–612.

Schroeder, T. (2004). *The Three Faces of Desire*. Oxford University Press.

Schroeder, T. (2006). Desire. *Philosophy Compass*, 1, 631–639.

Schroeder, T. (2020). Desire. In E. Zalta (ed.), *The Stanford Encyclopedia of Philosophy*. https://plato.stanford.edu/archives/sum2020/entries/desire/.

Schueler, G. (1995). *Desire*. MIT Press.

Schwarz, N. (1999). Self-reports: How the questions shape the answers. *American Psychologist*, 54, 93–105.

Schwitzgebel, E. (2002). A phenomenal, dispositional account of belief. *Noûs*, 36, 249–275.

Schwitzgebel, E. (2013). A dispositional approach to attitudes: Thinking outside the belief box. In N. Nottelmann (ed.), *New Essays on Belief*. Palgrave Macmillan.

Scott, M. (2013). Corollary discharge provides the sensory content of inner speech. *Psychological Science*, 24, 1824–1830.

Scott, R. & Baillargeon, R. (2017). Early false-belief understanding. *Trends in Cognitive Sciences*, 21, 237–249.

Scott, S. (2012). The computational and neural basis of voluntary motor control and planning. *Trends in Cognitive Sciences*, 16, 541–549.

Searle, J. (1983). *Intentionality*. Cambridge University Press.

Seeley, T. (1995). *The Wisdom of the Hive*. Harvard University Press.

Seligman, M., Railton, P., Baumeister, R., & Sripada, C. (2013). Navigating into the future or driven by the past. *Perspectives on Psychological Science*, 8, 119–141.

Seligman, M., Railton, P., Baumeister, R., & Sripada, C. (2016). *Homo Prospectus*. Oxford University Press.

Sescousse, G., Li, Y., & Dreher, J.-C. (2015). A common currency for the computation of motivational values in the human striatum. *Social Cognitive and Affective Neuroscience*, 10, 467–473.

Shafahi, A., Huang, W.R., Studer, C., Feizi, S., & Goldstein, T. (2020). Are adversarial examples inevitable? *International Conference on Learning Representations*. arXiv:1809.02104.

Shafer-Landau, R. (2003). *Moral Realism*. Oxford University Press.

Shapiro, L. & Spaulding, S. (2021). Embodied cognition. In E. Zalta (ed.), *Stanford Encyclopedia of Philosophy*. https://plato.stanford.edu/archives/win2021/entries/embodied-cognition/.

Sharot, T., De Martino, B., & Dolan, R. (2009). How choice reveals and shapes expected hedonic outcome. *Journal of Neuroscience*, 29, 3760–3765.

Sharot, T., Fleming, S.M., Yu, X., Koster, R., & Dolan, R. (2012). Is choice-induced preference change long-lasting? *Psychological Science*, 10, 1123–1129.

Sharot, T. & Sunstein, C. (2020). How people decide what they want to know. *Nature Human Behavior*, 4, 14–19.

Shea, N. (2018). *Representation in Cognitive Science*. Oxford University Press.
Shea, N. (2022). Concepts as plug & play devices. *Philosophical Transactions of the Royal Society B*, 378, 20210353.
Sheldon, S. & Moscovitch, M. (2010). Recollective performance advantages for implicit memory tasks. *Memory*, 18, 681–697.
Shenhav, A., Musslick, S., Lieder, F., Kool, W., Griffiths, T., Cohen, J.D., & Botvinick, M. (2017). Toward a rational and mechanistic account of mental effort. *Annual Review of Neuroscience*, 40, 99–124.
Shenhav, A., Straccia, M., Cohen, J.D., & Botvinick, M. (2014). Anterior cingulate engagement in a foraging context reflects choice difficulty, not foraging value. *Nature Neuroscience*, 17, 1249–1254.
Shenhav, A., Straccia, M., Musslick, S., Cohen, J.D., & Botvinick, M. (2018). Dissociable neural mechanisms track evidence accumulation for selection of attention versus action. *Nature Communications*, 9, 2485.
Shipstead, Z., Redick, T., Hicks, K., & Engle, R. (2012). The scope and control of attention as separate aspects of working memory. *Memory*, 20, 608–628.
Shizgal, P. & Conover, K. (1996). On the neural computation of utility. *Current Directions in Psychological Science*, 5, 37–43.
Shmuelof, L., Krakauer, J., & Mazzoni, P. (2012). How is a motor skill learned? Change and invariance at the levels of task success and trajectory control. *Journal of Neurophysiology*, 108, 578–594.
Shoda, Y., Mischel., W., & Peake, P. (1990). Predicting adolescent cognitive and self-regulatory competencies from preschool delay of gratification: Identifying diagnostic conditions. *Developmental Psychology*, 26, 978–986.
Shtulman, A. & Valcarcel, J. (2012). Scientific knowledge suppresses but does not supplant earlier intuitions. *Cognition*, 124, 209–215.
Sinhababu, N. (2013). The belief-desire account of intention explains everything. *Noûs*, 47, 680–696.
Small, D. & DiFeliceantonio, A. (2019). Processed foods and food reward: Processed foods compromise the fidelity of gut-brain signaling of food reinforcement. *Science*, 363, 346–347.
Smith, M. (1994). *The Moral Problem*. Blackwell.
Smolensky, P. (1988). On the proper treatment of connectionism. *Behavioral and Brain Sciences*, 11, 1–23.
Smolensky, P. & Legendre, G. (2006). *The Harmonic Mind* (2 volumes). MIT Press.
Smuts, A. (2011). The feels good theory of pleasure. *Philosophical Studies*, 155, 241–265.
Solomon, R. (1976). *The Passions*. Doubleday Anchor.
Sosa, E. (2011). *Knowing Full Well*. Princeton University Press.
Sosa, E. (2015). *Judgments and Agency*. Oxford University Press.
Southgate, V. & Vernetti, A. (2014). Belief-based action prediction in preverbal infants. *Cognition*, 130, 1–10.
Spelke, E. (2022). *What Babies Know*. Oxford University Press.

Spelke, E. & Kinzler, K. (2007). Core knowledge. *Developmental Science*, 10, 89–96.

Spivey, M. (2007). *The Continuity of Mind*. Oxford University Press.

Spreng, R., Mar, R., & Kim, A. (2009). The common neural basis of autobiographical memory, prospection, navigation, theory of mind, and the default mode: A quantitative meta-analysis. *Journal of Cognitive Neuroscience*, 21, 489–510.

Squire, L. & Zola, S. (1998). Episodic memory, semantic memory, and amnesia. *Hippocampus*, 8, 205–211.

Sridharan, D., Levitin, D., & Menon, V. (2008). A critical role for the right fronto-insular cortex in switching between central-executive and default-mode networks. *Proceedings of the National Academy of Sciences*, 105, 12569–12574.

Sripada, C. (2020). The atoms of self-control. *Noûs*, 55, 800–824.

Sripada, C. (2022). Impaired control in addiction involves cognitive distortions and unreliable self-control, not compulsive desires and overwhelmed self-control. *Behavioral Brain Research*, 418, 113639.

Sripada, C., Kessler, D., & Angstadt, M. (2014). Lag in maturation of the brain's intrinsic functional architecture in attention-deficit/hyperactivity disorder. *Proceedings of the National Academy of Sciences*, 111, 14259–14264.

Sripada, C. & Stich, S. (2006). A framework for the psychology of norms. In P. Carruthers, S. Laurence, and S. Stich (eds.), *The Innate Mind, Volume 2: Culture and cognition*. Oxford University Press.

Staffel, J. (2013). Can there be reasoning with degrees of belief? *Synthese*, 190, 3535–3551.

Staffel, J. (2017). Accuracy for believers. *Episteme*, 14, 39–48.

Stampe, D. (1987). The authority of desire. *Philosophical Review*, 96, 335–381.

Stanley, J. (2011a). Knowing (how). *Noûs*, 45, 207–238.

Stanley, J. (2011b). *Know How*. Oxford University Press.

Stanley, J. & Williamson, T. (2001). Knowing how. *Journal of Philosophy*, 98, 411–444.

Stanley, J. & Williamson, T. (2017). Skill. *Noûs*, 51, 713–726.

Stanley, M., Dougherty, A., Yang, B., Henne, P., & De Brigard, F. (2018). Reasons probably won't change your mind: The role of reasons in revising moral decisions. *Journal of Experimental Psychology: General*, 147, 962–987.

Starmans, C. & Friedman, O. (2020). Expert or esoteric? Philosophers attribute knowledge differently than all other academics. *Cognitive Science*, 44, e12850.

Stephens, D.W. & Krebs, J. (1986). *Foraging Theory*. Princeton University Press.

Sterelny, K. (1991). *The Representational Theory of Mind*. Blackwell.

Stevens, J.R. & Mühlhoff, N. (2012). Intertemporal choice in lemurs. *Behavioral Processes*, 89, 121–127.

Storbeck, J. & Clore, G. (2008). Affective arousal as information: How affective arousal influences judgments, learning, and memory. *Social and Personality Psychology Compass*, 2, 1824–1843.

Strawson, G. (2003). Mental ballistics or the involuntariness of spontaneity. *Proceedings of the Aristotelian Society*, 103, 227–256.

Striedter, G. (2005). *Principles of Brain Evolution*. Sinauer Associates.

Sutton, R. & Barto, A. (1998). *Reinforcement Learning*. MIT Press.

Sytsma, J. & Buckwalter, W. (eds.) (2016). *A Companion to Experimental Philosophy*. Wiley.

Tamietto, M. & de Gelder, B. (2010). Neural bases of the non-conscious perception of emotional signals. *Nature Reviews Neuroscience*, 11, 697–709.

Tappolet, C. (2016). *Emotions, Values, and Agency*. Oxford University Press.

Taylor, A., Elliffe, D., Hunt, G., & Gray, R. (2010). Complex cognition and behavioral innovation in New Caledonian crows. *Proceedings of the Royal Society B*, 277, 2637–2643.

Teodorescu, A. & Usher, M. (2013). Disentangling decision models: From independence to competition. *Psychological Review*, 120, 1–38.

Thelen, E., Schöner, G., Scheier, C., & Smith, L. (2001). The dynamics of embodiment: A field theory of infant perseverative reaching. *Behavioral and Brain Sciences*, 24, 1–34.

Thelen, E. & Smith, L. (eds.) (1993). *A Dynamic Systems Approach to Development*. MIT Press.

Thura, D. & Cisek, P. (2016). Modulation of premotor and primary motor cortical activity during volitional adjustments of speed-accuracy trade-offs. *The Journal of Neuroscience*, 36, 938–956.

Tian, X. & Poeppel, D. (2010). Mental imagery of speech and movement implicates the dynamics of internal forward models. *Frontiers in Psychology*, 1, #166.

Tian, X. & Poeppel, D. (2013). The effect of imagination on stimulation: The functional specificity of efference copies in speech processing. *Journal of Cognitive Neuroscience*, 25, 1020–1036.

Tiemann, L., Hohn, V., Ta Dinh, S., May, E., Nickel, M., Gross, J., & Ploner, M. (2018). Distinct patterns of brain activity mediate perceptual and motor and autonomic responses to noxious stimuli. *Nature Communications*, 9, 4487.

Ting, F., He, Z., & Baillargeon, R. (2021). Five-month-old infants attribute inferences based on general knowledge to agents. *Journal of Experimental Child Psychology*, 208, 105126.

Todd, P. & Gigerenzer, G. (2012). *Ecological Rationality*. Oxford University Press.

Toribio, J. (2011). Compositionality, iconicity, and perceptual nonconceptualism. *Philosophical Psychology*, 24, 177–193.

Toth, A., McNeill, E., Hayes, K., Moran, A., & Campbell, M. (2020). Does mental practice *still* enhance performance? A 24-year follow-up and meta-analytic replication and extension. *Psychology of Sport & Exercise*, 48, 101672.

Tracy, J. & Matsumoto, D. (2008). The spontaneous expression of pride and shame: Evidence for biologically innate nonverbal displays. *Proceedings of the National Academy of Sciences*, 105, 11655–11660.

Tracy, J. & Robins, R. (2008). The nonverbal expression of pride: Evidence for cross-cultural recognition. *Journal of Personality and Social Psychology*, 94, 516–530.

Tracy, J., Robins, R., & Lagattuta, K. (2005). Can children recognize the pride expression? *Emotion*, 5, 251–257.

Tsukahara, J., Harrison, T., Draheim, C., Martin, J., & Engle, R. (2020). Attention control: The missing link between sensory discrimination and intelligence. *Attention, Perception, & Psychophysics*, 82, 3445–3478.

Tulving, E. (1972). Episodic and semantic memory. In E. Tulving & W. Donaldson (eds.), *The Organization of Memory*. Academic Press.

Tulving, E. (1983). *Elements of Episodic Memory*. Oxford University Press.

Turing, A. (1950). Computing machinery and intelligence. *Mind*, 59, 433–460.

Tversky, A. & Kahneman, D. (1973). Availability: A heuristic for judging frequency and probability. *Cognitive Psychology*, 5, 207–232.

Tversky, A. & Kahneman, D. (1974). Judgment under uncertainty: Heuristics and biases. Biases in judgments reveal some heuristics of thinking under uncertainty. *Science*, 185, 1124–1131.

Uddin, L. (2015). Salience processing and insular cortical function and dysfunction. *Nature Reviews Neuroscience*, 16, 55–61.

Umanath, S. & Coane, J. (2020). Face validity of remembering and knowing: Empirical consensus and disagreements between participants and researchers. *Perspectives on Psychological Science*, 15, 1400–1422.

Umbach, G., Kantak, P., Jacobs, J., Kahana, M., Pfeiffer, B., Sperling, M., & Lega, B. (2020). Time cells in the human hippocampus and entorhinal cortex support episodic memory. *Proceedings of the National Academy of Sciences*, 117, 28463–28474.

Usher, M. & McClelland, J. (2001). The time course of perceptual choice: The leaky, competing accumulator model. *Psychological Review*, 108, 550–592.

Vadas, M. (1984). Affective and nonaffective desire. *Philosophy and Phenomenological Research*, 45, 273–280.

Vadillo, M., Gold, N., & Osman, M. (2016). The bitter truth about sugar and willpower: The limited evidential value of the glucose model of ego depletion. *Psychological Science*, 27, 1207–1214.

van Dantzig, S., Pecher, D., & Zwaan, R. (2008). Approach and avoidance as action effects. *Quarterly Journal of Experimental Psychology*, 61, 1298–1306.

van den Berg, R., Anandalingam, K., Zylberberg, A., Kiani, R., Shadlen, M., & Wolpert, D. (2016a). A common mechanism underlies changes of mind about decisions and confidence. *eLife*, 5, e12192.

van den Berg, R., Zylberberg, A., Kiani, R., Shadlen, M., & Wolpert, D. (2016b). Confidence is the bridge between multi-stage decisions. *Current Biology*, 26, 3157–3168.

Van den Stock, J., Tamietto, M., Sorger, B., Pichon, S., Grézes, J., & de Gelder, B. (2011). Cortico-subcortical visual, somatosensory, and motor activations for perceiving dynamic whole-body emotional expressions with and without striate cortex (V1). *Proceedings of the National Academy of Sciences*, 108, 16188–16193.

Van Essen, D., Andersen, C.H., & Felleman, D. (1992). Information processing in the primate visual system. *Science*, 255, 419–423.

Van Leeuwen, N. (2014). Religious credence is not factual belief. *Cognition*, 133, 698–715.

Vanderveldt, A., Oliveira, L., & Green, L. (2016). Delay discounting: Pigeon, rat, human – does it matter? *Journal of Experimental Psychology: Animal Learning and Cognition*, 42, 141–162.

Vasconcelos, M., Monteiro, T., & Kacelnik, A. (2015). Irrational choice and the value of information. *Nature Scientific Reports*, 5, 13874.

Vellante, M., Baron-Cohen, S., Melis, M., Marrone, M., Petretto, D., Masala, C., & Preti, A. (2013). The "Reading the Mind in the Eyes" test: Systematic review of psychometric properties and a validation study in Italy. *Cognitive Neuropsychiatry*, 18, 326–354.

Vijayakumar, N., Whittle, S., Dennison, M., Yücel, M., Simmons, J., & Allen, N. B. (2014). Development of temperamental effortful control mediates the relationship between maturation of the prefrontal cortex and psychopathology during adolescence: A 4-year longitudinal study. *Developmental Cognitive Neuroscience*, 9, 30–43.

Volle, E., Gonen-Yaacovi, G., Costello, A., Gilbert, S., & Burgess, P. (2011). The role of rostral prefrontal cortex in prospective memory: A voxel-based lesion study. *Neuropsychologia*, 49, 2185–2198.

Vuilleumier, P. (2015). Affective and motivational control of vision. *Current Opinion in Neurology*, 28, 29–35.

Wagner, U., Gais, S., Haider, H., Verleger, R., & Born, J. (2004). Sleep inspires insight. *Nature*, 427, 352–355.

Walasek, L. & Brown, G.D.A. (2024). Incomparability and incommensurability in choice: No common currency of value? *Perspectives on Psychological Science*, 19, 1011–1030.

Wallis, J. (2007). Orbito-frontal cortex and its contribution to decision-making. *Annual Review of Neuroscience*, 30, 31–56.

Watts, T., Duncan, G., & Quan, H. (2018). Revisiting the marshmallow test: A conceptual replication investigating links between early delay of gratification and later outcomes. *Psychological Science*, 29, 1159–1177.

Weiskrantz, L. (1986). *Blindsight*. Oxford University Press.

Weiskrantz, L. (1997). *Consciousness Lost and Found: A neuropsychological exploration*. Oxford University Press.

Westbrook, A., Lamichhane, B., & Braver, T. (2019). The subjective value of cognitive effort is encoded by a domain-general valuation network. *Journal of Neuroscience*, 39, 3934–3947.

Whitcomb, D. (2010). Curiosity was framed. *Philosophy and Phenomenological Research*, 81, 664–687.

Williams, B. (1970). Deciding to believe. In H. Kiefer & M. Munitz (eds.), *Language, Belief, and Metaphysics*, State University of New York Press.

Williams, B. (1981). Internal and external reasons. In *Moral Luck*. Cambridge University Press.

Williamson, T. (2000). *Knowledge and Its Limits*. Oxford University Press.

Williamson, T. (2007). *The Philosophy of Philosophy*. Blackwell.

Williamson, T. (2020). *Philosophical Method: A very short introduction*. Oxford University Press.

Wilson, G. & Shpall, S. (2012). Action. In E. Zalta (ed.), *The Stanford Encyclopedia of Philosophy*. https://plato.stanford.edu/archives/sum2012/entries/action/.

Winkielman, P., Berridge, K., & Wilbarger, J. (2005). Unconscious affective reactions to masked happy versus angry faces influence consumption behavior and judgements of value. *Personality and Social Psychology Bulletin*, 31, 121–135.

Winstanley, C. & Floresco, S. (2016). Deciphering decision making: Variation in animal models of effort- and uncertainty-based choice reveals distinct neural circuitries underlying core cognitive processes. *Journal of Neuroscience*, 36, 12069–12079.

Witkower, Z., Hill, A., Koster, J., & Tracy, J. (2021). Beyond face value: Evidence for the universality of bodily expressions of emotion. *Affective Science*, 2, 221–229.

Wolpert, D. & Flanagan, J. (2001). Motor prediction. *Current Biology*, 11, R729–R732.

Wolpert, D. & Kawato, M. (1998). Multiple paired forward and inverse models for motor control. *Neural Networks*, 11, 1317–1329.

Wong, A., Haith, A., & Krakauer, J. (2015). Motor planning. *The Neuroscientist*, 21, 385–398.

Woo, B. & Spelke, E. (2022). Eight-month-old infants' social evaluations of agents who act on false beliefs. *Proceedings of the Annual Meeting of the Cognitive Science Society*, 44, 1184–1189.

Woo, B. & Spelke, E. (2023). Toddlers' social evaluations of agents who act on false beliefs. *Developmental Science*, 26, e13314.

Wood, W. & Rünger, D. (2016). Psychology of habit. *Annual Review of Psychology*, 67, 289–314.

Woodward, J. (2003). *Making Things Happen: A theory of causal explanation*. Oxford University Press.

Wu, W. (2023). *Movements of the Mind: A theory of attention, intention, and action*. Oxford University Press.

Xia, Z., Hong, X., Gao, X., Feng, X., & Zhao, G. (2020). Spatiotemporal recurrent convolutional networks for recognizing spontaneous micro-expressions. *IEEE Transactions on Multimedia*, 22, 626–640.

Yang, S., Lengyel, M., & Wolpert, D. (2016). Active sensing in the categorization of visual patterns. *eLife*, 5, e12215.

Yarkoni, T., Poldrack, R., Nichols, T., Van Essen, D., & Wager, T. (2011). Large-scale automated synthesis of human functional neuroimaging data. *Nature Methods*, 8, 665–670.

Yarrow, I., Brown, P., & Krakauer, J. (2009). Inside the brain of an elite athlete: The neural processes that support high achievement in sports. *Nature Reviews Neuroscience*, 10, 585–596.

Yeomans, M., Leitch, M., Gould, N., & Mobini, S. (2008). Differential hedonic, sensory and behavioral changes associated with flavor-nutrient and flavor-flavor learning. *Physiology & Behavior*, 93, 798–806.

Zabelina, D., O'Leary, D., Pornpattananangkul, N., Nusslock, R., & Beeman, M. (2015). Creativity and sensory gating indexed by the P50: Selective versus leaky sensory gating in divergent thinkers and creative achievers. *Neuropsychologia*, 69, 77–84.

Zabelina, D., Saporta, A., & Beeman, M. (2016). Flexible or leaky attention in creative people? Distinct patterns of attention for different types of creative thinking. *Memory and Cognition*, 44, 488–498.

Zhang, R., Geng, X., & Lee, T. (2017). Large-scale functional neural network correlates of response inhibition: An fMRI meta-analysis. *Brain Structure & Function*, 222, 3973–3990.

Zhao, G., Li, X., Li, Y., & Pietikäinen, M. (2023). Facial micro-expressions: An overview. *Proceedings of the IEEE*, 10.1109/JPROC.2023.3275192.

Zwaan, R., Madden, C., Yaxley, R., & Aveyard, M. (2004). Moving words: Dynamic mental representations in language comprehension. *Cognitive Science*, 28, 611–619.

Zwaan, R. & Taylor, L.J. (2006). Seeing, acting, understanding: Motor resonance in language comprehension. *Journal of Experimental Psychology: General*, 135, 1–11.

Index

accumulator, neural, 33, 56
action, varieties of, 70–71
adaptation for argumentation, 38, 80, 109
addiction, 21, 120, 163
affect, science of, 46–51
agnosia, visual form, 25
alien-hand syndrome, 24
amnesia, 101, 144
  childhood, 140
analog-magnitude, 5, 11–12
  representation of likelihood, 169–71
  representation of value, 101, 116–18, 120
anger, automatic damage urge of, 64–65
aphasia, 35–36
appraisal, 47
arousal, 48–49
  degrees of, 164–65
  neural boost from, 164–65
attention, 16
  covert, 77–79
  default aversiveness of, 174–75
  overt, 77
  suppressive function of, 78, 112
  ventral network, 78, 81
attitude strength, intrinsic vs extrinsic, 158–60
autonoesis, 139

Barrett, Lisa Feldman, 51
Bayesian, 11, 172
Beddor, Bob, 41
belief, 135–43
  degrees of, 166–72
  distinct kinds of, 140–43
  embeds nonconceptual likelihood, 169–71
  episodic, 139
  nonconceptual forms of, 137–38
  reality of, 135–37
  semantic, 139–40
belief-desire psychology, 1
  failures of, 23, 34, 38, 58, 63, 75, 79, 90

blindsight, 26
Briscoe, Robert, 27

cerebellum, 31
Cochrane, Tom, 128
commitment, 88–89, 98–100, 150
computationalism, 11–12
consciousness, 67
  access, 29
  from ventral pathway, 26
  speed of, 27, 29
core knowledge, 137
cortex
  anterior cingulate, 82, 105
  anterior temporal / temporal pole, 41, 143
  dorsolateral prefrontal, 93, 105
  frontal eye-fields, 78
  insula, 81, 94
  intraparietal sulcus, 78
  medial temporal, 140
  motor, 26
  orbitofrontal, 94
  rostrolateral prefrontal, 93
  ventral parietal, 79
  ventromedial prefrontal, 94
creativity, 86–87
credences, 166–72
curiosity, 54, 55
  as metacognitive, 55
  as questioning, 51–52
  motoric theory of, 55–57
  seemingly instrumental behavior, 62–63

De Brigard, Felipe, 43–44
decision
  as accumulator boundary crossing, 32–34, 89
  not a mental action, 89–90
decision-making, 100–10
  push-push theory of, 160–61
  verbal, 108–10

deep-learning networks, 17
Dennett, Daniel, 6–7
desire, 118–24
  affective vs intention-like, 92–95
  as disposition to act, 129–30
  as nonconceptual representation of value, 122–24
  as perception of goodness, 130–31
  automatic approach urges, 63–64
  directed-attention account, 131
  mind-to-world direction of fit of, 130
  stored vs active, 91–93
  strength of, 162–63
  teleological theory of, 131–32
direction of fit, 2
  of belief, 130
  of desire, 5, 130
  of intention, 130
  of motor plans, 43
disgust, automatic avoidance urge from, 57–58
dualism, 9
dynamical-system, 18

ego-depletion, 174
embodied concepts, 17
embodied mind, 15–17
emotion, 3
  automatic expression of, 51–54
  direct non-instrumental expression, 54–59

fear, automatic behavior from, 58
forward model, sensory, 16, 30
Frankish, Keith, 150, 151, 167
future discounting, 105–7

habit, 20–24
heuristic, 103–4, 109, 172
hippocampus, 12, 41, 44
human nature, 37–38
Humeanism, 146, 147

Icard, Thomas, 172
imagination, 75–76
incentive-salience, 21, 61, 119–20
information, 12–15
intention, 2
  as belief, 98–100
  as desire, 96–97
  as inhibiting desire, 111–12
intentional content, 12–15
intentional stance, 7
intentionality, 10
inverse model, 30

judgment, 87–88, 148–49
  commitment-like forms of, 149–52

know-how, 39–40
knowledge
  concept of, 152–53
  not a mental state, 154–57

maps, mental, 14–15, 138
Marr, David, 10
memory
  constructive, 143–44
  declarative, 142
  episodic, 139, 140
  prospective, 93–94
  search, 76–77
  semantic, 11, 139–40, 141–42
  trace, 155
mental rehearsal, 72, 74–75
micro-expression, 53
mind-wandering, 82–86
model-based action, 59–60
model-free action, 60–61
moral internalism, 146

neuroeconomics, 104–5

object-file, 11, 138
optic ataxia, 25

paradox of the preface, 167–68, 172
Pavese, Carlotta, 41
personal / sub-personal distinction, 66–67
philosophical method, 180–84
physicalism about the mind, 8–10
placebo effect, 50, 146
pleasure, 114–18
  anticipatory, 114, 120
  as motivating feeling, 124–26
  as object of desire, 126–28
  as present-tensed, 127
  as representation of value, 116–18
  consummatory, 114–16
prospection, 100–4

realism about mental states, 6–8
representationalism, 10–11
responsibility, moral, 67–69
reward
  primary, 47, 50, 117
  secondary, 47, 50–51
risk preferences, 107–8

Scanlon, Thomas, 131
Schroeder, Tim, 128, 132–33
Schwenkler, John, 27
sensorimotor system
  decisions within, 32
  goal-sensitivity of, 30
  hierarchical, 30–31

Sinhababu, Neil, 97
skill, 29–34
  as distinctively human, 37–39
  not propositional, 40–43
  sequence chunking in, 31–32
speech
  as skill, 34–37
  competitive nature of, 34–36
  influences on, 35, 36
  inner, 73–74
  traditional model of, 34
standard model of action, 1–4
  failures of. *See* belief-desire psychology, failures
Stanley, Jason, 40
striatum, 60–61, 94
Stroop test, 36
synthetic philosophy, 183

temporal-difference model, 61–62
thinking, controlled, 79–82
Tulving, Endel, 139

utilization syndrome, 24

valence, 49, 105
  as common currency, 100
value
  common currency of, 104–5
  incommensurability, 102–3
  learning of, 51
  nature of, 47, 117
  phenomenology of, 117–18
vision
  dorsal stream, 25, 26–27
  Magnocellular vs Parvocellular pathways, 24–25
  ventral stream, 25–26
visual control of action, 27–29

Williamson, Timothy, 40, 152, 153
willpower
  as emotional intelligence, 175–76
  as strengthening prefrontal network, 176–78
Wu, Wayne, 66